TEACHING SCIENCE ONLINE

Current and forthcoming titles publishing in our
ONLINE LEARNING AND DISTANCE EDUCATION series
Edited by Michael Grahame Moore

TEACHING SCIENCE ONLINE

Practical Guidance for Effective Instruction and Lab Work

Edited by Dietmar K. Kennepohl

Series Foreword by Michael Grahame Moore

1996-2016 20TH ANNIVERSARY

Stylus
PUBLISHING, LLC.

STERLING, VIRGINIA

Published by Stylus Publishing, LLC.
22883 Quicksilver Drive
Sterling, Virginia 20166-2102

Library of Congress Cataloging-in-Publication Data
Names: Kennepohl, Dietmar Karl, 1961- author.
Title: Teaching science online : practical guidance for effective instruction and lab work / Dietmar Kennepohl.
Description: First edition. |
Sterling, Virginia : Stylus Publishing, 2016.
Identifiers: LCCN 2016003780 (print) |
LCCN 2016016277 (ebook) |
  ISBN 9781620361887 (pbk. : alk. paper) |
  ISBN 9781620361870 (cloth : alk. paper) |
  ISBN 9781620361894 (library networkable e-edition) |
  ISBN 9781620361900 (consumer e-edition) |
Subjects: LCSH: Science--Study and teaching (Higher) |
  Science--Computer-assisted instruction. | Web-based instruction. |
  Science--Study and teaching (Higher)--Case studies. |
  Science--Computer-assisted instruction. | Web-based instruction--Case studies.
Classification: LCC Q181 .K323 2016 (print) | LCC Q181 (ebook) |
DDC   507.8/2--dc23
LC record available at https://lccn.loc.gov/2016003780

13-digit ISBN: 978-1-62036-1870 (cloth)
13-digit ISBN: 978-1-62036-1887 (paper)
13-digit ISBN: 978-1-62036-1894 (library networkable e-edition)
13-digit ISBN: 978-1-62036-1900 (consumer e-edition)

Printed in the United States of America

All first editions printed on acid-free paper
that meets the American National Standards Institute
Z39-48 Standard.

Bulk Purchases

Quantity discounts are available for use in workshops and for staff development.
Call 1-800-232-0223

First Edition, 2016

10   9   8   7   6   5   4   3   2

To My Mother

CONTENTS

It is my privilege to introduce, as the newest addition to our Online Learning and Distance Education series, a book about science teaching. It is, of course satisfying to welcome every new book in our series, but the arrival of this particular book has been especially gratifying, for it provides evidence in a set of reported experiences of success in what has been regarded by many as subjects too difficult for teaching at a distance: the so-called hard sciences, principally chemistry, physics, biology, and geology. Although I am not a scientist ("real" scientists don't think much of my degree in economics!), during a lifetime in distance education, I have worked with many scientists, and I have become sensitive to their concerns about protecting what they see as the special character of scientific learning. These concerns about character have led to doubt regarding the suitability of distance teaching methods in their subjects. "It might be all right for English or even mathematics," they'll say, "but physics [or biology, chemistry, etc.] is different." Of course these subjects are different, but so is every subject. My own standard response to such skepticism has been that as a distance educator, I start with the assumption that in teaching the sciences, as in other fields, most difficulties are merely instructional design problems and therefore susceptible to instructional design solutions. It is true that in many courses in the sciences there is the key requirement that the student has hands-on experience of experimenting in a laboratory; yet, a good solution for many institutions was discovered several decades ago with the invention of the home experiment kit, a package of materials shipped to the distance learner that had been thoughtfully compiled to reproduce the kind of activity normally undertaken in the laboratory to help achieve the specific learning outcomes of a particular course. I say "thoughtfully" because it is the skill of identifying and matching up materials with content and instructional objectives through the combined skills of both science specialists and instructional design specialists that represents what I have in mind when I say that most problems are susceptible to instructional design solutions. However, to the scientist I am not a peer, and such assertions from nonscientists are not a sufficient foundation for the further development of distance teaching in the sciences. What scientists want to hear is what *other scientists* think and what have been *their* successful practices, and so we come to the core intent of this book—to pass on some recent real-life experiences of a selection of leading science educators. In these chapters, scientists show that sciences *can* be taught at a distance. Furthermore, learning at a distance can result in high-quality learning. The contributors specifically describe some of the methods and techniques they have used for achieving this learning.

It should be obvious from what has been said so far, but, to avoid any possibility of misunderstanding, let me say as clearly as I can: This book is not about science or about research in distance education. Rather, it is about *distance teaching in practice*. Being academics in the sciences, most authors introduce their chapters with a few references to pedagogical literature, but they have not set out to provide comprehensive reviews of literature or research and have limited such references to what helps underpin their proper focus: the *practice* of teaching. Going further, to clarify the character of the book, again to avoid misunderstanding, I would describe the general approach as focused on not only the *practice* of teaching but also the *practicalities*; in other words, the fundamentals that should be helpful for scientists who, though probably highly expert in their fields, are not yet experienced distance educators. To understand this, and some other points being made in this introduction, the reader need look no further than chapter 1, "The Basics of Getting Biology Courses Online." Don't be put off by the chapter's title if you are not a biology teacher. In this chapter, as in (nearly) every chapter of this book, examples are given from teaching a particular science, but the methods and techniques that are described are usually generalizable to other science subjects. I am not able to quote substantially to elaborate this point, but perhaps such generalizability can be illustrated by just the following part of one sentence from this volume: "It is perhaps worth noting here that students do not find PowerPoint slides unaccompanied by audio recordings helpful at all" (p. 12). Of course, in the chapter the authors expand on this assertion, including comments about how classroom students respond differently from distance learners in their responses to the same media. Another illustration comes from chapter 4, which states that

> those planning a distance education course will need to have in mind a realistic estimate of just how much reading, writing, or online interacting students can be expected to do. . . . Such are the demands of learning from even a well-written physics text that relatively slow reading rates of 150 words per minute are generally thought to be realistic. . . . Those preparing to write scripts for audio or video presentations should probably be planning on the order of three words per second. (pp. 71–72)

We then consider chapter 5, which is devoted specifically to determining how to provide the laboratory experience "at a distance." The most basic of pedagogical principles is restated in the following observation: "Often, the writing of learning objectives for laboratories is not done, which makes the evaluation of such experiences difficult to measure and assess" (p. 89). Amen to that!

That is not to say that every pedagogical technique is equally useful in every subject—or indeed in every course. On the contrary, one fundamental principle in distance education is that a tailor-made reconstituting of the contents of the pedagogical toolbox (technology, media, teaching technique, evaluation method, extent of dialogue between instructor and student and between student and student, degree of structure of its content) requires a mix-and-match procedure. I have been told, as an example, that in chemistry the instructor might want students to acquire a good grasp of relating macroscopic, molecular, and symbolic perspectives of a given system or reaction, for which outcome, such as a visualization technology (e.g., an app), would likely be valuable, and a discussion forum could be useless and lead to more misconceptions.

My point in citing these examples is to illustrate that these chapters, like others in this book, are about applications of the fundamentals of pedagogy in distance education, are usually not specific to only one science, are derived from real-life experience, and provide the basis for practical advice and guidance for improved teaching.

Lest I have overemphasized this focus on basic best practice in distance teaching, there is plenty in this book about innovation, especially application of certain new technologies. This includes, for example, chapter 8, with its discussion of computer-based laboratories "teaching what real laboratories cannot" (p. 132); chapter 6, written by instructors at The OpenScience Laboratory at The Open University in the United Kingdom, describing "cutting-edge tools for teaching practical biology at a distance" (p. 101); chapter 9, about "hands-on computer control of real laboratory equipment over the Internet" (p. 143); and chapters 10 and 12, which are focused on applications of mobile technology.

Teachers of science at the undergraduate college level have contributed most of the chapters in this book, but there are a few from other fields, and I want to mention two of these. Chapter 13 is about teaching in a field of science that has not been mentioned so far, namely, pharmacology, and reports the experience of European institutions that cooperated across national systems in a program of course design and delivery. This project should be of special interest as an example of the emerging organizational paradigm of virtual multi-institutional program design and teaching, the successor to both dual- and single-mode teaching institutions. It is also of special interest because it represents the enormously large and important field of continuing professional education. Too often educators at the college and university level, as well as in K–12 (elementary and secondary) schools, fail to appreciate how far ahead in pedagogical practice are some of the programs developed for learning in the professions, business and industry, the armed forces, and voluntary associations. Perhaps not enough has been said in this book on this topic (which perhaps will be the subject of at least one dedicated volume in this Stylus series in the future), but here and now I am glad to draw attention to its representation in chapter 13. Chapter 12 also addresses the need for professional development, and herein what I would argue is the most important profession of all, or at least the one in which the effects of training in distance education is likely to have the widest impact: the development of schoolteachers (K–12). If I were pressed to choose from among the many subjects raised in this book, it is this last, the training of teachers, that would be my personal choice as being of outstanding importance. This points to what should be one of the main ways in which this book will be used: as a resource for the training of future teachers and the retraining of serving teachers in the knowledge about and skills in distance teaching. Our colleges of education, almost without exception worldwide, continue to turn out teachers prepared to teach in a way very similar to how I was trained myself for teaching a half century ago, expounding content in front of a class, although nowadays with the additional resources available by way of the Internet—and sometimes with fewer books! How to actually design a distance learning course, or even how to collaborate efficiently with professional designers or how to facilitate learning in such a course, remains outside the core curriculum of too many teacher colleges, leading to a headwind of half-digested understandings that result in so many mediocre-quality programs. Thus, it is those who are responsible for training science teachers for the schools that should benefit from this book, at least as much as those who teach science at the college level. In this regard, our new book is especially timely, seen in light of the growing emphasis among educational policymakers, especially but not just in the United States, for measures to overcome the perceived general low level of knowledge about the science, technology, engineering, and mathematics (STEM) disciplines. As mentioned in Kennepohl's introduction to this book, it is now widely recognized that our schools must tackle the need not only to prepare more professionals in the STEM disciplines but also, and even more critically, to raise the level of science literacy among nonprofessionals. Surely these aspirations cannot be met by conventional classroom teaching alone, and there need not be such restrictions. As more and more colleges and schools learn the value of distance education for training professionals and the general public, we will finally dispel the prejudice that says "it can't be done in my field." As the stories told here will bear witness, it surely can.

And it is the vision that science can be taught with quality at a distance that has inspired Kennepohl, the editor of this volume. I extend thanks on behalf of the whole distance education community, thanking him not only for his vision but also for the tenacity with which he has worked to bring that vision to reality. I also thank every member of the team of authors, a team that only Kennepohl, with his great international reputation as the leader in this field, was able to assemble. Of course the more meaningful thanks for both the editor and his team will be that, resulting from their work, they see a significant spurt in understanding and practice of distance education in the sciences. That outcome now lies with our readers, and so now I must invite those of you who read this to go forward and, I hope, take up the challenge of teaching science and teaching science better—at a distance.

Michael Grahame Moore, Series Editor
The Pennsylvania State University

ACKNOWLEDGMENTS

I am grateful for being presented with the President's Award for Research and Scholarly Excellence (PARSE) from Athabasca University, which allowed me to bring this major project to completion.

I would also like to thank the reviewers of this book for their helpful comments and suggestions:

Mohamed Ally, *Athabasca University*
Farook Al-Shamali, *Athabasca University*
Sharon E. Brewer, *Thompson Rivers University*
Bruno Cinel, *Thompson Rivers University*
Edward Cloutis, *University of Winnipeg*
Zara Risoldi Cochrane, *Creighton University*
Robert G. Holmberg, *Athabasca University*
Md. Tofazzal Islam, *Bangladesh Open University*
Brian E. Martin, *The King's University*
Ken Munyikwa, *Athabasca University*
Barbie Panther, *Federation University Australia*
Lawton Shaw, *Athabasca University*
Peter Taylor, *The Open University*

INTRODUCTION

Setting the Stage

Dietmar K. Kennepohl
Athabasca University

Those who fall in love with practice without science are like a sailor who enters a ship without a helm or a compass, and who never can be certain whither he is going.

Leonardo da Vinci (1888)

Science[1] has become a vital component of almost every human endeavor in our modern world, and the global demand for higher education in the science, technology, engineering, and mathematics (STEM) disciplines is growing rapidly. Not surprisingly, science is a common part of many developing countries' national strategies for cultivating long-term economic growth and a higher standard of living. One can immediately imagine how that demand would be even more acute in countries where there is a lack of infrastructure and limited resources. What is surprising, if not totally unexpected, is that we also see evidence of the demand for higher education in the STEM disciplines in more affluent countries. Here the problem is not basic infrastructure or needed resources; it is the appeal of science itself. Quite simply, interest and participation in STEM disciplines, especially in higher education, is declining in industrialized countries. Science is not sexy.

Closing the Science Gap

Many are working hard to try to close this science gap, not only by increasing interest and engagement but also by removing any sort of barrier to access. In tackling this problem on many fronts, one quickly realizes that costs associated with traditional modes of higher education science are on the rise, and we really do not have the capacity globally, if we continue as we have in the past, to meet the demand. Online and distance education in the sciences presents a viable alternative to meet those challenges of capacity and access, while offering reduced cost and flexibility (Kennepohl, 2013). What's more, young people are vastly interested in technology, whether it is having ubiquitous access to the Internet; using mobile phones to text and share selfies; or playing with apps to pursue a variety of interests like creating music, athletic training, or digital art, to name a few. That excitement around technology can be a strong motivator for many; thus, as an "enabling tool," technology not only provides the connection but also engages the learner.

The Challenge

Teaching science online and at a distance is not a trivial undertaking. There are a variety of reasons for this complexity, of which the most obvious is dealing with the practical and applied components (laboratory, clinic, fieldwork, design project), as well as the skills that need to be developed there. Like any other discipline, science has its own culture. Students learn in the context of that culture; however, science is not just pure content or a collection of facts. At its roots, science is also a process or way of knowing. What makes the teaching of science unique is that science educators commonly use scientific methodology (which evolved from doing research) as their vehicle or approach. In the sciences, learners are expected to state problems; ask questions; make observations; keep records; offer explanations; create, design, or carry out experiments; reevaluate hypotheses; and communicate findings. This approach needs to be explicitly recognized, as it also underscores the important role of the teaching laboratory in science education. Really, the laboratory is the ultimate sandbox for learners in which scientific methodology can be explored. This book is written by practicing scientists from a variety of science-related disciplines who effectively employ online and distance education techniques. They provide not only their approach to teaching and learning but also practical information in dealing with the laboratory problem.

Appropriate Technologies

The other important thread that runs through many of these chapters is the integration of appropriate information and communication technologies (ICTs). Academics have a real love–hate relationship with new technologies. The science-related disciplines are no exception. We have already stated that global demand for science higher education is exceeding our capacity using our conventional systems. However, online and distance education not only allows us to meet the social mandate of access and education for all but also directly addresses basic capacity issues including cost, scalability, and physical space. Furthermore, ICTs are potentially a great enabling tool that can help us to more fully engage learners and transform how we do and how we think about education. ICTs not only offer enormous access to information and resources but also have the ability to transcend time and space (Kennepohl, 2012). Still, science educators must weigh what is needed for their own local situation, because they are in the best position to do so. Mandatory changes instigated by classroom outsiders, the chasing of new technology fads, or the wholesale importation of someone else's solution simply do not work. Conversely, adopting and adapting ideas from colleagues coupled with an understanding of what may be really required by their students seems to naturally draw educators and scientists. The chapter authors in this book provide guidance with some insights in their own effective approaches to incorporating ICTs in designing their science courses, as well as frank and practical information. As scientists who teach, they have found ICTs to be not only useful but also relatively simple to incorporate.

Who Should Read This Book?

This book is intended for people with a passion for higher and continuing education in any science-related discipline and who care how higher education might look and be approached in the twenty-first century. This would include college instructors, school-teachers, university professors, and learning designers who are continuing their own professional development, working with new teaching technologies and multimedia, delivering courses and labs at a distance, or just exploring blended learning to complement traditional lecture settings. It also provides useful knowledge for institutional and government administrators who might be searching for alternative approaches to learning from logistics, financial, and policy perspectives.

With restructuring of higher education systems around the globe, an increased emphasis on and demand for education in the STEM disciplines, rapidly growing knowledge economies, availability of enhanced ICTs, and more mobile populations, the only thing that seems constant is change itself. In this context, what should our modern teaching and learning of sciences look like to achieve success? Online and distance education offer some tangible advantages and will be an important part of that vision.

The Basics of Getting Science Courses Online

The book opens with four foundational chapters that discuss biology, chemistry, earth science, and physics, respectively. They answer the most common initial questions about teaching science online and at a distance. Each of these chapters provides the reader with an introduction and up-to-date reference sources for study and research within the context of that specific science discipline. More important, these chapters deal with many of the practical considerations for getting a course or laboratory up, including applied methodology and teaching, considering appropriate learning technologies and suggesting specific software for that particular science discipline, engaging the students, and avoiding common mistakes. They also highlight emerging trends to build context and provide a broader perspective by discipline. Although they do not exhaustively cover every science discipline, these four chapters provide a solid base for examining the subsequent chapters.

Applications: Case Studies and Special Topics

Next, we reach the case studies and special topics portion of the book. Here, established science educators around the globe present successful approaches employed in a variety of science-related disciplines from different educational jurisdictions. Each of these chapters uses real situations to highlight and illustrate concepts in delivering online and distance education science courses.

In chapter 5, "Science Online: Bringing the Laboratory Home," we immediately introduce a discussion on the importance and delivery of the laboratory experience in a variety of science disciplines at a midsize dual-mode college that serves mostly working adults. We then turn our attention to chapter 6, "Practical Biology at a Distance: How Far Can We Go With Online Distance Learning?" to focus on a single discipline within a mega open and distance learning (ODL) university, highlighting the range of practical skills and outlining the extent to which they can be achieved without directly supervised hands-on practical classes. Although also set in a single-mode ODL environment, the practical skills problem in a different discipline at a smaller institution is examined in chapter 7, "Assessment in Physics Distance Education: Practical Lessons at

Athabasca University," which features laboratory kits where all experiments are carried out at home.

The next chapters in this section concentrate on the use of technologies to create new learning environments. The technological focus in chapter 8, "Computer-Based Laboratory Simulations for the New Digital Learning Environments," begins with a piece on employing simulations, demonstrating how both laboratory and classroom can be enhanced. Then in chapter 9, "Remote Access Laboratory Equipment for Undergraduate Science Education," we investigate the approach of crafting a virtual laboratory environment by remotely accessing real experiments in real time. Last, in chapter 10, "Situated Science Learning for Higher Level Learning With Mobile Devices," we explore the use of portable technologies that can create, complete, or shape learning environments.

In the final chapters of this section, we venture away from the idea of learning exclusively in the traditional framework of a classroom or laboratory, irrespective of the latest technological advancements, to learning in the field and in the workplace. We do find excellent methodologies for online laboratory work in chapter 11, "Online Delivery of Field- and Laboratory-Based Environmental and Earth Sciences Curriculum," but we are also introduced to handling fieldwork, which is essential to some science disciplines. The next case study in chapter 12, "Enabling Remote Activity: Widening Participation in Field Study Courses," offers a very creative scheme to allow students with physical disabilities to carry out fieldwork. Although meant to target a particular issue, the approach to increased access has universal implications. We also see examples of online and distance applications in reaching out to learners already in the workplace. Chapter 13, "Collaborative e-Learning in Pharmacy: Design, Evaluation, and Outcomes of a European Cross-Border Project," describes a successful international collaboration among multiple traditional institutions in which graduate pharmacists continue their studies online while serving in clinical placements off campus. Finally, a critical review and assessment of in-service programs that augment the knowledge and skills of practicing science teachers is presented in chapter 14, "Online Professional Development for Australian Science Teachers: Developing and Deploying a Curriculum Evaluation Model." The book concludes with a final summary section and two appendices with further resources.

Getting Inspired

When getting started, know that changing everything all at once is not necessary or even desired; you can often just change components of a course or an activity. More important, it is good to know that others with your background and interests in teaching and learning are already doing this, including the authors of this book. Quite frankly, if we can do it, anyone can. Finally, to make sense and get the best out of the veritable smorgasbord of information and experiences presented in these chapters, you should remember that there is no one right way in doing any of it. Each discipline, course, or laboratory session has its own requirements. There is no ultimate technology or silver bullet. Usually it is a combination of approaches with the right mix that leads to success. Getting the right mix means being inspired and exposed to new ideas, being willing to experiment, and knowing what your students really need in the first place.

Although the particular mix of teaching and learning modes really depends on the specific situation, experience has shown that certain learning activities are better suited to different approaches. For example, exploiting ICT automation works well to support and provide feedback for cognitive activities, particularly in simple exercises, drills, and quizzes. To assist you in finding your own right mix, Appendix A provides a first glimpse of some issues to take into account for the learning activities in your course. It is far from exhaustive, but it is illustrative of some of the many considerations you may have in forming your own approach.

As you decide what online or ICT components to integrate into your science course, it will be important to keep some basic practices and principles in mind. The following section includes a top-10 list of effective practices and principles based on practitioners' many years of experience in delivering tertiary science courses (including laboratory components) at a distance.

Effective Practices and Principles

In our experiences, the following are the most effective methods to employ when teaching tertiary science courses remotely:

1. Engage the learner early and often.
2. Focus on science concepts and content rather than on the technology.
3. Take a team approach in developing and delivering courses. Scientists already collaborate in areas of research, so extend that to teaching.
4. Exploit open educational resources (OERs) wherever possible, and build on what is already there. This includes adopting and adapting approaches that are already successful elsewhere.
5. Avoid cognitive overload by providing content and technology sparingly. Teaching is about lighting a fire, not filling a bucket.
6. Use technology with which you are comfortable and for which you have technical support.
7. Select proven technologies rather than the latest technologies.
8. Both students and teachers need training in any learning technologies employed. Do not assume knowledge or expertise.
9. Exploit technology where it will have the greatest impact to learning, or at the very least provide substantial practical advantages like saving time through automation.
10. Expect students to use the technology in unexpected ways. Incorporate this into the teaching and newer iterations of the course (Kennepohl, 2012, p. 384).

You will notice these chapters identify, introduce, and discuss key concepts, delivery modes, and emerging technologies that inform teaching online and at a distance, with an emphasis on providing practical approaches used by established science educators around the globe. Because experimentation and practical work are regarded as a fundamental part of the education and training of most scientists, because the approach to teaching and learning in the sciences often tries to reflect scientific methodology or process, and because practical work at a distance is so challenging, this book has a special emphasis on research and practice in teaching laboratories.

Whether designing laboratory experiments, employing new technologies, or reframing a method of learning, you have plenty of opportunities to discover new ideas that will engage both you and your students. I invite you now to come and explore these pages and see for yourself some approaches to teaching and learning science in the twenty-first century!

References

da Vinci, L. (1888). *The notebooks of Leonardo da Vinci* (Vol. 2). Trans. J. P. Richter. Retrieved from www.gutenberg.org/ebooks/5000

Kennepohl, D. (2012). Pitfalls and prospects: Integrating ICTs in tertiary science education. In J. Peterson, O. Lee, T. Islam, & M. Piscioneri (Eds.), *Effectively implementing information communication technology in higher education in the Asia-Pacific region* (pp. 371–388). New York, NY: Nova.

Kennepohl, D. (2013). Teaching science at a distance. In M. G. Moore (Ed.), *Handbook of distance education* (3rd ed., pp. 670–683). London: Routledge.

Note

1. *Science* includes not only the natural and physical sciences but also mathematics, technology, and many science-related fields such as engineering and allied health disciplines.

PART ONE

The Basics of Getting Science Courses Online

1

THE BASICS OF GETTING BIOLOGY COURSES ONLINE

Wendy Wright, Jennifer Mosse, and Barbara C. Panther
Federation University Australia

Abstract

The online environment provides great flexibility in teaching and learning. In this chapter, we describe an incremental approach to the development of online biology courses, starting with traditional teaching and learning materials. The need for clear course objectives, particularly regarding the role and purpose of practical activities, is highlighted. The ability to tailor the online biology course to provide a student-centered approach, thereby catering to a wide range of student abilities and interests, is discussed. The need to seek out and respond to student feedback to ensure that online courses remain relevant and useful is emphasized.

Biology is, of course, the study of life. Teaching and learning in biology are distinguished by the importance of communicating and understanding concepts that span various scales and dimensions and often exhibit complex networks of connectivity.

Most students are familiar with the biological hierarchy that extends from molecules and cells; through tissues and systems; to individuals, populations, communities, and ecosystems. Most of the laboratory-based biological disciplines (molecular biology, cell biology, histology) are located at the microscopic end of this size-based hierarchy, whereas the field-based biological disciplines (population biology, ecology) are at the opposite end of the spectrum. Mayr (2004) argued that because emergent properties arise at each hierarchical level, the reductionist approach used so successfully in other scientific disciplines is of limited use in biology. He defined the concept of *emergence* as the idea that the entire system may exhibit properties that are not deducible from knowledge of the individual components of the system (the whole is greater than the sum of the parts). In biological systems, the organization of component parts—the way in which things are put together—is as important as the component parts themselves. For example, the structure and function of the kidney cannot be understood from knowledge of its component molecules, and an ecosystem cannot be understood by knowledge of its individual species and abiotic constituents.

For this reason, when discussing the biological function of DNA, teachers and learners do not limit their exploration to the molecular scale, only considering structure of the molecule, the importance of the order of nitrogenous bases in coding for proteins, and the cellular machinery that "reads the code." Instead, the mechanisms of genetic inheritance and the interactions between the genome and the environment across several generations are also discussed. The complexity itself is of interest.

Timescales are also important. For example, consideration of evolutionary processes requires students to appreciate the cumulative effect of small changes over very long periods of time. Many evolutionary processes are also located spatially (particularly geographically), and so the interactions between space and time are also important.

Appreciating the multifaceted relationships that exist between and within living systems and their individual components and the environment is another challenge for students and teachers of biology. Relationships are scaled, in that they exist within and across hierarchical levels, but they also have dimensional aspects, because they may also occur in space and/or time. The issues of scale, dimensions, and connectivity are critically important in biological sciences. Teachers and learners must grapple with and apply these concepts, whether interacting face-to-face or online.

How to Get Online

Clearly understanding and articulating the motivations for the development of an online course, the needs of the particular class, and the appropriate approach to practical work are necessary to ensure good design of an online biology course. It is assumed that this work has already been done, along with careful consideration and alignment of learning outcomes and teaching activities and (where relevant) decisions about appropriate evaluation. Here, the focus is on moving an already established course into the online environment. Answers to the questions posed as subheadings in this section are useful to keep in mind when developing online materials.

Why Go Online?

The two major drivers for online delivery are flexibility for time-poor students and potential for increased student engagement and superior learning outcomes. Bromham and Oprandi (2006) contended, "Unlike a large face-to-face class, online activities generally allow students to undertake tasks at their own pace, in a time and place that suits them" (p. 21). This supports our own, and other, studies that indicate that well-designed e-learning tools encourage student-directed learning.

Reducing institutional costs is now well understood to be a poor reason for the development of online courses (Allen & Seaman, 2013). In addition to considering costs associated with technology and technology support, effective online teachers must be fully engaged with their online students and continue to invest in maintenance and updating of the site materials. Meyer (2014) made the important distinction between *cost-efficiency* and *cost-effectiveness*, defining *cost-efficiency* as "the provision of education at either less cost or more students at the same cost" and *cost-effectiveness* as "the provision of more or better learning at the same or lower cost" (p. 38). When educators design an online course, cost-effectiveness should be the aim.

The nature of the class must be considered. When the online course is intended to provide a supplementary learning environment for students who participate in face-to-face classes, it may be sufficient to set up an electronic storehouse—a place where students can go to find copies of handouts, explanations for assignments, and perhaps recordings of lectures they may have missed. Discussion, exploration, and elucidation can occur in the classroom rather than online.

When the online environment is intended to support students who learn entirely (or almost entirely) without attending classes, a different approach is needed. These students need more than a storehouse; for them, the online environment *is* the classroom. It must be a place where they can engage with the learning materials, their teachers, and their peers.

In many cases, multiple classes may access the online learning environment, so it must serve both on-campus and off-campus students simultaneously. In this blended approach, the online environment must be all things to all students.

What Tools Are Available to You?

Most institutions currently deliver online content via web-based learning management systems (LMSs) such as Moodle, Blackboard, or Desire2Learn. Such systems allow a stepped approach to the development of an online course, because course authors may take advantage of a range of facilities to support learners, from the very basic to the more advanced. From the students' perspective, the LMS becomes their interface with the learning institution. They can access content, obtain direction, submit assignments, receive feedback, and communicate with peers and with teachers via the LMS. From the teacher's perspective, the LMS provides an adaptable delivery platform, along with automated administrative systems for receipt and return of assessment tasks and recording of grades. From an institutional perspective, the LMS facilitates a standardized approach to delivery.

Advances in the capabilities of mobile devices such as smartphones and tablet computers have led to a significant increase in the number of people using these devices to access the Internet. Already, in many countries, mobile devices are the default method of accessing the Internet (Benson & Morgan, 2013). This makes it extremely important that the chosen LMS is designed for use on both desktop and mobile devices and that learning materials are designed in such a way that they are effective regardless of the device being used.

It is also worth considering the role of social media tools in moving to an online course. These tools support everyday communication and collaboration and in many cases offer greater ease of use and increased functionality compared to LMSs.

What Do the Students Want?

An online learning environment can support a broad diversity of learning styles. Khan (2012–2013) provided an excellent analysis of a set of online activities and their relationship to Bloom's Taxonomy of Learning. In Khan's online classroom, students were able to select from a range of different media activities that matched their learning styles, and this resulted in higher-than-usual motivation. Khan (2012–2013) concluded that the "use of multiple sources works to include more learning styles and thus engage and motivate more students" (p. 171).

Research into the resources preferred by our own students (Panther, Wright, & Mosse, 2012) also indicated that students value a wide range of materials and use different resources in different ways. Our off-campus students ranked their assigned textbooks (in this case, not linked to the online learning environment), text-based study guides (available for download online), and recorded lectures (linked to the LMS) as their most useful learning tools. Around half of the students we surveyed preferred to use study guides and textbooks as their primary source of information, turning to lecture slides and lecture recordings to fine-tune and revise. These students were highly organized and had a linear approach to their study. The remaining students tended to begin with lecture slides and recordings, using the lecturer's teaching framework to structure their learning (Panther et al., 2012). The breadth of online resources available catered to these very different learning styles.

It is perhaps worth noting here that students do not find PowerPoint slides unaccompanied by audio recordings helpful at all (Elder, 2009). PowerPoint slides that may be well constructed for use in a face-to-face classroom where the presenter provides explanation and supporting information may not be useful in isolation. Posting slides online provides students with mere glimpses of the information they are required to understand. Without the context, rationale, details, and explanations for each "dot point," the information is inaccessible, and students are unable to connect the dots into a coherent picture. It is also important to remember that although the missing context can be provided to students via audio recording, most off-campus learners use recorded lectures quite differently than do on-campus students who were in the classroom during the lecture. For example, off-campus students typically make full use of the ability to pause, fast-forward, and rewind the recording; many report that they sometimes pause the lecture recording to further explore a particular concept, using the textbook or other resources (Panther et al., 2012). On-campus and mixed-mode students are more likely to use recorded lectures for clarification or revision of content. They may also use the recorded lecture as a replacement for lectures missed due to scheduling or traveling difficulties (Panther et al., 2012).

How to Handle the Labs

Hands-on experiences such as examining specimens in the field, conducting dissections, or isolating DNA from tissue samples are one (very effective) way in which the issues of scale, dimensions, and connectivity, peculiar to an understanding of biological systems, can be addressed and explored. Hands-on experiences are also important ways in which students can develop field or laboratory skills to complement their knowledge of biological systems (Sukhontapatipak & Srikosamatara, 2012). MacQueen and Thomas (2009) identified the hands-on experience as a key requirement for teaching and learning biology and explained that the adherence of The Open University's biology program to a compulsory residential school is driven by a firm view that "nothing can truly substitute for the tactile experience of getting one's hands dirty in the laboratory or the field" (p. 142). This approach is not unusual among off-campus biology programs.

A clear understanding of the student group can assist in addressing the questions of whether and how much hands-on biology should be included as part of, or in addition to, an online biology course. Notwithstanding its peculiarities of scale, dimensions, and connectivity, the "knowledge" of biology is perhaps more easily taught and learned using online resources than are the "skills" required by professional biologists. The discipline-specific skills of a field- or lab-based biologist may indeed be best learned by practice and mastery, as is the case for skills in many other fields. However, not all biology students intend to become professional biologists. Indeed, not all biology courses are intended to produce professional biologists. A careful examination of the objectives of a course and the possible professional destinations of the students can therefore help to determine the balance of the lab and theory components of the course and may influence the extent to which hands-on components of the curriculum should be included.

Much has been written regarding the inclusion or exclusion of dissections in the practical program of biology courses (e.g., Franklin, Peat, & Lewis, 2002; Kinzie, Strauss, & Foss, 1993). Offner (1993) argued that dissections are a fundamental experience for students of biology. Again, the reason for including the dissection in the program at all should be carefully considered. The increasing costs of dissection, the lack of suitable materials, and the emotional conflicts for students and teachers have all contributed to the need for alternatives to dissection (Hart et al., 2008). Although dissection promotes excitement and engagement, Hart and colleagues (2008) reported that the experience of dissection does not seem to result in improved learning by students when compared with the use of alternative teaching materials, such as interactive software, reusable models and specimens, and other resources.

If the inclusion of hands-on experiences is considered necessary, the nature of each learning activity should be carefully aligned with desired course outcomes. This is a helpful way to decide whether traditional supervised activities such as on-campus lab classes or group field trips could be replaced, either with online activities or with independent (off-line) activities in which students carry out practical work at a time and place that best suits them. Use of experimental kits is one approach that provides a hands-on experience without relying on attendance at the campus (Mosse & Wright, 1999).

Table 1.1 explores the purposes of hands-on activities in teaching and learning biology and indicates the relative advantages and disadvantages of online activities, independent activities, and supervised activities. Particularly where skill development is an important learning objective, the inclusion of traditional supervised laboratory or field-work activities may be required.

Taking It Online

The development of an online biology course requires careful consideration, taking into account the issues of scale, hierarchy, and complexity in biological systems and the various ways in which learners can be supported. Simply posting materials developed for the face-to-face learning environment onto a web-based platform is unlikely to be adequate, for either distance learners or mixed-mode classes. The planned online environment should be a custom fit, so that the requirements of the particular students are met. However, the capacity of the course developer will also dictate the nature of the online

TABLE 1.1
Comparison of Alternative Delivery Modes for Teaching Biology

Purpose	Online Activities: Simulations and Virtual Experiences	Independent Activities: May Involve Experimental Kits	Supervised Activities: On Campus, Field Trips
To illustrate theory and aid conceptual understanding	+ These activities are often superior to lab exercises, as there are no time or place restrictions. + They can move freely from the microscale to the macroscale. + They can help students "visualize" complex processes. * Boundaries between models (unknown) and reality (known) must be clearly defined.	* Useful, but they rely on clear, unambiguous directions. * They can be supported by asynchronous discussion forums and video materials. * Safety concerns must be addressed.	+ They ensure key messages are clear. + They allow exploration of unexpected results and discussion of difficult concepts. + Biological variation can be explored. + They occur in real time.
To highlight scale	+ They can move rapidly from the microscale to the macroscale. * They must be specifically designed, as images are often designed to "fill the screen" so relative scale is not always obvious. * They need to provide points of reference for comparison.	* Hands-on activities ensure scale is clear, but within one activity, scale range is usually restricted (e.g., microscale lab work, macroscale field trips).	
To demonstrate connectivity	+ High-quality simulations allow students to rotate molecular images, explore underlying anatomical structures, traverse expansive landscapes, and so on.	* They typically occur within a restricted scale (e.g., cellular structures, anatomical structures, bounded landscapes).	
To develop discipline-specific skills (dissection, microscopy, fieldwork, etc.)	+ Students may observe others performing skills. + Students can "practice" skills in a virtual environment, may be able to manipulate instrument controls, select techniques, and so on. – Students' ability to demonstrate and master skills is limited.	+ Students can practice skills using simple equipment. – Errors in technique may not be identified.	+ Students are exposed to a wider range of more complex equipment. + Students can practice skills under supervision. + Errors in technique can be rectified, so skills can be mastered.
	+ Online simulations can be used to support, prepare, or augment skill development in independent and supervised activities.		

Note. The questions of whether and how best to include practical activities in an online biology course can be informed by a clear understanding of the purpose of the activities. Here, the advantages (+), disadvantages (–), and "points to watch" (*) for each mode and purpose are identified.

course. Many course developers have other responsibilities within their institutions, and levels of familiarity with online systems vary. Clearly, course designers will work within many constraints; time and skills may be limiting factors. It is important that the course developer is not overwhelmed by the prospect of the task.

In many instances, the content and pedagogy of an online course may be limited by the LMS in use. This is often outside of the control of the individual course designer, because decisions about the LMS usually reside at an institutional level. For example, synchronous events may not be supported by some systems, ruling out the option of web-based tutorials. In addition, institutional limitations (including copyright restrictions) may be placed on the use of online resources external to the university, including social media and mobile applications. Despite these limitations, which will vary in each circumstance, the online teaching and learning environment can be used extremely effectively to support learning activities.

Often, development of online resources occurs incrementally. Where time or funding is limited, course developers may not have the luxury of creating a fully online course from first principles and may be asked to convert an existing course, originally designed for face-to-face teaching and learning, to online delivery or for the blended learning environment (Gedik, Kiraz, & Yasar Ozden, 2013).

Getting Started: First Steps

The first step in creating an online biology course could be fairly simple, perhaps as straightforward as pulling together a series of directed readings (study guides) that may include activities designed to illustrate key concepts or to develop skills. It is important that this information be bundled with instructional text that clearly highlights how students are required to use the learning objects and materials. Clear expectations regarding assessment should also be provided. We use assignment guidelines to ensure that students understand the requirements of each assignment. This information may include guidance on structure and word count, assessment rubrics or grading forms, and exemplars of appropriate standards of work. Appropriate time frames for completion of assignments and of the various sections of the course must also be provided so that the learner can plan his or her approach (Gedik et al., 2013).

Provision and active facilitation of an online discussion forum is also extremely useful, enabling multiway communication between and among students and teachers. Participation can also be encouraged by personal and individual contact from the teacher at the beginning of the teaching period and by including discussion items as a small part of the assessment for the course. However, one useful function of the discussion forum is for students to work collaboratively to assist one another in their learning; this can be inhibited by awarding marks for students' contributions. Our own observations indicate that students feel more comfortable using the online discussion forum once they have developed a sense of belonging within the class (Panther et al., 2012). For example, we have observed an increase in the use of discussion groups by off-campus students after attending residential programs.

Basic course content and scheduling information could take the form of a series of text-based files posted online, perhaps supplemented by recorded (only audio or audio plus visual) lectures. When the course is also taught in face-to-face mode, recordings of lectures can often be obtained without too much difficulty.

If working in an environment where there is no institutional support for recording of lectures, teaching staff may use a small digital recording device to capture audio and then make recorded audio files available for students to use in conjunction with a copy of the PowerPoint file. Programs such as Camtasia and iMovie can be used to record sound and screen visuals concurrently from a laptop or desktop computer, which can then be uploaded to the online environment. Many institutions use lecture capture systems that teaching staff may elect to activate in their classrooms. These systems record a speaker's computer presentation and voice and integrate these into an audiovisual package that can be uploaded onto a server and viewed asynchronously by distant students. EchoSystem (formerly Lectopia) is an example of such a system.

Video vignettes are also commonly used to support content. Rather than record the entire lecture, staff create short videos of key concepts and place them online. These may include slides and audio, as in recorded lectures, but are usually more focused on key concepts. The content of one face-to-face lecture may become three or four separate vignettes online.

When recording an on-campus lecture for distribution to off-campus students, lecturers should explicitly acknowledge the off-campus class during lectures. For example, questions from students in the physical class will need to be repeated and/or rephrased by the lecturer so that they are captured for the virtual class. The lecturer should face the camera (virtual class) and directly address members of the virtual class, as well as those physically present in the lecture room.

Students whose only experience of the lecture is via the recording may become frustrated when a lecturer explains a complex process using an ad hoc sketch on the classroom whiteboard, which the distant student cannot see. Digitally inking PowerPoint slides allows annotations and explanatory sketches to be captured and made available to all students (Panther et al., 2012). Alternatively, supplementary material can be posted on the LMS before or after the lecture, or the recording can be enhanced using editing software such as Camtasia or iMovie.

Thus, an acceptable starting point for the development of an online biology course could include the following:

- Basic content (text-based and/or recorded lectures) including instructional material
- Course outline and information regarding assessments
- Online discussion forum

Already Online: What Now?

Further development of an online biology course from the basic provision of essentially text-based learning materials to a carefully constructed course comprising a mixture of text-based material, visual representations (including simple and complex diagrams, photographs and video images, animations and simulations), and hands-on practical activities can take place incrementally. It is largely a matter of collecting and making available relevant materials that enhance student learning. "It is not the technology, but the instructional implementation of the technology that contributes to learning effectiveness" (Tang & Austin, 2009, p. 1243).

Course developers wishing to progress to an intermediate or advanced online learning environment can create a layered approach that allows students of diverse backgrounds to select an accessible entry point into a particular topic. Looped structures within each topic then allow students to refresh, revise, and/or consolidate their understanding, providing an environment that can be uniquely tailored to the needs of each student.

Many LMSs include tools, such as lessons, books, and quizzes, that allow students to follow their own path through the material. For example, there may be a reading or video followed by a short quiz. The student may then be led to different resources based on his or her answer to the quiz question; perhaps back to review content or forward to the next topic. This type of lesson can be quite sophisticated and intentionally developed to address common biology misconceptions. Specifically designed quiz questions can identify misconceptions that exist for an individual student, who is then led to particular content to address the error in understanding.

Another useful student-centered activity is the use of embedded links to supporting material throughout the content, allowing students to access background material or an alternative representation of the content.

These sorts of personalized online lessons require a significant investment in time to set up, but once designed, they require little time on the teacher's part while giving students the type of personalized learning experience advocated by Tanner (2011) in her analysis of quality teaching in secondary-level biology.

Online quizzes and analytics can also be used to inform the teacher of student progress in particular topic areas. In a "flipped classroom" approach to online learning, students are given content to study prior to scheduled classes for each topic and are then quizzed on their understanding. The teacher can use the results of the quiz to identify aspects of the topic with which students are comfortable and aspects that require further input from the teacher. This understanding then informs the choice of subsequent classroom activities.

Link Outside Your LMS

A range of high-quality animations, stock images, videos, and interactive activities are available online for all areas of biology. Links to relevant and well-designed software can bring these excellent learning resources into your online course and may be the best way for students to achieve learning objectives. For example, visualizations of cell processes, population dynamics models, and virtual dissections are widely available and can be embedded directly into an LMS.

Digital Frog International (www.digitalfrog.com) is an example of online software suitable for inclusion in online biology courses. The products range from interactive virtual frog dissections to digital field trips exploring locations such as wetlands and rain forests. In the digital field trips, students can move around within the environment; observe flora and fauna; and click on links for further information, visualizations, or data about a location. These trips often include animations such as how the location would change in the event of a flood or with a change in predator numbers.

The National Association of Biology Teachers (a U.S.-based group) provides many free teaching resources in topics including animals, bioethics, biotechnology and genetics, ecology and environment, education, evolution, general biology, health and safety, and stem cells. Resources include links to videos, animations, nest cameras, and "Ask a Scientist" interactive discussions (www.nabt.org). Web-based courses, such as those available via the Khan Academy (www.khanacademy.org), can be a useful source of videos, animated whiteboard sketches, and alternative explanations. The Howard Hughes Medical Institute (www.hhmi.org) is another source of high-quality online materials, including interviews, lectures, animations, video clips, images, and more.

Social Media

In addition to web-based resources, there are many possibilities for the use of social media in the biology classroom. Social media are platforms in which users create an individual profile and then engage with others in an online network. Educational options include communicating and interacting with communities via platforms such as Facebook and Twitter; bookmarking or recommending digital content via platforms such as Delicious and Pinterest or via RSS feeds; or obtaining content from student- or teacher-generated web pages, wikis, podcasts, or blogs. Regardless of the platform used, it is important to ensure that any use of social media aligns with the policy of the educational organization and that guidelines for use are explicitly discussed with both students and staff.

When trying to understand how social media may assist in your classroom, you will find it useful to observe and establish comfort with the media to understand the types of interactions expected and how the particular platform could be useful. O'Brien (2012) provided a helpful summary of some of the ways that social media can be used in teaching.

An Australian secondary school teacher, Andrew Douch, created a very popular series of weekly biology podcasts titled Douchy's Biology Podcast (biologyoracle .podomatic.com), which is followed by high school biology students across the country. In each podcast, he spends about five minutes discussing one biology topic. Often the topics are those suggested by students who submit questions to his Facebook page.

There are a number of examples of using Twitter in the biology classroom: #Scistuchat is a monthly Twitter chat in which students can pose a question to be answered by a scientist practicing in a relevant discipline area. Recent topics have included evolution and cloning. Students have used Twitter for note taking and back-channel discussion as they watch documentaries (Russo, 2013; Sample, 2010). At the University of Connecticut, Twitter is used in the ornithology class; students tweet their bird observations outside of class (Revkin, 2011). Sample (2010) provided a useful framework for teaching with Twitter.

Apps are applications specifically designed to run on mobile devices such as telephones and tablets. A wide range of useful apps is available to biology teachers, some of which are free of charge. For example, in the field of cell biology, the OnScreen Gene Transcription app includes an interactive three-dimensional (3D) DNA model and a simulation of the transcription process. Students can move and rotate the image and zoom in and out. WholeSlide is an app that allows users to interact with high-quality slide images from all areas of biology, including histology and neuroanatomy. For example, students can look at a whole range of cross sections of the rodent brain. The Bacterial Identification Virtual Lab walks students through the process of extracting, purifying, amplifying, sequencing, and analyzing a DNA sample. Finally, students can access a 3D tour through a cell using the iCell app.

Maintenance

Whether the online learning environment that you build is basic or advanced, its content should change over time, and your site will require maintenance. Unlike authors of textbooks, who at some point declare their work complete and send it off for publication, authors of online content can continue to revise and tweak their work beyond the date of publication. This capacity to revise materials in response to developments in biological science allows teachers to demonstrate the dynamic nature of science and explicitly discuss how knowledge is created. Opportunities to engage students by linking course content to popular media stories or to trending social media posts can also be maximized in the online environment.

Feedback from students provides useful guidance about which aspects of the online learning environment are effective from the learners' perspective and why. Feedback can be sought formally (e.g., a class survey) or informally during class discussions, either face-to-face or online.

Unique Challenges for Getting Your Biology Class Online

There are a number of considerations unique to the discipline when delivering biology content in an online mode. These include taking care with the use of diagrams and models and ensuring that the language of biology is accurately represented in the online environment.

Addressing Complexity via Diagrams and Models

Tsui and Treagust (2013) discussed the importance of multiple representations (including analogies, metaphors, visualizations, discourses, models, multilevel representations, and multimodal representations) in teaching and learning about biological concepts across hierarchical levels. They identified visualizations or visual representations, including drawings, pictures, photographs, diagrams, animations, and simulations, as particularly important in biology (Treagust & Tsui, 2013). Many of these illustrations represent complex biological relationships across scales (Griffard, 2013), and understanding them can be a problem for the online learner.

Griffard (2013) found that learners use complex diagrams more successfully when teachers are able to assist them to (a) engage with a clear goal and (b) identify prior relevant knowledge. The importance of teachers' modeling the appropriate decoding of the information was also noted. Because so much of biology is taught using visual representations, the inclusion of such commentary in the online biology classroom is critical.

Visualization tools are powerful aids to understanding, but they can sometimes lead to misunderstanding when they are used without interpretation and explanation. For example, diagrams commonly used to show the highly structured nature of the eukaryote cell and its organelles are (necessarily) oversimplified. Without an explicit discussion of the representative nature of such diagrams, many students develop misunderstandings, such as construing that there are only two or three mitochondria in any given cell in the body, because only a small number of these organelles are shown in the diagram. This misunderstanding is just as likely to develop from a textbook diagram as from a 3D image available online or embedded in an app.

Teachers should also be vigilant about less obvious examples of confusion when using visualization tools. For example, amino acids are usually represented as similar-sized objects in diagrams and animations. This is a useful shortcut and arguably is of little importance when discussing the primary structure of a protein; however, appropriate understanding of the tertiary structure is easier if students understand that the 3D arrangement of the amino acid chain is influenced by the different sizes of the amino acid R groups and the interactions among these.

In many instances, more complex diagrams are presented to students as a single image. Consider the example of a biochemical pathway. In a face-to-face scenario, the lecturer can guide the student through the diagram, pointing out and further explaining the items of interest to the student. However, for the online student, all of the information on the diagram or image is presented at once, which can be overwhelming or distracting.

The use of digital ink in combination with recorded lectures allows teachers to annotate or even create complex diagrams, explicitly modeling the development of complex representations and higher order thinking skills for the online learner (Harrison, 2013; Venema & Lodge, 2013). The diagram can begin as a simple image, growing in detail with sequentially added information using digital ink. Students who see a complex process diagram developing as they hear an explanation are arguably in a better position to understand the relationships described than those who see only the finished diagram.

A strategically placed link to a well-designed online visualization can increase understanding and engagement. In many cases, online visualizations can provide a better representation of scale and connectivity than an actual laboratory (see Table 1.1). An excellent example is "The Scale of the Universe" animation (Huang & Huang, 2012). This interactive animation allows students to explore scale in a meaningful way that would be unachievable in traditional print-based or classroom approaches to teaching and learning.

Online materials may be purchased individually, obtained as freeware, or associated with a biology textbook. A number of publishers now offer fully interactive packages along with their text, which can be embedded into a learning management platform. These packages may include an online version of the text, video, and visualizations, as well as interactive activities such as quizzes, virtual labs, and simulations. Course designers and teachers may choose to use all or some of the materials available, depending on their alignment with course learning objectives.

Facilitating Acquisition of Vocabulary and Pronunciation of Key Terms

Students of biology must rapidly build a new vocabulary to be able to understand and communicate biological concepts. It is generally understood that acquisition of vocabulary is enhanced when students both hear and read new terms (Krashen, 1989), so there is an argument for providing access to audio and/or video recordings that allow students to hear new terms spoken in context. One simple way to do this is the inclusion of an audio glossary within the online resources for a subject in which terms are linked to an audio file. When the student clicks on a word, an audio file of the correct pronunciation is played. Audio glossaries (in a range of languages) are commonly provided with the online resources for major textbooks. Teachers also model pronunciation, and this can be captured in recorded lectures. Scutter, Stupans, Sawyer, and King (2010) reported that students use recorded lectures explicitly to review both the meaning and the pronunciation of new terms.

Many biological terms are pronounced differently in different regions. For example, English and Australian biologists would emphasize the second syllable in the word *capillaries*, whereas North Americans would emphasize the third. As Australian teachers, we have found that many of the available online resources use North American narrators, and in the past, our students sometimes acquired American pronunciations. The situation is now less common since the use of recorded lectures has increased.

Future Trends

Online learning resources are becoming more readily available, more sophisticated, and more easily integrated into online learning platforms. Course designers will increasingly be able to obtain high-quality materials to use in their online courses without the need to do their own software development. Increasing demands for access to further and higher education, but fewer available resources, are likely to lead to extensive cooperation among institutions in developing course structures and content (Phoenix, 2002). A survey of campus information technology officers in the United States (Campus Computing, 2013) indicated that many American institutions are outsourcing various components of their online programs. Institutions are now commonly purchasing modules for learning content or administration of learning content to "mix and match" into their own institutional packages. In fact, there are a growing number of businesses that develop new content (or reuse existing content) and/or refine, automate, and enforce learning administration processes for incorporation into LMSs (Kerschenbaum & Biehn, 2009).

The development of massive open online courses (MOOCs) is also changing the nature of online education. Bernstein (2013) reported that the funding available for the development of MOOCs has provided some academics with resources for the development of high-quality online tools and described two vastly different approaches. One academic who built his own online environment and created content using a cartoonist and a composer required 100 to 200 hours of production time for each hour of produced content. In contrast, another academic producing content on a lower budget created video lectures, estimating that each minute of video for his course required six minutes of production time. In both cases, the products were used not only by the MOOC but also in the academics' face-to-face and blended learning classes. The MOOC experiment is as yet incomplete, with serious concerns about their effectiveness for instruction highlighted in the U.S. campus information technology officers report (Campus Computing, 2013).

Teachers and students are already using the Internet for communication via e-mail, newsgroups, and discussion lists. The roles of Internet-based conferencing (Peat & Fernandez, 2000), apps, and social media (Gosper, Malfroy, & McKenzie, 2013) are likely to increase. Campus Computing (2013) also noted the increasing uptake of mobile apps by tertiary institutions in the United States. It is likely that students will increasingly expect to be able to access and interact with learning materials via smartphones and tablets rather than via laptop computers. However, Gosper and colleagues (2013) warned that keeping up with the pace of technological change and the accompanying changes in social, work, and study behaviors can be costly and argued that the introduction of new communication technologies should be balanced against the potential benefits for students.

Online environments are well suited to facilitate student participation in real-world science collaborations, ranging from those in which students can make real-time observations to inform their studies to those in which students make meaningful contributions to data collection and analyses. Peat and Fernandez (2000) noted the participation of Australian primary and secondary biology students in programs such as Global Learning and Observations to Benefit the Environment (GLOBE), a worldwide science and education program that allows students to participate in international group work that is focused on specific issues (www.globe.gov).

Conclusion

Biology deals with issues of scale, dimension, and connectivity—and teachers of biology must help their students to navigate and understand these aspects of the discipline. The online environment can be a useful space in which to explore these concepts, because it provides opportunities to depart from linear and two-dimensional explanations and representations of biological concepts. Animations and 3D models can provide powerful insights for students of the discipline; however, teachers should be vigilant in regard to the development of misunderstandings and be ready to facilitate correct interpretations of tools used to access these complex concepts.

Getting a biology course online can seem daunting. We recommend an incremental approach, beginning with a basic set of teaching and learning tools to provide content suited to the classes and the objectives of the course. The extent to which hands-on practical activities are included will vary depending on the nature and purpose of the course. There are several ways in which to incorporate such activities if they are considered appropriate.

The basic online biology course can be augmented and developed over time, as the course designer gains confidence and discovers useful and relevant materials. There is scope to tailor the online biology course so that it is highly student centered, with loops and links to suit students who struggle with particular aspects of the course, and other loops and links to extend those who move through the basic content easily. Links may take students outside the LMS to relevant sites, apps, and social media tools, many of which are available to course designers at no cost, but care should be taken to ensure that such additions augment, rather than distract from, the broader aims of the course.

The online course is never completed, and the course designer has unlimited opportunities to refine the style, presentation, and content of the course. Regular monitoring of the materials and tools provided, together with feedback from students, can help the online course to continually evolve in the direction most suited to the objectives of the course and the needs of the students.

References

Allen, I. E., & Seaman, J. (2013). *Changing course: Ten years of tracking online education in the United States.* Oakland, CA: Babson Survey Research Group and Quahog Research Group.

Benson, V., & Morgan, S. (2013). Student experience and ubiquitous learning in higher education: Impact of wireless and cloud applications. *Creative Education, 4*(8A), 1–5.

Bernstein, R. (2013). Education evolving: Teaching biology online. *Cell, 155*(7), 1443–1445.

Bromham, L., & Oprandi, P. (2006). Evolution online: Using a virtual learning environment to develop active learning in undergraduates. *Journal of Biological Education, 41*(1), 21–25.

Campus Computing. (2013, October). Campus IT officers affirm the instructional integration of IT as their top priority, offer mixed reviews on IT effectiveness and outsourcing for online education. *The Campus Computing Project.* Retrieved from www.campuscomputing.net/sites/www.campuscomputing.net/files/CampusComputing2013_1.pdf

Elder, L. (2009, October 21). Why you shouldn't use PowerPoints in (most) online courses [Northern Arizona University's E-Learning Center web log post]. Retrieved from nauelearning.wordpress.com/2009/10/21/nopptonline/

Franklin, S., Peat, M., & Lewis, A. (2002). Traditional versus computer-based dissections in enhancing learning in a tertiary setting: A student perspective. *Journal of Biological Education, 36*(3), 124–129.

Gedik, N., Kiraz, E., & Yasar Ozden, M. (2013). Design of a blended learning environment: Considerations and implementation issues. *Australasian Journal of Educational Technology, 29*(1), 1–19.

Gosper, M., Malfroy, J., & McKenzie, J. (2013). Students' experiences and expectations of technologies: An Australian study designed to inform planning and development decisions. *Australasian Journal of Educational Technology, 29*(2), 268–282.

Griffard, P. B. (2013). Deconstructing and decoding complex process diagrams in university biology. In D. F. Treagust & C.-Y. Tsui (Eds.), *Multiple representations in biological education: Models and modeling in science education* (Vol. 7, pp. 165–183). Dordrecht, the Netherlands: Springer.

Harrison, N. (2013). Using the interactive whiteboard to scaffold a metalanguage: Teaching higher order thinking skills in preservice teacher education. *Australasian Journal of Educational Technology, 29*(1), 54–65.

Hart, L. A., Wood, M. W., Wiley, D., Hamann, B., Molinaro, M., Meyers, S., . . . Storm, W. A. (2008). BioSafaris: A rationale for educational software on human biology and health in precollege as an alternative to dissection. In *Proceedings of the 6th World Congress on Alternatives and Animal Use in the Life Sciences*, special issue of *Alternatives to Animal Testing and Experimentation* (Vol. 14, pp. 243–248). Tokyo, Japan: Japanese Society for Alternatives to Animal Experiments.

Huang, C., & Huang, M. (2012). *The scale of the universe.* Retrieved from htwins.net/scale2

Kerschenbaum, S., & Biehn, B. T. W. (2009). *LMS selection: Best practices* (White Paper). Indinapolis, IN: Adayana. Retrieved from www.trainingindustry.com/media/2068137/lmsselection_full.pdf

Khan, R. L. (2012–2013). A taxonomy for choosing, evaluating and integrating in-the-cloud resources in a university environment. *Journal of Educational Technology Systems, 41*(2), 171–181.

Kinzie, M. B., Strauss, R., & Foss, J. (1993). The effects of an interactive dissection simulation on the performance and achievement of high school biology students. *Journal of Research in Science Teaching, 30*(8), 989–1000.

Krashen, S. (1989). We acquire vocabulary and spelling by reading: Additional evidence for the input hypothesis. *The Modern Language Journal, 73*(4), 440–464.

MacQueen, H., & Thomas, J. (2009). Teaching biology at a distance: Pleasures, pitfalls, and possibilities. *American Journal of Distance Education, 23*(3), 139–150.

Mayr, E. (2004). *What makes biology unique? Considerations on the autonomy of a scientific discipline.* Cambridge, UK: Cambridge University Press.

Meyer, K. A. (2014). An analysis of the cost and cost-effectiveness of faculty development for online teaching. *Journal of Asynchronous Learning Networks, 18*(1).

Mosse, J., & Wright, W. (1999, April 9). Mum can't come to the phone right now: She's in the laundry doing a rat dissection. In *Proceedings of the UniServe Science Flexible Learning Tools Workshop* (pp. 34–36). Sydney, Australia: UniServe Science.

O'Brien, L. (2012, April 4). Six ways to use social media in education [Duke University Center for Instructional Technology web log post]. Retrieved from cit.duke.edu/blog/2012/04/six-ways-to-use-social-media-in-education/

Offner, S. (1993). The importance of dissection in biology teaching. *The American Biology Teacher, 55*(3), 147–149.

Panther, B. C., Wright, W., & Mosse, J. A. (2012). Providing a flexible learning environment: Are on-line lectures the answer? *International Journal of Innovation in Science and Mathematics Education, 20*(1), 71–82.

Peat, M., & Fernandez, A. (2000). The role of information technology in biology education: An Australian perspective. *Journal of Biological Education, 34*(2), 69–73.

Phoenix, D. A. (2002). Education partnerships: The way of the future? *Journal of Biological Education, 36*(3), 108–109.

Revkin, A. C. (2011, May 5). On birds, Twitter and teaching [The *New York Times* opinion pages web log post]. Retrieved from dotearth.blogs.nytimes.com/2011/05/05/on-birds-twitter-and-teaching/?_php=true&_type=blogs&_php=true&_type=blogs&_r=1

Russo, C. (2013, September 9). Guest post: Creating scientists in 140 characters [The Public Library of Science web log post]. Retrieved from blogs.plos.org/scied/2013/09/09/guest-post-creating-scientists-140-characters/

Sample, M. (2010, August 16). A framework for teaching with Twitter [*The Chronicle of Higher Education* web log post]. Retrieved from chronicle.com/blogs/profhacker/a-framework-for-teaching-with-twitter/26223

Scutter, S., Stupans, I., Sawyer, T., & King, S. (2010). How do students use podcasts to support learning? *Australasian Journal of Educational Technology, 26*(2), 180–191.

Sukhontapatipak, C., & Srikosamatara, S. (2012). The role of field exercises in ecological learning and values education: Action research on the use of campus wetlands. *Journal of Biological Education, 46*(1), 36–44.

Tang, T. L.-P., & Austin, M. J. (2009). Students' perceptions of teaching technologies, application of technologies, and academic performance. *Computers and Education, 53*(4), 1241–1255.

Tanner, K. D. (2011). Reconsidering "what works." *CBE Life Science Education, 10*(4), 329–333.

Treagust, D. F., & Tsui, C.-Y. (2013). Conclusion: Contributions of multiple representations to biological education. In D. F. Treagust & C.-Y. Tsui (Eds.), *Multiple representations in biological education: Models and modeling in science education* (Vol. 7, pp. 349–367). Dordrecht, the Netherlands: Springer.

Tsui, C.-Y., & Treagust, D. F. (2013). Introduction to multiple representations: Their importance in biology and biological education. In D. F. Treagust & C.-Y. Tsui (Eds.), *Multiple representations in biological education: Models and modeling in science education* (Vol. 7, pp. 3–18). Dordrecht, the Netherlands: Springer.

Venema, S., & Lodge, J. M. (2013). Capturing dynamic presentation: Using technology to enhance the chalk and the talk. *Australasian Journal of Educational Technology, 29*(1), 20–31.

2

TEACHING UNDERGRADUATE CHEMISTRY BY DISTANCE AND ONLINE

Lessons From the Front Line

Peter Lye and Erica Smith
University of New England

Abstract

At the University of New England, in regional Australia, it is possible to complete a science-based bachelor's degree by distance. We first began teaching chemistry by distance in 1992 and over the past 20 years have gained immeasurable experience in delivering distance courses, working with distance students, and covering laboratory content. In this chapter, we outline some of the key issues that must be considered and addressed before the successful delivery of an online or distance chemistry program can be considered. These are the combined thoughts and experiences of chemistry practitioners at the front line of delivering distance tertiary chemistry education.

By its very nature, teaching is about change. Typically change comes about as a result of feedback from colleagues and students and personal reflection by the teachers. However, change in the classroom can also be a reflection of larger technological and societal changes. Although all of these inputs are important, the last two are of particular relevance to online teaching.

We should first define the terms *distance* and *online education* or *teaching. Distance education* is when a student completes a course or entire program remote to the teacher or institution. *Online education* is when a student completes part or the entirety of a course or program of study remote to the institution with his or her only institutional contact being via electronic communication. Typically courses and programs are a mix of the two; for example, an off-campus student may need to visit the institution or an on-campus student may need to complete an assessment online. This mix is referred to as a *blended* or *hybrid* program. The differentiation between and the review of these modes is not the aim of this chapter; however, we direct the reader to recent books in this area (Anderson, 2008; Kennepohl & Shaw, 2010; Moore & Kearsley, 2012). We will use the term *distance* in a holistic sense to refer to students who are studying off campus and complete some assessments online.

Although we have drawn on experiences from elsewhere, this chapter focuses on the history of, or change in, the blended chemistry distance educational experience offered at the University of New England (UNE) in regional New South Wales, Australia. UNE offers complete science-based bachelor's degrees by distance. This means that all courses, or units, that contribute to a university degree can be completed through on-campus or off-campus (distance) modes. We aim also to give practical advice in regard to getting online and strategies for covering laboratory work with distance students from academics who have many years of experience in delivering distance courses and working with distance students.

Any study of science is inevitably predicated by a thorough grounding in the disciplines of chemistry, physics, and mathematics. Of these, chemistry is universally denoted as the "central science" or the "enabling science" (National Research Council, 2007, p. 3). On the other hand, the required rigor of the subject has often proved a learning hurdle in the pathway of aspiring scientists. Our key objectives, as teachers of chemistry at UNE, have been to make chemistry as accessible as possible and to enthuse and instill in our students a passion for lifelong learning. Through offering a full suite of chemistry courses, from bridging and foundation courses, introductory to advanced courses, at all undergraduate levels and in both on-campus and distance modes, we have made it possible to obtain a full science degree, with a major in chemistry, entirely through distance education study. UNE was one of the first universities in Australia to offer such a program of study. The curricula and resources that have been developed through an integrated team approach continue to enhance and influence teaching and learning opportunities for distance education students of science where chemistry is the major focus, either through a full chemistry major or through specific courses that enhance and service other branches of fundamental and applied sciences.

When we consider change, it is important to recognize the nature of the change or innovation being proposed. Raine (2002) wrote

> My experience is that resistance to change occurs where it creates tension in the integration, often where innovation threatens to fracture the sense of community. Where innovation creates win-win situations, or at least offers the prospect of such, I have not experienced open antipathy to it. (p. 87)

This reinforces the idea of a community of inquiry put forward by Garrison, Anderson, and Archer (1999, 2010) where, as educators, we need to view the educational experience around a framework that includes social, cognitive, and teaching inputs that involve both the students and the teaching staff. The idea of a community of inquiry is pursued further in the section "Handling the Laboratory Component," later in this chapter.

Although some science-based courses were available at UNE in the distance education mode, prior to 1992 the Department of Chemistry had not been involved in distance teaching. In 1992, the UNE Department of Chemistry introduced full, first-year undergraduate, rigorously science-based chemistry courses in distance mode. These courses were the forerunners of a whole suite of chemistry courses that exist today at higher levels.

In 2014, we had approximately 710 distance education students in undergraduate chemistry courses at UNE: 560 at first-year level, 125 at second-year level, and 25 at third-year level. Note that most undergraduate science degrees in Australia are three years in duration. An optional fourth year of research and higher level courses enables graduation with honors. We are also teaching more than 800 on-campus students over equivalent year levels. Our distance education students come from every state and territory in Australia. Some students come from even further, as Australian citizens working or living internationally. Many distance students undertake their chemistry study while balancing part- or full-time employment and demanding family situations. For almost all distance education students, the challenges are greater than those experienced by on-campus students, particularly in understanding and mastering chemical concepts in isolation.

Recognizing that student-focused learning is essential for such a conceptually and factually based discipline as chemistry, we focus on engaging our students through activity-centered curricula that builds on their previous knowledge, maintains their interest, assists in their knowledge retention, and instills confidence in their understanding. In essence, we can equip students best for their careers not by teaching them about the methods of chemistry but by giving them a framework of knowledge onto which they can build in the future. As the available technology has developed, we have continued to incorporate the latest advances into our distance education and on-campus courses. Over the years these have included in-house-produced videos of laboratory techniques; audiotapes including conversational and question-and-answer-style discussions specifically designed for noninteractive listening; excerpts from commercially available software and video packages; CD-ROM–based materials including interactive learning resources; course notes and interactive software with online testing and feedback based on learning management software; and complete lecture PowerPoint slides with animations, movies, commentaries, and notes embedded in the package. This is in addition to the range of ancillary packages accompanying the set texts for each course, including solutions to exercises, interactive web-based activities, databases, and resources.

Courses such as chemistry that involve a high level of conceptual, visual, and practical content (laboratories) pose particular problems in the distance education mode. Although the use of home experimental kits, online interactive activities, and videotaped experiments has been effective in enabling some of this content to be covered at home (Boschmann, 2003; Dalgarno, Bishop, & Bedgood, 2003; Kennepohl, 1996; Mawn, Carrico, Charuk, Stote, & Lawrence, 2011), there is still, in our view, a substantial requirement for an on-campus component in these courses for distance students. Meeting this requirement to be on campus for one part of the course can be both difficult and costly for students living long distances from the university. However, as will be discussed, distance students and staff consider some on-campus experience to be valuable.

Hands-on laboratory training in real, modern, well-equipped chemical laboratories is achieved by on-campus intensive schools for most courses, where distance students are exposed to an intensive period of laboratory, tutorial, or workshop sessions. For each course, the intensive schools can range from two to five days. However, far from being an impediment and a disincentive to undertaking chemistry by distance education, we insist on making this aspect a focus of each course and a high point of student involvement and participation in an active learning process. The involvement of postgraduate and honors students as laboratory demonstrators is integral and completes the intensive school experience. Invariably over the years we have received primarily encouraging and complimentary feedback from our students for these intensive schools. For example, the following was feedback from a second-year distance student: "I just wanted to thank you both for a great res [*sic*] school. I certainly felt I learned a lot and the others all said the same."

The overwhelmingly positive comments received highlight the real advantages and satisfaction for students in being able to experience chemical principles in action and especially the opportunities of having one-on-one interactions with their fellow students, instructors, and laboratory demonstrators. We believe it is important that the distance students derive more than completing laboratory exercises at the intensive schools and that they gain a university experience (Garratt, 2002). For each intensive school, a complete set of practical experiments based on the existing on-campus course are developed in parallel, with any necessary adaptations carefully incorporated to take into account the intense nature of the intensive schools. Typical student feedback from intensive school experience includes comments like the following: "Lectures and labs were both useful. The labs that involved repeated tests of important ideas helped me understand better" and "I don't think it would be easy to do better."

The Royal Australian Chemical Institute (RACI) is the professional association for chemists in Australia. As part of its charter, the RACI has put in place a system of accreditation of chemistry courses, and graduates of accredited courses are eligible for full membership of the RACI. To ensure that our graduates meet the full accreditation (so that they can be registered as Chartered Chemists in Australia), we have been particularly mindful not only of the need for laboratory training through intensive schools but also of offering a range of units that meet the needs of future employers. Toward this end, courses that span both pure and applied aspects of chemistry are offered and allow our students the opportunity to either upgrade their qualifications or retrain for a future career while they are still in the workforce, ensuring open access without the need for full-time on-campus attendance, which would be beyond their capacities.

Although the concept of open access to higher education training and certified achievement in chemistry is commendable, the reality is often somewhat tempered by the limitations imposed by potential students' lack of prior knowledge or scientific literacy. We have sought to redress this with the introduction of bridging or foundation-level courses in chemistry. In 1997, we initiated the development of a so-called foundation course in chemistry. It was set up to operate entirely in distance education mode and is offered in two out of three trimesters each year. More recently, we have introduced a modified version of this course as a three-week online intensive bridging course. The bridging course caters to students who are unable to count the foundation chemistry course to their degree or for students who just need a refresher course in chemistry.

Chemistry is the central science and as such is integral to the training of scientists in a host of disciplines. Toward this end, the provision of a comprehensive range of chemistry courses in the distance education mode provides accessible career and study path options that may have previously been denied to a large proportion of the student population, namely, those whose choice is distance and flexible study.

The following sections outline some of the key issues that must be considered and addressed before the successful delivery of an online or distance chemistry program can be considered. These are the combined thoughts and experiences of chemistry practitioners at the front line of delivering distance and online tertiary chemistry education.

How to Get Online

In higher education today, the differentiation between distance and online delivery of courses is minimal. If a course is offered online, theoretically anyone can enroll in it. If a course is offered via distance, the likelihood that it is not delivered via some kind of online portal is minimal. To deliver chemistry courses online and via distance, practitioners must utilize some kind of online learning environment.

Learning Management Systems

There is an abundance of educational technology ideas available for online delivery of education courses; however, the one application that seems to have the most prevalence is the *learning management system* (LMS), also known as a *virtual learning environment*. An LMS is a software application that provides infrastructure, framework, and tools to facilitate online learning or training and that is used by educational institutes for teaching blended, online, and distance classes.

An LMS serves as a place to store content in such a way that only enrolled students can access the material; however, an LMS also provides facilities to (a) create and deliver online quizzes and self-tests, (b) automate the grading of assessments and feedback, (c) e-submit assignments to a central location, (d) store and publish grades, (e) conduct remote tutorials, (f) manage learning groups, (g) track the progress of students, (h) promote interactive and collaborative learning through social-media-type interaction, and (i) generate data for analytics.

There are commercial and open-source LMSs available; however, an institution using an open-source (free) version of an LMS will still incur costs in the provision of in-house or contracted support and associated costs including setup fees, hosting costs, hardware administrative costs, and feature upgrade costs. Like all software, things can go wrong, and expertise is required to manage and ensure the smooth running of an LMS. Some commonly used LMSs are Moodle, Sakai, Blackboard, Desire2Learn, and eCollege; however, there are many more available. It is more than likely that your university or college already has an LMS in place.

An LMS provided and supported on an institutional level contains links to each class in which a student is enrolled. Different institutions will have their own set of requirements for each class "site," varying from free rein to design and deliver as the instructor sees fit to being quite prescriptive as to how a site is set out (perhaps to build brand or for ease of student navigation).

For classes that require students to utilize software (e.g., a computational chemistry unit), an online class can be constructed on a server, which acts like a remote desktop. The server can host web pages of content like a traditional LMS but also allows students to access and run any software required for the class.

Course Design

Using a web page or LMS solely as a repository for materials and resources is a realistic option only for chemistry courses taught using blended learning where students also attend regular face-to-face sessions such as lectures, tutorials, problem-solving sessions, and laboratories. The provision of online platforms to discuss concepts, ask questions, and collaboratively problem solve is essential if instructors wish to encourage these types of activities in fostering student engagement and learning for distance and online students.

There are any number and combinations of resources that can be provided and pedagogical theories to inform the class design, and, as with face-to-face or blended instruction, the design and provision of materials is largely dependent on the prescribed learning outcomes of the class, the particular cohort of students, and the individual instructor's pedagogical philosophy and experience. The major factors to consider when designing an online chemistry course are the size of the class, stage of the program, subject (e.g., first-year general chemistry or higher level theoretical chemistry), and level of student preparedness and motivation for taking the class (e.g., compulsory or elective, chemistry or life science majors). Types of materials, resources, and support to consider providing include the following:

- Expectations and responsibilities
  - Welcome "screen capture" video
  - Practice quiz on expectations and responsibilities
  - Diagnostic testing and concept inventories
  - Simple outline of assessment details and key dates
- Content
  - Study timetable and study guide
  - Topic notes and content summaries
  - Recorded lectures (with PowerPoint slide files provided)
  - Homework problems (hard copy and/or online)
  - Links to alternative resources (suggestions are provided at the end of this chapter)
- Online assessments (multiple choice, calculations, and short answer)
- Support
  - Webinar-type "live" tutorials and lectures
  - Discussion boards
  - Chat rooms
  - Frequently asked questions

Expectations and Responsibilities

Learning chemistry in an online environment can present several challenges for students, in particular for those who are in their first year of tertiary study, who may not be computer or Internet savvy, or who have had an absence from formal study (or any combination of these). In light of this, it is advisable to include as a first port of call on the class site a short video with screen captures (e.g., using Camtasia) showing real-time navigation of the online learning environment and pointing out the main features of the site. This will serve not only to welcome students but also to engage and reassure students.

New or returning students may also hold misconceptions or be ignorant of the expectations and responsibilities that higher education study entails. This is another common cause of stress for students enrolling in online courses. Therefore, it is essential that students be provided with a clear and precise description of expectations and responsibilities appropriate for themselves and also for their instructors.

A good way to do this is to first provide content on expectations and responsibilities (a short document or video) and then generate a short online quiz that will have the look and feel of an actual online assessment students may encounter within the class and that contains questions on expectations and responsibilities. The quiz can be assigned a nominal grade percentage to encourage student completion. Another option is to make completion of the quiz mandatory with a grade of 100% but allow students multiple attempts, with the result not counting toward the final assessment. This is simple to administer, as it can be set up automatically in the LMS, and access to content can be conditional upon task completion. This way, students are forced to engage with the material and, it is hoped, begin their study with appropriate expectations. In our experience, this approach to the dissemination of information on appropriate expectations is effective and ultimately reduces stress levels of both students and staff.

Because of the often broad range in prior skills and knowledge of students enrolling in online courses and considering the wide range of backgrounds from which students come to the course (prospective students enrolled in a degree program or in the chemistry course as a stand-alone activity), consider utilizing diagnostic or concept inventory activities.

Voluntary self-diagnostic tests are useful for courses that do not have entrance requirements or do not require students to undergo placement tests and have been shown to be useful in allowing students to independently measure their potential for success (Kennepohl, Guay, & Thomas, 2010). Concept inventories are designed less to assess student preparedness for, and subsequent likelihood of success in, a course but more to demonstrate the extent of student confusion about some basic concepts and consequently direct the instructor and student toward activities to help address any misconceptions. There are a number of concept inventories that have been created in different areas of chemistry (Adams & Wieman, 2011; Luxford & Bretz, 2014; McClary & Bretz, 2012; Treagust, 1988; Wren & Barbera, 2013) and also some evaluation and analysis studies of the effectiveness of these knowledge surveys and confidence inventories (Barbera, 2013; Bell & Volckmann, 2011).

Finally, provision of a simple and clear outline of key dates will help students in cyberspace orient themselves to something concrete at the beginning of the course.

Content

With traditional distance education modalities, supported through online learning managements systems, content is relatively easily presented to students in a number of ways, such as lecture presentations in a PowerPoint format, content summaries, study guides, access to library readings or notes, and Internet-based resources. The level of the course and preferences of the instructor will dictate the design and choice of these types of resources, and the material provided would typically be no different from what would be provided to on-campus students.

The relationship between structure and properties is regarded as an overarching concept in chemistry, and it has been suggested that students have great difficulty in making this connection (Cooper, Underwood, & Hilley, 2012; Kozma & Russell, 1997; Shane & Bodner, 2006). Students undertaking studies in chemistry need to be able to translate the two-dimensional representations of molecules into three dimensions to visualize aspects of the behavior and properties of molecules, such as their stereochemistry, chirality, and reactivity.

One of the differences for content delivery when considering students studying by distance or solely online is the opportunity to attend live lectures and tutorials. Without the use of effective online resources, these students are left with utilization of two-dimensional resources, such as their textbooks and the instructors' PowerPoint presentations. The challenge for chemistry academics is to provide adequate resources to those students who are accessing learning materials via an online environment. Reflections from a recent European Union working group (Eilks & Byers, 2010) summarized the 10 key innovations required in chemistry education in which they referred to "the uniqueness of chemistry" (p. 236) and the notion that academics need to develop visualization approaches that foster student confidence to constantly shift among the three levels of thinking (Johnstone, 1982) required in chemistry (i.e., the macromolecular, submicro, and symbolic representations).

Fortunately, teaching chemistry in an online environment provides an excellent opportunity to utilize well-developed molecular-level animations such as the constructivist VisChem Learning Design (Tasker & Dalton, 2006). The VisChem research and development project has been designed to probe the mental model that a student has of a reaction or substance at the molecular level before showing animations portraying the phenomenon. The work on the VisChem project has indicated that animations and simulations can effectively communicate many key features about the submicro (molecular) level and that these ideas can link the macroscopic (laboratory) level to the symbolic level.

Delivery of "live lectures" to distance and online students is possible via technology that produces videos of live lectures (e.g., Echo360 Personal Capture). This technique is reportedly well received by students (D'Angelo, 2014), although the strategies reported were developed to enhance the engagement and learning of technologically savvy on-campus students. For distance students, we have found the production of special purpose recordings of either entire lectures or key concepts using screen capture technology, such as Camtasia and an interactive tablet, to be highly successful (Smith, Lye, Greatrex, Taylor, & Stupens, 2013). Feedback from distance students indicated that recordings of live lectures were often difficult to follow because of issues such as background noise. Also, we believe that utilizing a tablet for detailed screen capture during a live lecture may reduce the ability of the instructor to effectively engage the live lecture audience.

Consequently, special purpose recordings are produced in the instructor's office. The screen capture technology allows live screen capture of the lecturer's "pointer" and any written work presented, as well as the possibility to utilize a webcam to capture the manipulation of molecular models. In other words, real-time three-dimensional explanations of concepts and working of problems can be provided as they would be to the on-campus students during regular face-to-face lectures and tutorials.

These special purpose recordings provide a framework, in addition to accessing PowerPoint lecture slides and audio recordings, that enables distance students to navigate course learning materials as if they were participating in face-to-face sessions. This approach potentially addresses issues identified in previous research that compared recorded lectures with face-to-face lectures. The work identified that students attending lectures have some advantages inherent in the face-to-face mode, including the opportunity to ask questions; general motivation; and, interestingly, viewing whiteboard diagrams (Panther, Mosse, & Wright, 2011), which could include calculations and worked examples. It has also been reported that online video tutorials have been shown to increase the learning of difficult concepts in chemistry courses (He, Swenson, & Lents, 2012).

The utilization of purpose-made lecture recordings provides a nice segue into the concept of the "flipped" or "inverted" classroom. This technique is useful for incorporating online elements into an on-campus course and is currently a popular strategy to address some of the weaknesses of traditional teaching (Lancaster & Read, 2013). The general idea is to record short lecture "snippets" that students watch online before coming to class, where students will work problems (Arnaud, 2013). This is not to be confused with blended learning where some in-class instruction is replaced with online instruction. In a flipped classroom, the number of in-class hours remains the same (Christiansen, 2014).

The provision of online homework and practice problems that go beyond downloadable documents with lists of questions is an effective engagement tool for on-campus and distance students. However, they have obvious advantages for distance students who cannot attend live tutorials or peer-supported study sessions. Most textbook publishers provide test banks of questions that are compatible with LMSs and are suitable for use in constructing online practice homework and assignments. Commercial Internet-based homework resources that contain a range of activities are also available. Activities can range from traditional question-and-answer test banks to more sophisticated resources, including adaptive and dynamic mastering exercises, cartoon simulations of molecular processes, simulated laboratory experiments, assignments, grade books, and tutorials.

The benefits of online homework in first-year general chemistry courses are well established and have been thoroughly reviewed (Richards-Babb, Drelick, Henry, & Robertson-Honecker, 2011). Reviews of the commercially available online chemistry learning resources have also been published (Evans, 2009; Harris, 2009; Hendrickson, 2009; Miller, 2009; Rowley, 2009; Shepherd, 2009; Zhao, 2009). Studies in undergraduate organic chemistry have shown online homework might be effective for improving student learning, experiences, and success in such courses but that even for the most motivated students some degree of external influence (e.g., extra credit) may be necessary to improve the likelihood of benefit (Parker & Loudon, 2013). Studies have also indicated that interactions and feedback an individual receives may play a crucial role in the advancement of student knowledge (Malik, Martinez, Romero, Schubel, & Janowicz, 2014).

The automation of online homework has the potential to be particularly valuable in large-enrollment introductory and first-year courses in which the student need for additional help places a high demand on instructors.

Online Assessments

An LMS offers a wide variety of features to support online assessment of students. Instructors may offer formative and summative assessment tasks, and there are also numerous ways to track the participation, engagement, and success of students in the course assessment tasks.

Instructors can create assignment e-submission portals where students can submit documents electronically. The documents can then be downloaded for marking either in hard copy or by using electronic marking technology. There are also facilities to generate and manage peer review assignments, as well as functionalities for recording and presenting grades and detecting of plagiarism.

Online tests or quizzes can also be used to assess the learning occurring in the course, and they have some distinct advantages. Using either published question banks (e.g., from the textbook publisher) or questions generated by the instructor, online tests can be designed so that each student receives a unique set of questions that can then be automatically marked with question-specific feedback provided.

Many question types are supported by LMS quiz facilities, including (but by no means limited to) true–false, short answer, numerical, calculated formula (where numbers in the question change for each student), essay, fill in the blanks, and matching. As chemistry instructors, we have found one disadvantage in our LMS, which is that for the question categories that can be automatically marked, the system does not support subscripting or superscripting of numbers or symbols in the space where students type their answers. It is possible for the short-answer-type questions; however, these require manual marking.

The main concern for online assessment using an LMS is the temptation for students to utilize the Internet or alternative sources for help in answering questions. Dealing with this issue will depend on the goal of the individual instructor for each assessment task. For example, for formative assessment tasks, the instructor may desire that students utilize resources for help in answering questions, thereby assisting students in achieving their learning outcomes. However, for summative assessment, the issue can become complicated.

For obvious reasons, assessing student outcomes via proctored examinations is not straightforward for solely online and distance education students who are not in the locale of the campus. Many institutions have systems in place for students to take exams in almost any location around the world; however, as this is administratively time-consuming and expensive, there is an increasing use of remote proctoring of examinations in many higher education institutions around the world, in particular in the United States. There are several commercially available technologies (Eduventures, 2013), and some universities have developed their own technology (Hillier, Fluck, & Emerson, 2014). Technologies available include video monitoring of students (recorded or live streaming) and also the ability to monitor whether the Internet has been accessed during an examination.

Web-based video was recently reported as being utilized as an assessment tool for student performance in organic chemistry (Tierney, Bodek, Fredricks, Dudkin, & Kistler, 2014). Students made video responses to specific questions as part of the assessment process and were required to utilize a molecular modeling kit. The method of assessment allowed the instructor to see a student's higher order thinking, and the authors concluded that it appeared to be a viable additional tool for grading student performance.

The Internet opens up many possibilities for online learning opportunities. Recent innovations include a game-based approach to a physical chemistry course (Daubenfeld & Zenker, 2015), multiplayer games, and a gaming program to resolve protein structures that have eluded researchers (Franco, 2012). The latter gaming program can be utilized as a problem-based learning assignment for the understanding of protein folding, interactions, and structure and allows student contributions to significant research. The ability to work on real research problems significantly increased student interest in the assignment.

Support

It is tempting to think that online provision of chemistry courses will open opportunities for institutions of higher education to enroll a large quantity of students and provide instruction with minimum effort. In higher level chemistry classes, which generally have prerequisite entry conditions, once the initial time investment in setting up the course is completed, this may be true to some extent. However, for large general chemistry classes where there is limited or no control of the background knowledge and skills of enrolling students, the time investment required by the instructor in engaging and dealing with student queries and issues can be substantial.

One of the most challenging aspects of teaching a chemistry class online is a direct result of the microscopic, abstract, and three-dimensional nature of the material being taught. Teaching chemistry "live" gives instructors the opportunity to work through sample problems, use models, and conduct demonstrations, as well as show simulations of molecular processes and engage students in discussions and peer-assisted learning activities. As previously discussed, this can be effectively done online using lecture capture technology with webcams, tablets, embedded video, and simulations. However, it cannot replace the need for interaction between the instructor and the student (whether remotely or in person) in probing and addressing confusion and misconceptions.

It is important to remember that teaching and learning is not just about provision of content. It is well documented in the literature that frequent student–instructor contact is the most important factor in student motivation and involvement (Chickering & Gamson, 1987). This is particularly advantageous in an online or distance learning environment where the Internet can be utilized to develop and improve the communication and interaction not only between the instructor and the student but also among the students themselves to build a sense of community within the course. It is therefore essential that the design of the learning support mechanisms within an online or distance chemistry course be carefully considered.

One method is to utilize synchronous learning activities such as live and interactive online tutorials, lectures, or chats (often called *webinars*) using a tablet and video-conferencing software (e.g., Adobe Connect or Microsoft Lync). However, there are several factors and limitations that need to be considered. A class with high enrollments is difficult to run via video-conferencing, with the maximum number for an effective and interactive learning experience being about 20 students. Even in the in-person environment, interactive learning is easier to achieve in a small classroom versus the large lecture theater. There are also limitations that are technology dependent. For example, communication in webinars is usually very structured, and though the instructor may answer questions, the participants are typically not able to talk to one another. Realistically only one participant can have his or her microphone active at a time, and students are usually required to type their questions and comments into a chat box.

Internet and personal computer issues with microphones and speakers cause all sorts of frustrations, and the synergy that can be found within a group of people who are interacting "in person" is usually lost over the phone or online. Other issues with live online tutorials or webinars are that two of the main cohorts of online students are those who are utilizing this method of study that fits in with work and personal commitments and those who are anxious about learning "in public." Consequently, finding a time that suits (Seery, 2012) or even the courage to attend (Lye, Smith, Rosser, & Dillon, 2016) is problematic, and hence attendance can be low. However, successful synchronous learning in organic chemistry using Doceri software for iPad, which allows greater flexibility with features like drawing on PowerPoint slides, was recently reported (Silverberg, Tierney, & Bodek, 2014).

The other main vehicle for student learning support in an online or distance chemistry course is asynchronous learning activities such as discussion forums and e-mail communication, which can be facilitated through an LMS or via web-based social media. These are usually set up and monitored by the instructor, and there is a wealth of information available on building these, from content to online communities (Watwood, Nugent, & Deihl, 2009) and comparisons of synchronous and asynchronous online learning (Hrastinski, 2008). Undoubtedly, asynchronous learning communities provide a great opportunity for online and distance learning of chemistry.

Still, the increase in communication and changes in communication technology and accessibility means that students can ask a question and often expect to receive an answer at almost any time of any day (D'Angelo, 2014). The appropriateness of an expectation of an immediate response is highly debatable, and the timing or availability of instructor interaction within learning communities is something that individual instructors must decide on and make clear to students.

Factors to consider in setting out the expectations, responsibilities, and desired learning outcomes for students in utilizing discussion forums are the level of the course, the background and number of students, and the amount of time the instructor can commit to monitoring discussions and answering questions. Salmon's five-step model for e-moderating (Salmon, 2000, 2011) is a good place to start when considering the inclusion of discussion forums to ensure student engagement in discussions is productive and constructive for learning and teaching (Seery, 2012).

It is useful to note that students may initiate their own discussion forum space (e.g., making their own Facebook group). If an instructor chooses not to play a role in such a group (probably because he or she has already provided a discussion forum), these discussion forums provide possible avenues where misconceptions may flourish. However, the risk of misconceptions being floated is no different than for on-campus students undertaking private group study. If students are aware that instructors will not monitor the forum, then a decision on the balancing act between the desire to discuss concepts free of the instructor's watchful eye and the quality of the discussion is down to the individual student. In our experience, if students feel supported and encouraged to voice their queries, and the quality of instruction is high, then students will generally not feel the need to form their own group.

Handling the Laboratory Component

Although course content is an important factor in any course design process, too often the critical questions are overlooked; that is, what do we want our students to learn, and how do they learn? Furthermore, we don't want students just to memorize content so they regurgitate it at exam time; we want the students to be able to use and apply the knowledge that they have acquired. Garratt (2002) put this beautifully when he stated, "Our graduates need to know their subject so that they can explain, exploit and extend it; universities need to provide a triple X experience" (p. 40). Expressing the same view, de Bono (1968) stated, "It must be more important to be skilled in thinking than to be stuffed with facts" (p. 7). It has been suggested that, to their disadvantage, the sciences have failed to take these ideas seriously. Science courses are often taught in a manner that gives students the impression that there is a right answer for everything, which results in the public having misconceptions about what science can and cannot do (Finster, 1989). This is where the importance of laboratory work cannot be underestimated.

Offering a laboratory component for even on-campus science courses is a moot point for some (Garratt, 2002; Hawkes, 2004). However, this is not the place to argue the pros and cons of laboratory work to a science graduate, in particular for a chemistry graduate. We take the view that laboratory work is critical to student learning at all stages in students' chemistry major or course. However, as will be pointed out in this section, it is perhaps even more important for distance students.

As most chemistry courses offered at UNE require students to complete a laboratory component, we require distance students to complete their experiments either remotely or by attending an intensive school. Intensive schools involve distance students coming onto campus for between two and five days to complete primarily the laboratory component of a unit. However, students derive much more from attending an intensive school than simply completing laboratory-based experiments. They experience face-to-face interaction with teaching staff and fellow distance students. This interaction is very important because the online environment within an LMS-organized course can be socially isolating and impersonal for many distance students.

Therefore, a social presence, for both the students and the instructor within a course, is important when teaching online. The formation of a "community of inquiry," or learning community, contains three critical elements: cognitive presence, social presence, and teaching presence. This has been well recognized as an integral part of engaging online students with their subject (Garrison et al., 1999, 2010; Mathieson & Leafman, 2014). The challenge is, how can we foster the social presence and/or interaction? Intensive schools provide a vehicle to enhance the social presence of both the student and the instructor beyond LMS forums.

Some institutions prefer laboratory kits, which are sent to a student's home, or utilize virtual or remote labs (Baran, Currie, & Kennepohl, 2004; Kennepohl, 1996; Mawn et al., 2011). Although these approaches may be adequate for refresher or elementary chemistry courses, we don't see them as appropriate for mainstream chemistry courses. We have introduced remote laboratories in a second-year physical chemistry course; however, we do believe students overwhelmingly benefit from the social interaction provided through an intensive school.

A blended approach can work for both on-campus and distance students. This could involve the completion of preliminary laboratory (prelab) questions online. This requires students to revise or work ahead to cover the material relevant for the experiment to be completed (Chittleborough, Mocerino, & Treagust, 2007; Gregory & Di Trapani, 2012). This approach also allows students to practice and, we hope, build confidence with mathematical operations and/or chemistry concepts that will be required to complete the laboratory exercise (Schmid & Yeung, 2005). Many distance students have very low opinions of their own abilities in terms of basic math and chemistry. Thus, completing prelab questions before arriving at the lab or intensive school takes away some of the mystery and requires the students to engage with the course. It also encourages students to post questions on forums where other students can help, which can promote peer tutoring.

We have made prelab questions a key component of the laboratory experience for both first-year courses and require that they be completed before students start an experiment. Students are able to attempt the questions multiple times until all sections are answered correctly. Therefore, the emphasis is on learning, not on achieving the highest mark possible. It should be noted that we require on-campus and distance students to complete prelab questions online. Questions covering laboratory safety and assessing risk can be included in the prelabs. This broadens the learning outcomes that can be covered for distance students at the intensive school.

The inclusion of online prelabs in chemistry courses at second and third year varies. However, in the senior laboratory classes, all students must complete a risk assessment for the experiment they are to complete before entering the laboratory. Again this is required of both on-campus and distance students. The completion of a risk assessment, prior to arriving at an intensive school, is made possible through online access to chemical material safety data sheets (MSDSs). This exercise serves a dual purpose. It requires the students to carefully read through each of the experiments they will complete (before arriving in the laboratory) so they can identify and assess any risks involved and determine the correct disposal of chemical wastes. In the process of prereading the laboratory notes, students may need to refer to course notes and/or the textbook to clarify terms or concepts covered. Therefore, the process of completing a risk assessment engages the students with the content being covered in the course. When students arrive at the laboratory (on campus or distance), their risk assessments are returned in the laboratory with comments appended, and further discussion between the demonstrator and the students is possible.

An alternative to requiring students to attend an intensive school is to offer the ability for students to complete experiments remotely. The term *remote labs* can mean different things. It could be that students acquire data in the lab and process the data remotely, or, as is done at UNE, students control equipment remotely to acquire data and ultimately complete experiments (Baran et al., 2004; Wallace, Miron, Murphy, & Brown, 2013). This latter approach has been used in engineering courses for a number of years, as the equipment and the experiments are suited to automation (see links to Labshare and Weblabs at the end of the "Online Chemistry Resources" section at the end of this chapter). Therefore, the experiments that have been targeted at UNE have been second-year physical chemistry experiments that lend themselves to automation. These experiments are completed remotely by both on-campus and distance students, with the students able to repeat the experiments as many times as they like. Although not all students take advantage of the possibility of repetition, those who do have found that it enhances the learning experience.

Intensive schools, by definition, are intense for students and staff alike. An issue that should be seriously considered when planning and running an intensive school is student burnout. This can result from having a high cognitive load or simply trying to fit too much into too short a time period. There are certain things that can be done to relieve the stress and make the experience more rewarding for both students and staff—and the key to this is preparation. This can be achieved, in part, by students completing preliminary laboratory questions in first year or risk assessments in higher level courses before attending the intensive school. Having students read through the laboratory manual can help to reduce some of the anxiety students experience while attending the intensive school. At the first-year level, we have prepared videos showing the physical laboratory environment and running through the use of common equipment and procedures that students will be required to use and perform at the intensive school. This approach has been reported to benefit students through familiarizing them with the laboratory (Dalgarno et al., 2003). The skill and assistance of the laboratory demonstrators is also very important. Typically, students are organized into groups based on their prior knowledge of chemistry. We have found that this removes issues that can develop between laboratory partners and also helps the demonstrator set the level of assistance and terminology used. All of these strategies can help reduce student anxiety.

Even with the strategies discussed, intensive schools can be very intimidating for students, especially for those who dislike large groups. Intensive schools can range from approximately 200 students at first year to 10 students at third year. The distance cohort is made up of a range of personality types; however, as may be expected, more introverted personality types gravitate toward distance study. This student cohort can find intensive schools particularly challenging. However, from our experience, following the strategies outlined previously can help to alleviate most of the anxiety experienced by distance students.

Feedback and comments received from students suggest that being able to talk with other students, face-to-face, actually relieves anxiety as they realize their fellow students are finding the content challenging as well and/or they realize that they understand more than they thought they did. Some also find that having something explained one-on-one "flicks the switch" or that having a problem worked through in front of them brings the thought processes together and adds understanding. Yes, it can be expensive for students; yes, it can cut into annual leave; and yes, it can cut into family time. However, the majority of students understand the importance of the entire intensive school experience beyond simply completing experiments. Some students actually value the time away from work and/or family that they can devote to their studies, whereas others bring their families along.

Future Trends

The future of online and distance learning will be largely dependent on the evolution of technology and the utilization of this technology as a vehicle to implement principles of effective teaching (Chickering & Gamson, 1987). The education technology analysis website Edutechnica (see edutechnica.com/2014/01/07/a-model-for-lms-evolution) recently predicted that the next generation of LMS technologies will leverage network effects, have advanced analytics capabilities, provide a seamless user experience across content and devices, and support the trend of empowering choices relating to content and tools to the user level in a "bring your own learning tools" or "create your own learning experience" type of way.

Edutechnica also predicts that the next generation of LMSs will be characterized by (a) adaptive paths and content that support remediation and reinforcement, as well as exploration of interests; (b) predictive analytics that reactively support instructors; (c) content subscription and syndication capabilities; (d) mobile capabilities that seamlessly move across content delivered from multiple places, learning tools from different providers, and navigation across multiple devices; (e) integrated store-like content and learning tools; (f) the ability to support personal learning networks, lifelong social capabilities, and ongoing communities of practice; and (g) off-line, device-specific capabilities such as syncing content to tablets.

It is also clear that with evolving technology, the growth of remote laboratories will increase and thus increase the opportunity for distance students to complete even more of the laboratory component of science-based courses from the comfort of their own home. However, we must not forget or ignore the importance of the social presence in the learning experience.

Conclusion

We have presented one institution's experience with delivering a comprehensive chemistry major online and by distance. Others' experiences have been compared and contrasted with our own methods and experiences. However, the reality is that each institution and each course will have unique requirements and idiosyncrasies that will require modified or new approaches to course delivery. As we stated at the very beginning of this chapter, teaching is all about change, and when linked with technology, change will be constant if not inevitable. Although we may like stability, there is always the next version of an LMS or a completely different paradigm to consider. So we will leave you by saying that teaching chemistry online can be very rewarding and sometimes frustrating—however, it is never boring.

Online Chemistry Resources

ChemCollective (www.chemcollective.org): Collection of virtual labs, scenario-based learning activities, tutorials, and concept tests organized by a group of faculty and staff at Carnegie Mellon who are interested in using, assessing, and creating engaging online activities for chemistry education.

Chemical Education Digital Library (www.chemeddl.org): Digital resources, tools, and online services for teaching and learning chemistry.

JCE Web Software Collection (www.jce.divched.org/jce-products): Suite of subscription online tools for *Journal of Chemical Education* Xchange subscribers.

Labshare (www.labshare.edu.au): Labshare is a consortium of Australian universities promoting the sharing of remotely accessed science and engineering laboratories.

Multimedia Educational Resource for Learning and Online Teaching (chemistry.merlot.org): MERLOT, a program of the California State University System, is a free and open peer-reviewed collection of online teaching and learning materials.

National Science Foundation (www.nsf.gov/news/special_reports/chemistrynow): Videos on the science of everyday things, developed by the NSF for the International Year of Chemistry 2011.

Royal Society of Chemistry (www.rsc.org/learn-chemistry): Simulations.

The Concord Consortium (mw.concord.org/modeler/showcase/chemistry.html): Simulations of molecular behavior.

UC Davis ChemWiki (chemwiki.ucdavis.edu): Free dynamic chemistry e-textbook.

University of Colorado Interactive Simulations (phet.colorado.edu): Interactive simulations for teaching chemistry.

VisChem (www.vischem.com.au): Research and development project to study the effectiveness of molecular-level visualization, produce animations of chemical structures and processes at this level, and develop effective learning designs for a deep understanding of chemistry.

Weblabs (como.cheng.cam.ac.uk/index.php?Page=Research&Section=Weblabs): Weblabs is a University of Cambridge group producing remotely accessible laboratories.

References

Adams, W. K., & Wieman, C. E. (2011). Development and validation of instruments to measure learning of expert-like thinking. *International Journal of Science Education, 33*(9), 1289–1312.

Anderson, T. (Ed.). (2008). *Theory and practice of online learning* (2nd ed.). Edmonton, Canada: AU Press.

Arnaud, C. H. (2013). Flipping chemistry classrooms. *Chemical and Engineering News, 91*(12), 41–43.

Baran, J., Currie, R., & Kennepohl, D. (2004). Remote instrumentation for the teaching laboratory. *Journal of Chemical Education, 81*(12), 1814–1816.

Barbera, J. (2013). A psychometric analysis of the chemical concepts inventory. *Journal of Chemical Education, 90*(5), 546–553.

Bell, P., & Volckmann, D. (2011). Knowledge surveys in general chemistry: Confidence, overconfidence, and performance. *Journal of Chemical Education, 88*(11), 1469–1476.

Boschmann, E. (2003). Teaching chemistry via distance education. *Journal of Chemical Education, 80*(6), 704–708.

Chickering, A. W., & Gamson, Z. F. (1987). Seven principles for good practice in undergraduate education. *AAHE Bulletin, 39*(7), 2–6.

Chittleborough, G. D., Mocerino, M., & Treagust, D. F. (2007). Achieving greater feedback and flexibility using online pre-laboratory exercises with non-major chemistry students. *Journal of Chemical Education, 84*(5), 884–888.

Christiansen, M. A. (2014). Inverted teaching: Applying a new pedagogy to a university organic chemistry class. *Journal of Chemical Education, 91*(11), 1845–1850.

Cooper, M. M., Underwood, S. M., & Hilley, C. Z. (2012). Development and validation of the implicit information from Lewis structures instrument (IILSI): Do students connect structures with properties? *Chemistry Education and Practice, 13*(3), 195–200.

Dalgarno, B., Bishop, A. G., & Bedgood, D. R., Jr. (2003). The potential of virtual laboratories for distance education science teaching: Reflections from the development and evaluation of a virtual chemistry laboratory. In K. Placing (Ed.), *Proceedings of Improving Learning Outcomes Through Flexible Science Teaching Symposium*, October 3, 2003, the University of Sydney (pp. 90–95). Sydney, Australia: Uniserve Science.

D'Angelo, J. G. (2014). Use of screen capture to produce media for organic chemistry. *Journal of Chemical Education, 91*(5), 678–683.

Daubenfeld, T., & Zenker, D. (2015). A game-based approach to an entire physical chemistry course. *Journal of Chemical Education, 92*(2), 269–277.

de Bono, E. (1968). *The 5-day course in thinking.* London, UK: Allen Lane, Penguin Press.

Eduventures. (2013). *Remote exam proctoring: Current state of the market for voice proctoring, facial recognition, and other new technologies.* Retrieved from www.eduventures.com/whitepapers/remote-exam-proctoring-white-paper/

Eilks, I., & Byers, B. (2010). The need for innovative methods of teaching and learning chemistry in higher education: Reflections from a project of the European Chemistry Thematic Network. *Chemistry Education Research and Practice, 11*(4), 233–240.

Evans, J. A. (2009). OWL (Online Web-Based Learning) (published by Cengage-Brooks/Cole). *Journal of Chemical Education, 86*(6), 695–696.

Finster, D. C. (1989). Developmental instruction: Part 1. Perry's model of intellectual development. *Journal of Chemical Education, 66*(8), 659–661.

Franco, J. (2012). Online gaming for understanding folding, interactions, and structure. *Journal of Chemical Education, 89*(12), 1543–1546.

Garratt, J. (2002). Laboratory work provides only one of many skills needed by the experimental scientist. *University Chemistry Education, 6*(2), 58–64.

Garrison, D. R., Anderson, T., & Archer, W. (1999). Critical enquiry in a text-based environment: Computer conferencing in higher education. *The Internet and Higher Education, 2*(2–3), 87–105.

Garrison, D. R., Anderson, T., & Archer, W. (2010). The first decade of the community of inquiry framework: A retrospective. *The Internet and Higher Education, 13*(1–2), 5–9.

Gregory, S. J., & Di Trapani, G. (2012). A blended learning approach to laboratory preparation. *International Journal of Innovation in Science and Mathematics Education, 20*(1), 56–70.

Harris, H. (2009). Electronic homework management systems: Reviews of popular systems. *Journal of Chemical Education, 86*(6), 691.

Hawkes, S. J. (2004). Chemistry is not a laboratory science. *Journal of Chemical Education, 81*(9), 1257.

He, Y., Swenson, S., & Lents, N. (2012). Online video tutorials increase learning of difficult concepts in an undergraduate analytical chemistry course. *Journal of Chemical Education, 89*(9), 1128–1132.

Hendrickson, S. M. (2009). WebAssign (published by WebAssign). *Journal of Chemical Education, 86*(6), 698–699.

Hillier, M., Fluck, A., & Emerson, M. (2014). *Transforming exams: A scalable examination platform for BYOD invigilated assessment.* Retrieved from transformingexams.com

Hrastinski, S. (2008). Asynchronous and synchronous e-learning. *EDUCAUSE Quarterly, 31*(4), 51–55.

Johnstone, A. H. (1982). Macro- and micro-chemistry. *School Science Review, 64,* 377–379.

Kennepohl, D. (1996). Home-study microlabs. *Journal of Chemical Education, 73*(10), 938–939.

Kennepohl, D., Guay, M., & Thomas, V. (2010). Using an online, self-diagnostic test for introductory general chemistry at an open university. *Journal of Chemical Education, 87*(11), 1273–1277.

Kennepohl, D., & Shaw, L. (Eds.). (2010). *Accessible elements: Teaching science online and at a distance*. Edmonton, Canada: AU Press.

Kozma, R. B., & Russell, J. (1997). Multimedia and understanding: Expert and novice responses to different representations of chemical phenomena. *Journal of Research in Science Teaching, 34*(9), 949–968.

Lancaster, S. J., & Read, D. (2013). Flipping lectures and inverting classrooms. *Education in Chemistry, 50*(5), 14–17.

Luxford, C. J., & Bretz, S. L. (2014). Development of the bonding representations inventory to identify student misconceptions about covalent and ionic bonding representations. *Journal of Chemical Education, 91*(3), 312–320.

Lye, P. G., Smith, E. J., Rosser, A., & Dillon, W. (2016). *Looking for answers; why do or don't distance education students in first year chemistry units utilize online tutorials?* Manuscript in preparation.

Malik, K., Martinez, N., Romero, J., Schubel, S., & Janowicz, P. A. (2014). Mixed-methods study of online and written organic chemistry homework. *Journal of Chemical Education, 91*(11), 1804–1809.

Mathieson, K., & Leafman, J. S. (2014). Comparison of student and instructor perceptions of social presence. *Journal of Educators Online, 11*(2).

Mawn, M. V., Carrico, P., Charuk, K., Stote, K. S., & Lawrence, B. (2011). Hands-on and online: Scientific explorations through distance learning. *Open Learning, 26*(2), 135–146.

McClary, L. M., & Bretz, S. L. (2012). Development and assessment of a diagnostic tool to identify organic chemistry students' alternative conceptions related to acid strength. *International Journal of Science Education, 34*(15), 2317–2341.

Miller, S. (2009). SmartWork (published by WW Norton). *Journal of Chemical Education, 86*(6), 697.

Moore, M. G., & Kearsley, G. (2012). *Distance education: A systems view of online learning* (3rd ed.). Belmont, CA: Wadsworth Cengage Learning.

National Research Council. (2007). *The future of U.S. chemistry research: Benchmarks and challenges*. Washington, DC: The National Academies Press.

Panther, B. C., Mosse, J. A., & Wright, W. (2011). Recorded lectures don't replace the "real thing": What the students say. In M. Sharma, A. Yeung, T. Jenkins, E. Johnson, G. Rayner, & J. West (Eds.), *Proceedings of the Australian Conference on Science and Mathematics Education: Teaching for Diversity—Challenges and Strategies,* September 28–30, 2011, University of Melbourne (pp. 127–132). Sydney, Australia: UniServe Science.

Parker, L. L., & Loudon, G. M. (2013). Case study using online homework in undergraduate organic chemistry: Results and student attitudes. *Journal of Chemical Education, 90*(1), 37–44.

Raine, D. J. (2002). Independent learning for the unwilling. *University Chemistry Education, 6*(2), 84–88.

Richards-Babb, M., Drelick, J., Henry, Z., & Robertson-Honecker, J. (2011). Online homework, help or hindrance? What students think and how they perform. *Journal of College Science Teaching, 40*(4), 81–93.

Rowley, S. (2009). ARIS (Assessment, Review, and Instruction System) (published by McGraw-Hill). *Journal of Chemical Education, 86*(6), 691.

Salmon, G. (2000). *E-moderating: The key to teaching and learning online*. London, UK: Kogan Page.

Salmon, G. (2011). *E-moderating: The key to teaching and learning online* (3rd ed.). New York, NY: Routledge.

Schmid, S., & Yeung, A. (2005). The influence of a pre-laboratory work module on student performance in the first year chemistry laboratory. In A. Brew & C. Asmar (Eds.), *Higher Education in a Changing World: Proceedings of the 28th HERDSA Annual Conference,* July 3–6, 2005, Sydney, Australia (pp. 471–479). Milperra, Australia: HERDSA.

Seery, M. K. (2012). Moving an in-class module online: A case study for chemistry. *Chemistry Education Research and Practice, 13*(1), 39–46.

Shane, J. W., & Bodner, G. M. (2006). General chemistry students' understanding of structure-function relationships. *The Chemical Educator, 11*(2), 130–137.

Shepherd, T. D. (2009). Mastering chemistry (published by Pearson/Prentice Hall). *Journal of Chemical Education, 86*(6), 694.

Silverberg, L. J., Tierney, J., & Bodek, M. J. (2014). Use of Doceri software for iPad in online delivery of chemistry content. *Journal of Chemical Education, 91*(11), 1999–2001.

Smith, E., Lye, P., Greatrex, B., Taylor, M., & Stupens, I. (2013). Enriching learning for first year chemistry students: Introduction of Adobe Connect. *European Journal of Open, Distance and e-Learning, 16*(1), 94–101.

Tasker, R., & Dalton, R. (2006). Research into practice: Visualisation of the molecular world using animations. *Chemistry Education Research and Practice, 7*(2), 141–159.

Tierney, J., Bodek, M., Fredricks, S., Dudkin, E., & Kistler, K. (2014). Using web-based video as an assessment tool for student performance in organic chemistry. *Journal of Chemical Education, 91*(7), 982–986.

Treagust, D. F. (1988). Development and use of diagnostic tests to evaluate students' misconceptions in science. *International Journal of Science Education, 10*(2), 159–169.

Wallace, A., Miron, D., Murphy, A., & Brown, T. (2013, June). *Remote chemistry laboratory to enhance science learning and access.* Paper presented at the Digital Rural Futures Conference, University of New England, Armidale, Australia.

Watwood, B., Nugent, J., & Deihl, W. (2009). *Building from content to community: [Re]thinking the transition to online teaching and learning.* Richmond, VA: Virginia Commonwealth University.

Wren, D., & Barbera, J. (2013). Gathering evidence for validity during the design, development, and qualitative evaluation of thermochemistry concept inventory items. *Journal of Chemical Education, 90*(12), 1590–1601.

Zhao, N. (2009). WileyPLUS with CATALYST (published by John Wiley and Sons, Inc.). *Journal of Chemical Education, 86*(6), 692–693.

3

DEVELOPING ONLINE EARTH SCIENCE COURSES

Kevin F. Downing
DePaul University

Abstract

This chapter provides an overview of practices and innovations to take into consideration if you are developing an online earth science course from the bottom up or are updating components of an existing course. It begins with a glance at the state of earth science education and then reviews factors that impact the character of online instruction. Following this, technological trends and pedagogical approaches that support teaching earth science online are reviewed. In the final sections, specific instructional elements and techniques, including effective communication and assessment structures, are appraised to provide a road map to taking an earth science course online.

Earth science is the study of the interconnections among the lithospheric, atmospheric, hydrospheric, and atmospheric systems. It is not surprising that news from earth science fields captures daily attention and often headlines in media outlets because of the close interdependence of human society with physical geography, natural resources, natural disasters, global environmental change, and other phenomena that impact daily life. One might presume that because of its relevance to human well-being, education and research on earth science would be an indispensable and healthy enterprise within higher education institutions. Unfortunately, this is not actually the case, and many geoscience and earth science departments have been shuttered in the past few decades. For example, from 1989 to 2002, the number of U.S. geology departments decreased by 16% and earth science departments by 22% (L.E. Davis, 2012). They simply do not appear to hold the unquestioned right to exist as do many other departments in vogue in academic culture. It is within this general contraction of support for earth science that you will be developing your online course activities and should therefore take into consideration in course design and purpose that—in at least a small way—your efforts are important to sustaining and reinvigorating the importance of the earth sciences to students and society.

It is difficult to ascertain and quantify the degree to which online earth science instruction or even online science instruction has penetrated the U.S. higher education market. Certainly there has been marked growth along with the general expansion of online learning. Nevertheless, national surveys to date, like the annual Online Learning Consortium surveys (e.g., Allen & Seaman, 2013), are coarse focusing on the broad patterns of enrollment rather than on the granular trends within disciplines. When they have been undertaken, studies of specific disciplines within geoscience programs such as paleontology suggest that earth science divisions show low participation, low interest, and little strategic planning in terms of online learning (Downing & Holtz, 2012). A glimpse of online earth science course enrollment patterns is available at the level of community college instruction for the state of Washington. Xu and Jaggers (2013) found that 10% of all community college enrollments in Washington were online, and 8.42% of total online enrollments were in the natural sciences. Astronomy and geology were counted as the most common at 39% and 19%, respectively. This study also found that students taking natural science courses online performed relatively better in those courses than in other disciplines represented online, although low student persistence in earth science courses was problematic. The authors recommended that colleges provide screening and early warning systems for student performance, as well as broad scaffolding to support learning assignments. One other notable area where online earth science instruction is being pursued is at the high school level, where students are being provided opportunities to take advanced placement courses such as environmental science online (Missett, Reed, Scot, Callahan, & Slade, 2010). Overall, there is much potential to grow the online earth science offerings at all levels.

General Factors Impacting Your Instructional Design

You may encounter several challenges during the development and implementation of your online science course related to (a) the validation level of the online learning format by your colleagues and students, (b) the learning management system and corresponding tools provided by your institution to publish the course, (c) the student perceptions of online learning, and (d) the institutional and course strategies to support student retention in the online learning environment.

Validation Level of Online Learning

Faculty generally continue to be concerned about whether students in online learning courses will achieve the same level of competence as they would in a face-to-face course. The literature is replete with studies that demonstrate similar student outcomes for both online and on-site formats, and research for online earth science courses is concordant with this generalization. For example, in a comparison of performance of online students versus on-site students on identical exams in an introductory earth science course for nonmajors, no significant difference was detected (Werhner, 2010). Despite the regular validation of online science instruction, one of the potential challenges of developing an online earth science course is overcoming your college's internal skepticism to the online format.

Learning Management Systems and Standardization

There are some general trends in the evolution of online learning that will impact the way your course is devised. For example, most institutions offering online learning have purchased a learning management system (LMS) such as Blackboard, Moodle, Desire2Learn, Angel, and others that will be the course canvas on which you will paint. Each LMS offers an inclusive and growing suite of features for course development, content delivery, and communication with each brand, paying increasing attention to tools for social learning, multimedia integration, data analytics for tracking student learning, mobile learning, recording and broadcasting, and interoperability with external learning resources. In fact, in the area of interoperability, there are increasing calls for standardization between educational service providers, content providers, and so-called brokers that locate educational resources (e.g., Anido-Rifón et al., 2014), with the goal that the faculty end user can smoothly integrate extensive digital resources into a course to enrich the student learning experience. For online earth science instruction, enhanced interoperability of LMSs is important to optimize the rich archives of multimedia available at digital libraries.

Just as the online platform used for developing and teaching your online earth science course will have standardized features, it is also likely that your host institution has generated or adopted standard requirements for courses that will regulate the character of your earth science design efforts. For instance, many institutions have adopted the fee-based Quality Matters program (for details, see www.qualitymatters.org) that sponsors a best practices rubric, founded on scholarly research addressing online pedagogy and best practices for online and blended courses. Under such rubrics, courses must adhere to predetermined best practices in the area of quality teaching (syllabi, grading, materials, interaction, resources) but also attend to the particular considerations of the technology mitigating teaching to ensure students have the skills, information, and experiences to succeed in the online learning environment.

Student Perceptions of Online Learning

Naturally, some studies assessing student achievement of outcomes in online earth science courses indicate unfavorable and poorer results than are achieved with on-site learning. In a study of student perceptions of earth and ocean science from novice to expert levels that compared online students and distance learners and a variety of other demographics, Jolley, Lane, Kennedy, and Frappé-Sénéclauze (2012) found that distance learning was not as effective for student learning as on-site versions. The authors postulated that some students might be self-selecting for distance education because of a lack of interest in the subject (i.e., they just need it for a requirement) or that the face-to-face students indeed had a better learning experience. Jolley and colleagues (2012) suggested that a regular census of student perceptions may help to inform revisions of pedagogy to engage even the least motivated student. On the whole, this study reminds us that even the most carefully designed learning environment may not connect with all students, and that some students may have self-selected the online course environment for the "wrong" reasons.

Another important consideration for your course design is revealed by recent investigations indicating that there is often a disparity between student perception of online learning and that of faculty around the qualities of the online learning environment and experience. Faculty assumed that their presence online was important and that their guidance obviated the need for students to elevate and rely on their self-directed learning skills. However, a survey by Otter and colleagues (2013) contrasting both student and faculty perceptions in traditional and online environments revealed that in contrast to the faculty conviction, students judged they had to teach themselves more, felt they were more disconnected from the learning experience, and viewed faculty as having a lesser role in their learning. Similarly, using the community of inquiry (COI) paradigm that relates the impact of social, cognitive, and teaching factors on the educational experience, Morris (2011) evaluated community college student perception of the online environment through a questionnaire and interviews. The conclusion of this study was that social connection should be built in courses through mandatory and regular participation tasks and clear instructional design and that instructor promptness on formative assessment and individualized feedback was crucial in enhancing learning and student perceptions of the online learning experience. Group size also bears on student perceptions and connectivity online. Breaking students into smaller subgroups for discussion forums and corresponding active encouragement from the instructor enhances student interactivity in the form of elaboration and negotiation (J. Kim, 2013). As you build and conduct your online learning in the earth sciences, a key message for instructional practice from these studies is that your students' perception of what you are doing is going to be different from your own. However, there are concrete strategies you can utilize to improve student perception and corresponding retention, such as offering clear instructional design that fosters self-directed learning, requiring regular participation, and developing opportunities for more "intimate" participation in small groups.

Strategies to Support Student Retention

One of the great nemeses of the online learning enterprise is student retention, which regularly underperforms in comparison to the on-site learning format. Therefore, as you undertake developing your earth science learning activities and as much as an instructor has a degree of control over retention factors, it will be imperative to consider how course activities sustain students in the online earth science learning environment. Lee and Choi (2011) compiled published research on the reasons why students drop out of online courses and uncovered 69 principle factors, further grouping them into three main categories involving student, course-program, and environmental variables. Student factors, such as academic background, time management, and psychological attributes, were considered the principal reasons for online course dropout but were notably the hardest to address by an instructor or institution. Likewise, environmental factors such as having a supportive home and work environment were crucial but are largely beyond an instructor's influence. In a comparable study, Hart (2012) found that satisfaction with online learning, motivation to learn, belonging to a learning community, peer and family support of learning, time management, and regular use of the instructor were central to student persistence in online courses. As a course developer and instructor, you need to "accept the things you cannot change" and focus on the course and program factors that can support the optimum online science learning experience.

Emphasizing course-program factors for improving the retention of online learners, Lorenzetti (2013) concluded that the following strategies will improve retention: conveying that the instructor has subject matter expertise, limiting the amount of assignments and readings, providing orientation to online learning, and providing opportunities to students to preemptively self-assess to determine if online learning is a good match. Additional recommendations are to provide thorough technological assistance and training, supplemental scaffolding for topics, flexibility on assignments to accommodate student issues, and good program advising.

Because a student's self-directed learning competence is a crucial retention factor, especially elevated in online learning, it is important to explore models that promote the development of this skill through the character of the learning system itself. R. Kim, Olfman, Ryan, and Eryilmaz (2014) described a personalized learning system that promotes self-directed learning using the social media application Media Wiki. Using this system, students can customize their content according to learning goals (i.e., competencies), locate appropriate learning resources, assess their performance, and revise learning strategies. Although the system takes some time to employ, R. Kim and colleagues (2014) concluded that students can learn to be more effective self-directed learners while gaining subject mastery.

Technology Trends and Your Approach to Teaching Earth Science Online

Technological innovation has been a continuous consideration throughout the evolution of online learning and has required regular adaptation of courses to *useful* emerging educational technologies; not all of them are useful, so discriminating functionality from fad is imperative. Some authors have characterized the current state of technological capability as a so-called Third Generation of distance education that advances the online learning format from one of "Internet-based courses" to "technology-enabled learning environments" with added dimensionality through expanded connections and breadth of potential experiences (Moller, Robison, & Huett, 2012, p. 2). Because of technical limitations and content scarcity, the early generations of online learning were inadequate for supporting multimedia such as video, animations, communication interactivity, and rich media that enables a student to interact with content (e.g., simulations, games, three-dimensional [3D] virtual worlds). The core premise of the Third Generation concept is that increased capability of the Internet to facilitate learning has fostered a greater emphasis on learning experience design versus simple information presentation approaches, so that students interact with content and are immersed in social and collaborative circumstances (Moller et al., 2012). The implication here is that your vision for online earth science activities should include the affordances of Third Generation technologies, such as ubiquitous connectivity and virtual reality, as students who have grown up with these technologies will expect them.

Teaching Earth Science: Big Picture Approaches

Whether you are teaching online or on-site and as you are constructing your learning activities, it is helpful to consider what the earth science community collectively considers its principal educational objectives to convey to students and society. Manduca and Kastens (2012a) endorsed the idea that geoscience instruction should emphasize the overarching themes of time (geologic), space (dimensional visualization), systems, and fieldwork. In terms of teaching about natural systems, concepts should be multidimensional, active reasoning should be linked to learning earth science systems, and there should be attention to the practical application of earth science concepts (Stillings, 2012). In the same way, Wysession and colleagues. (2012) developed a set of earth science literacy principles around the so-called big ideas that earth science can convey as functional student competencies, including scientific reasoning as a way of knowing, the vast age of the earth, earth processes as systems, the earth as dynamic and transforming, the earth as fundamentally a water planet, evolving life, human dependence on earth resources, human modification of the earth's surface, and the earth's production of geological hazards for humans.

The expanding volume of information in earth science makes it impossible for students to achieve broad-spectrum expertise; therefore, instructional design strategies have been advanced to achieve focused expertise to solve problems. With this in mind, one paradigm advanced to help encourage learning is the idea of employing knowledge integration (KI) to learn geosciences through the synthesis of interdisciplinary information. KI pedagogy strives to bring about student competence and skills efficiently without the necessity for the review of voluminous information. In the geosciences, KI can be advanced through using (a) place-based examples that are relevant to the student, (b) broad themes and big ideas to bind the learning experience (e.g., evolution), (c) societally important issues, (d) the practice of scientists (e.g., authentic experiences), and (e) models that bring together key topics with relevant data (Manduca & Kastens, 2012a, 2012b). The pedagogical point of KI is that instruction in the earth sciences does not have to be encyclopedic to be effective and that instructors should center earth science assignments on representative examples and earth science models.

Although general pedagogical models for teaching earth science like KI are available, educational research on a discipline-by-discipline basis within earth science can be scarce or inconclusive. For example, there is some question as to the relative merits of traditional approaches to teaching physical geography. A comprehensive review of teaching practices in physical geography conducted by Day (2012) concluded that many of the standard active learning approaches such as fieldwork, service learning, and inquiry-based and problem-based learning had little validation in formal studies. Moreover, this study also determined that the effectiveness of virtual field trips was equivocal and that the main innovations in teaching physical geography are the supplementary animations and simulations sponsored by textbook publishers, incorporation of lecture podcasts, and LMS features adopted to facilitate learning.

Taking Earth Science Learning Online

A good starting place for teaching earth science courses is provided by the National Association of Geoscience Teachers (NAGT) under the link for teaching resources at the NAGT website (nagt.org/nagt/teaching_resources/index.html). NAGT provides resources on geoscience literacy, teaching materials, and topical resources. In particular, the NAGT-sponsored workshops, "On the Cutting Edge," have generated numerous helpful resources for teaching online geoscience courses. Topics include pedagogy, course design and course delivery, specific online course activities, and exemplary course materials (see serc.carleton.edu/NAGTWorkshops/online/index.html).

Selecting an Online Earth Science Course Approach

The degree to which online science learning is utilized in support of earth science instruction is a spectrum from simple administrative facilitation of an on-site course to full-service courses where learning is completely facilitated online and a student situated thousands of miles from the host institution may never visit the campus. A choice for many earth science departments with a strategic goal of developing distance options and flexibility for their students is to offer hybrid courses that have a mixture of traditional on-site learning activities coupled with strategic online modules or exercises. There are many reasons why programs choose to offer hybrid options, from institution-based rationales (e.g., cost, scale, and faculty workload), to pedagogical goals (e.g., expanding discussion, increasing participation, and using multimedia affordances available online), to student factors (e.g., offering pace flexibility, accommodating adult work-life balances, and keeping student costs down). As with studies of fully online courses, student achievement in hybrid courses has been investigated and they have been found to produce comparable learning results to those of on-site courses. For example, online student performance was comparable to that of students taking an on-site version of an earth and space course directed to elementary science instructors, and faculty teaching the course actually found that their workload was reduced for the online sections (Cervato, Kerton, Peer, Hassall, & Schmidt, 2013).

Some colleges take a one-dimensional approach to offering distance education by simply transmitting recorded or live streamed webcasts of lectures and employing standard testing as the mode of instruction for a course. This is sometimes coupled with discussion groups and active tutoring. This chapter maintains, however, that such a simplistic approach is not optimal for teaching earth science online. That is not to say that webcasted lectures are without value as a supplementation strategy when supporting online, hybrid, and on-site earth science courses. For example, Traphagan, Kucsera, and Kishi (2010) evaluated the impact of lecture webcasting on on-site attendance and overall learning for a large-enrollment geology course. This study established that webcasting lectures lowered on-site attendance but nullified performance reduction observed for normal absenteeism. They determined that students who viewed webcasts reported positive learning experiences and scored higher on performance measures. These findings suggest that student learning can improve through passive webcasting—students can use them as accompanying notes to other course materials and review concepts until understanding is achieved; therefore, it is worth considering recording lecture-type presentations to further supplement and engage students in your online earth science course whether hybrid or fully online.

There are numerous examples in the literature describing Third Generation–style approaches to online STEM education and to accomplish a more student-centered approach to online learning. For example, in an archetypal online introductory earth science course online from a decade ago, Dong and Hubble (2004) emphasized interactivity through online multimedia supporting labs and field trips and also created online tutorials and practical exams. More recently, in teaching an online statistics course, Yang (2013) employed a combination of problem-based learning and case studies, synchronous (e.g., office hours, instant messaging) and asynchronous faculty interactivity with students (e.g., discussion forums, e-mail), video demonstration of concepts, and embedded social presence via a faculty introductory video. In another example described by Hariri (2013), the Blackboard LMS was used for teaching a graduate structural geology course. This online graduate course successfully used Blackboard's online tools for e-mail, announcements, and grading and emphasized asynchronous discussion for student interaction, as well as case studies and article summaries as a share of assessed assignments.

The general model for developing earth systems science instruction online in China is noteworthy and serves as a good example of an integrated approach. The overarching goal, summarized by Dong, Xu, and Lu (2009), is to develop a sustainable instructional design framework around a student-centered model. They defined the model as one of *multivisualization*, where instructional design emphasis is to make knowledge both visible and interactive by combining online multimedia with detailed visualization-supporting graphics such as 3D models, animations, and video clips with narration. Their earth systems science course specifically incorporates geodatabases built around an adaptable LMS called Skyclass. Students in this Chinese earth systems science model are placed in an immersive earth science learning environment, as the authors considered a predominantly verbal learning environment insufficient.

To summarize, there are numerous approaches that one can take to develop an online earth science course depending on the course topic, learning objectives, and desired mix of interactivity and assignments. However, to a large degree, LMSs have induced a convergence of course "shape" to the standard qualities and features of contemporary LMS environments. It is easy to feel bound by the LMS, but this can be overcome by extending the environment to external multimedia and authentic activities, as discussed later in this chapter.

Incorporating Student Research

A concern for both on-site and online science instructors is how their students use online information—popular versus peer-reviewed academic sources—to learn concepts and conduct original research within a course. It is typical that students, particularly in their formative years, will use basic resources returned from popular search engines for research papers and other learning activities unless there is deliberate training and instructions to cultivate students' effective use of academic search engines and corresponding unearthed quality information. Improving students' use of online resources by directly teaching them information literacy skills can be accomplished by providing scaffolding to students to direct them to authoritative disciplinary sources. To make this an imperative, their course assessment should be tied to the quality of resources they use in assignments (Kirkwood, 2008). Therefore, a best practice consideration in your online earth science course is to make room for students to read and use excerpts from scholarly papers (Wenk & Tronsky, 2011). Ensure, however, that they are provided with direct instruction on how to obtain them from the library.

Another effective way to promote student learning in an online course is to have students conduct authentic research. Whether in support of general education requirements or for science majors, study of the earth science principles through research provides a sound educational platform for conveying and honing student inquiry skills. In an online science course format, there are several approaches to engage students in practical research. One option is to develop student-directed field exercises in a student's local area. For example, Clary and Wandersee (2014) described the effective use of informal field sites by students to conduct their own paleontology research. They determined that it was important to streamline field assignments and have activities apply principles directly related to course content. Another way to have students conduct research is for them to use real data available online. Using online data has been confirmed to improve the conceptual knowledge of preservice science teachers completing an earth tides exercise (Ucar & Trundle, 2011). In this study, students pursuing guided inquiry using web-based data showed better understanding than those taught by traditional instruction with a simulation and markedly outperformed (by 29%), students taking traditional instruction.

Uncovering and Incorporating Outstanding Earth Science Multimedia

There are an expanding number of online resources for earth science instructors to integrate into course activities. One example of a useful archival source that applies a metadata standard (e.g., Sharable Content Object Reference Model, or SCORM) to science resources is the National Science Digital Library (NSDL) (nsdl.org) sponsored by the U.S. National Science Foundation. Users of this resource library can search for items based on key characteristics such as the topic, the intended academic level, and the type of media or multimedia desired. Another approach being used to generate quality resources around a particular earth science subject that is not a part of the national efforts such as the NSDL or Digital Library for Earth System Education (DLESE) is a system of faculty peer review of online resources. Gold and colleagues (2012) described how the Climate Literacy and Energy Awareness Network (CLEAN) overlaps with and expands the criteria of review of archived resources used by the national-sponsored digital libraries, including faculty review, more stringent curation, and additional rating criteria that improve the quality of the linked resources.

Of course, many exceptional multimedia resources, typically independent efforts by individual faculty, do not end up in a prominent archive but if discovered provide earth science instructors with excellent instructional opportunities. A recent example, described by M. G. Davis and Chapman (2012), permits students to extract real-time meteorological and geothermal data from the Emigration Pass Observatory in Utah. Using this site, students are able to complete exercises that make use of authentic data. The dilemma for the science instructor going outside of the sponsored libraries like the NSDL to secure earth science multimedia to build components of an online course is that searching with a general engine like Google or Bing can take an inordinate amount of time. Accordingly, start your multimedia search with the curated archives.

Identifying and Using Informal Resources

As earth science concepts are often presented as educational displays at museums and other public science institutions, these informal educational resources can be readily tapped to provide online science students with hands-on exercises. The chief limitation of employing informal resources is whether all students will have access to suitable institutional resources locally and whether they can be efficiently coordinated through a generic exercise for student use. Sellés-Martinez (2013) described how informal resources were employed to address a gap in the Argentine educational system in the area of geosciences. The strategy for this effort was to provide learners a multifaceted assortment of learning opportunities using exhibitions, lectures, earth science weeks, and museum exhibits to introduce key concepts of earth science. In my own courses, I use a similar informal educational strategy for assignments, typically a self-directed field trip assignment to a museum exhibit (e.g., Chicago's Field Museum of Natural History) where students are directed to analyze the morphological characteristics and ecological and evolutionary relationships of fossil specimens following a field trip rubric. It is a worthwhile and constructive use of your instructional design time to catalog a variety of informal earth science resources available to you locally and when possible to enlist your "very distant" online students to develop a list of potential resources available to them (e.g., museums, natural history areas, landforms).

Considering m-Learning Options and Applications

The popularity and widespread use of mobile devices by students for everyday communications and other purposes has triggered the development of instructional design efforts around incorporating mobile-learning (m-learning) affordances into online instruction, including in the earth sciences. For example, Weng, Sun, and Grigsby (2012) described an application called Geotools developed for Android phones that permits students to use the device in place of traditional field tools used by geologists, such as a pocket transit compass and a device to capture GPS information, video, and audio. Podcasts of lectures were adopted early in m-learning, and they remain a solid resource supplement to incorporate into college science, although they do lower attendance for on-site courses (Holbrook & Dupont, 2011). Podcasts and other m-learning affordances will become more commonplace as LMSs become more interoperable with them. Accordingly, in the design of online earth science activities, you must keep in mind that some students will undertake the greater part of their course through these devices.

Not every new m-learning device or its applications will be a useful innovation for education. A case in point, in their examination of the use of iPad technology in the classroom and field, Wallace and Witus (2013) found that in-service K–12 teachers facilitating an earth science course did not increase content knowledge in comparison to standard instruction without the devices. Students were distracted by the devices and used them for alternative purposes. So m-learning should be incorporated with specific intent, and its parameters of use and cost should be justified by the proportional learning value.

Structuring Intentional Communication and Interactivity

As an online earth science instructor, you will typically have fewer opportunities for interaction to address spontaneous student questions unless an instructional dialogue is strategically planned to initiate instructor–student–peer interactions for specific course activities (Gorsky & Caspi, 2010). In particular, one of the areas of teaching practice in the geosciences that is receiving more attention in recent publications is the affective domain of the learner. There is a call for more purposeful production of learning activities that foster discussions and collaborations that evoke emotion, participation, motivation, values, and so on. On the basis of motivation and emotion theory, van der Hoeven Kraft, Srogi, Husman, Semken, and Fuhrman (2011) contended that for geoscience students to succeed, they need to (a) interact socially, (b) think they can be successful, (c) model expert thinking processes, and (d) undertake assignments that connect them to content through the learning experience and local places. They maintained that instructors can accomplish this with an instructional approach that "connects" students to the earth using peer groups during cooperative learning and local field-based experiential learning. As an earth science instructor teaching with the affordances of online learning's Third Generation, you have the opportunity to use the vast communication technology options to shape affective learning activities.

It is clear from numerous studies that students usually do appreciate opportunities to interact with each other and the instructor and to learn from quality online multimedia rather than a text- and lecture-driven course format (Boling, Hough, Krinsky, Saleem, & Stevens, 2012). So it is critical in your instructional design to consider how you are strategically building a social learning environment. With this in mind, however, there are differences between disciplines, and this can bear on the balance of teaching, social, and cognitive presence optimal to a particular earth science course (Arbaugh, Bangert, & Cleveland-Innes, 2010). If, for example, you are developing an earth science course that will be heavy on discourse and debate over pressing societal issues (e.g., pollution, global environmental change, natural resources) with less emphasis on the acquisition of detailed subject matter and techniques, it is reasonable to elevate the degree of activities that engage student-to-student interaction and critical analysis of these issues and avoid an overload of resources that scaffold basic concepts. If your course objectives involve detailed subject matter and techniques, however, scheduling too much social interaction can actually be a distraction and deleterious to student progress and learning.

Another course interaction strategy is "just-in-time" course modification, where student feedback to the instructor results in rolling modifications to course activities. In onsite courses, polling using clickers can be conducted in real time or input can be gathered asynchronously after class from online questionnaires. Of course, an online course using a sophisticated LMS has built-in functions that can act to generate just-in-time modifications to improve student learning. Tong (2014) described an electronic feedback system in a geophysics course that generated custom electronic study packages from a general resource database of links on course topics. If you desire to work just-in-time elements into your online science course, you can set up the LMS to open forums where students can provide timely feedback for ongoing course activities to engage you as an instructor and provoke modifications where warranted.

One of the characteristics of student discourse that many of us who regularly teach science online observe is that the frequency and overall quality of student argumentation in asynchronous discussion forums exceeds that of synchronous on-site classrooms. Research on student argumentation in an online physical science course confirms that the quality and complexity of student argumentation is improved online and that this may be largely attributed to greater investment of time on the part of students (Lin, Hong, & Lawrenz, 2012). Therefore, the structure of your planned online discourse among students through discussion forums is a seminal part of their learning and must be well considered in terms of the general balance of student assignments (e.g., written assignments compared to participation in discussion forums) during course design to promote deeper learning. To accomplish this, you should pose questions and problems to students that provoke thorough exchanges. In my courses, students achieve this by providing several examples drawn from course readings, finding corroborating or contradicting online information, and responding to multiple classmates' submissions. The discussion activities are facilitated by providing students with a detailed set of instructions and rubric for discussion entries. For example, in the discussion forum on mountain formation in my course Exploring Earth's Physical Features, students are required to research two examples of mountain belts, provide pictures of each, describe how geologists interpret the origin and evolution of each, and respond to at least two classmates' contributions to the forum.

Planning for Balanced Assessment Strategies

When configuring how student learning will be assessed in your online earth science course, consider that a traditional system of summative practical exams may be unsuitable, particularly as it will not capture or motivate aspects of social presence. A diverse approach to course assessment that I have found effective in my online earth science courses involves the following categories: participation in discussions, laboratory reports, virtual field trip reports, a self-directed field trip report, an original research paper, and an essay-style practical exam. The key is to find a sound weighting of categories appropriate to the cumulative course activities.

One of the helpful affordances of online learning is the ability of an instructor to build in regular self-assessment for students as they progress through learning activities. Kerton and Cervato (2014) investigated patterns of assessment in an earth and space science course for elementary education majors and determined that students generally did not use self-assessments effectively and spent a relatively short amount of time on online exams. Their conclusion and recommendation is that embedded self-assessments should occur frequently throughout course materials, and students should perceive self-assessment as an integral part of a course and not just a terminal activity at the end of a unit.

Extending on-site learning experiences with follow-up online assignments has been a mainstay affordance of distance learning. A robust study of large enrollment introductory science classes by Arasasingham, Martorell, and McIntire (2011) demonstrated that online homework assignments lead to higher scores on exams, particularly when the online activity enhanced visualization of concepts difficult to communicate statically, such as molecular structure. Therefore, if you are considering embellishing an on-site earth science course or are developing a hybrid course online, follow-up assignments that are formally assessed toward a grade are very suitable for improving student achievement.

Engaging Students in Online Practical Work in Earth Science

Teaching an online science course does not require setting aside the hands-on activities so crucial to learning science and promoting scientific reasoning. There are many practical work strategies that have been validated as reliable means to achieve student competence in the earth sciences through online learning formats. In the following discussion, several of these strategies are reviewed, including online-facilitated laboratory work, at-home laboratory kits, online simulations, Google Earth activities, remote labs, and virtual and online-facilitated field trips.

Online-Facilitated Laboratory Work

One of the largest hurdles to bringing your earth science instruction online is providing students with practical work learning outcomes comparable to those reached by on-site students. The importance of including practical work and the best practices for accomplishing it have been discussed at length, with many examples in Downing and Holtz (2008), Kennepohl and Shaw (2010), and Jeschofnig and Jeschofnig (2011). These resources should be reviewed for creative ways of incorporating laboratory and fieldwork into online learning activities in the earth sciences. The following discussion reviews representative examples of recent recommendations for structuring online practical work.

Based on a three-year study of virtual labs, Flowers, Moore, and Flowers (2011) identified several best practices for online science courses, including require some group work if possible, use simulations, provide clear instructions regarding lab procedures and assessment, provide quality presentations and videoconferencing, and use strong assessment tools. On the basis of several examples reviewed, including an exercise on analyzing cemetery demographics for an environmental issues course, Mawn, Carrico, Charuk, Stote, and Lawrence (2011) suggested that for online labs to be effective, they should have clear process-related objectives, involve a discussion forum, and be reasonably open ended so that students can expand their learning. Cloutis (2010) pointed out that it is particularly important to develop online practical work in the form of laboratories or field-based studies where a core goal of the earth science course is to convey professional techniques.

At-Home Laboratory Kits

At-home science kits have proven very useful in conjunction with teaching science at a distance, particularly for introductory-level courses. A lab kit can be a useful way of having students engage in authentic experimentation. For example, in my Prehistoric Life course, students work with a general fossil kit to investigate specimen morphology, classification, and preservation. Likewise, instruction around basic chemistry and mineralogy can also be facilitated through the use of lab kits (Lyall & Patti, 2010). Feig (2010) presented a comprehensive summary of the components of an online physical geology laboratory on rock specimen identification and classification using a mineral kit that yielded student learning outcomes comparable to those in a face-to-face version of the same lab. The strategy employed for this lab involved the Blackboard LMS, asynchronicity, rock kits, online tutorials, and image-processing freeware. Assessment involved security-controlled quizzes taken after labs were completed. This physical geology laboratory is an example following the Quality Matters rubric.

Online Simulations

Online simulations using real tabular data are a very effective strategy for encouraging the application of higher order cognitive thinking in science students. Barclay, Renshaw, Taylor, and Bilge (2011) developed a volcano crisis simulation for a natural hazards course that requires students to analyze eruption information in tables rather than just interpret a summative graphic representation of information. Using tables as a part of a simulation was determined to result in student learning higher than that achieved through more passive simulations. There are a growing number of simulations available for earth science instruction online that approximate the characteristics of lab instrumentation. One example is the virtual microscope explained by Whalley, Kelley, and Tindle (2011) that allows students to observe real specimens and share visualizations with other students. Such simulated instruments can provide an immersive learning environment for both technological training and content knowledge; however, they are very time-consuming to develop from scratch and must be available to the general academic teaching community.

Google Earth Activities

If you are teaching earth science concepts that involve visualizations of the earth's physical features or distributions of regional data, you may find a combination of the attributes of Google Earth with data tabulated in Microsoft Excel to be an effective approach. In fact, Google Earth is becoming a core facet of instruction in many of the earth sciences, such as physical geography and geology, to investigate geologic features and the spatial relationships of features of the natural environment. Bailey, Whitmeyer, and De Paor (2012) identified four chief areas for the use of Google Earth in the geosciences: data visualization, digital geological mapping, virtual field experiences, and support of education models and their corresponding learning methods and assessment. For example, to show geometric 3D relationships of geological fold features in structural geology, structured data can be visualized by placing them on virtual globes with embedded symbols in Google Earth (Blenkinsop, 2012). The features of Google Earth that make it a useful tool for instruction are 3D perspective visualization tools, data quantification affordances, and students' ability to overlay geologic information over the earth's physical features (Monet & Greene, 2012). Another Google Earth example reported is a simulation that combines the application's visualization features with various views of landforms (e.g., oblique and planimetric) to approximate aerial photography analysis ordinarily conducted with stereoscopic tools in on-site geomorphology labs (Palmer, 2013). Suffice it to say that there are many creative ways to employ Google Earth to teach earth science concepts to online students.

Remote Labs

A more authentic form of an online science lab than a simulation is a remote lab that provides a learner with the ability to control an actual experimental environment at a distance. Kennepohl (2010) described the desired character of a remote lab as one in which real results from real objects are yielded so that students can draw meaningful conclusions. Moreover, it was noted that a remote lab does not have to be designed to be identical to on-site ones. The key is that a student will achieve the desired competence by using the remote experiment. Mathers, Goktogen, Rankin, and Anderson (2012) described a recent example of a remote experiment environment that approximates a mission to Mars. Students in the remote experiment are able to control a model Mars rover, monitor its systems, and collect data. Missions are conducted following a problem-based approach. An elaborate remote fieldwork system using mobile technology is used at The Open University to facilitate students in a geology field course in Scotland (Collins, Gaved, & Lea, 2010). The system provides a temporary wireless connection that can relay photographs and videos taken by researchers at remote localities to online students. As technology facilitating distance education increases in capability, it is becoming more feasible for real-time oversight of student practical work and remote experiments by an instructor. For example, Reddy (2014) used interactive television to provide real-time student–instructor interaction while students conducted online labs.

Virtual and Online-Facilitated Field Trips

Çaliskan (2011) discussed the use and affordances of virtual field trips in earth and environmental science and suggested that the cost of authentic geology field trips is causing them to become a less viable option for learning, so virtual field trip options should be explored. Online-facilitated field trips can be characterized as either passive, where students are just observers of information, or active, where students take on a more participatory role. (This author considers active field trips to be the more favorable option). Granshaw and Duggan-Haas (2012) summarized the characteristics and educational use of virtual field environments (VFEs) in geoscience. They defined *virtual field work* as "observation, data gathering and problem solving using a computer generated representation of an actual field site" (p. 286). The VFEs differ from a standard virtual field trip in that they do not follow a linear pathway, and thus they permit students a large degree of freedom in exploring the dimensional nature of the virtual environment. Effective VFEs will have the spatial and visual characteristics of the actual field area so students can collect data and measurements.

Student-led field trips are another potential approach to practical work for online or on-site earth science students. Todd and Goeke (2012) described a student-led field trip model for advanced geology courses where geologic features are investigated. Students conduct preparatory research, communicate their investigation to classmates through a presentation, and develop a report to be assessed by their instructor. Another approach to enhance student field research is to provide interactive virtual field trip guides (VFGs) that students can review before going out into the field or consult through a mobile device while in the field. Stott, Litherland, Carmichael, and Nuttall (2013) described several examples of VFGs. One example investigated the Ingleton Waterfalls Trail as a part of an introduction to geosciences course. The Virtual Alps exploration supported a physical geography course. Included in these supportive VFGs are 360° panoramas of the physical features of the study area, video clips, and color images. Stott and colleagues also indicated the potential to link data to the VFG for students to use during their field study.

Anticipating the Future of Online Earth Science Instruction

It is important to recognize at the onset that the online learning you plan to develop for your students occurs amid a decade of intense and ongoing revolutionary change in higher education involving the rapid growth in student and institutional participation in the online learning format (Allen & Seaman, 2013); implementation of innovative online technologies to teaching (Downing & Holtz, 2008; King & Cox, 2011); pronounced adjustments to both the teaching responsibilities and the skills repertoire for the online professor; and deepened attention to particular online learner success factors such as competence in self-directed learning, technological proficiency, and time management skills. All of these significant changes in the maturing online teaching environment can impact the way you approach your instructional design strategies.

Along with the upheaval in the character of college instruction driven by the demand for and rapid expansion of online learning, an interrelated economic conflict is looming in the higher education industry, particularly in the United States, pitting the student and parent consumer against the traditional higher education industry as the cost of a college degree and the amount of student indebtedness has soared to unsustainable levels (Smith, 2013). Although most online courses are still built to be confined to their home institutions and students, the traditional brick-and-mortar framework of higher education is itself on the precipice of a wave of creative destruction that has begun to destabilize the castle keep. Online learning modalities such as the nearly free massive open online courses (MOOCs) make it possible to offer quality education broadly and cheaply to the public. Indeed, were it not for universities' current accreditation fortifications around the awarding of degrees, the price of higher education could conceivably tumble, facilitated by online learning courses that meet universal measures of disciplinary competence.

But is there a MOOC future for online earth science courses? Will the MOOC colossus not only tear down the brick-and-mortar universities but also cannibalize individual college faculty's online earth science course efforts? A recent study of trends of MOOCs by Jordan (2014) sheds light on whether your efforts in the online earth science arena will be soon in vain. Students are migrating in droves to MOOCs as elite universities with large endowments offer what could be called massively open online degrees (MOODs). Jordan's timely study found that the average completion rate of students taking recent MOOCs was only 6.5%; that MOOC students very often already hold degrees; and that the format actually requires a high degree of technological literacy, so it is not an egalitarian educational panacea as sometimes portrayed. Earth-science-themed MOOCs are still rare and center on sustainable agriculture, global energy, and astrobiology rather than core traditional courses. So at this point, MOOCs represent little competition to individual efforts to teach earth science online. On the other hand, this MOOC gap in the earth science area raises the possibility that you could be the one to create the first MOOC in your area of expertise.

Notably, if MOOCs are to play an increasingly significant role in the future of online learning, a large hurdle for MOOCs is how quality assessment will occur at a vast enrollment scale, especially for writing-intensive assignments or practical work assignments in science. One emerging strategy is automated essay scoring using algorithms that learn and model scoring based on how faculty have previously scored exams. Another strategy is calibrated peer reviews where students are trained and conduct the assessment of work based on rubrics for the assignments (Balfour, 2013).

In terms of the technological future of teaching earth science online, improvements in virtual reality headsets like the Oculus system show promise for supporting even more immersive online learning environments that facilitate simulations and instruction through 3D virtual worlds. The improved headset imaging systems have the potential to replace screens as the dominant way to learn at a distance and would enhance the quality of scientific visualization so central to instruction in many of the earth sciences.

Conclusion

The state of earth science instruction is precarious in higher education despite its relevance to society. Yet, the outreach of an online learning format provides faculty an opportunity to popularize earth science broadly to a global student audience. With the emergence and adoption of quality control criteria (e.g., Quality Matters) and institutional reliance on LMSs, online courses, including earth science ones, are converging in their characteristics to conform to a standard suite of LMS tools and pedagogical structures. Innovation and creativity in instructional design will best manifest itself in specific assignments and discussions. There are specific instructional design measures that can be taken by the online earth science instructor to improve students' perceptions of their learning experience, performance, and retention. Third Generation affordances of the Internet make it possible to use rich multimedia and complex communication structures in online earth science courses, including extending the learning environment to m-learning applications. Formal archives of earth science multimedia contain bountiful resources that are easily incorporated into learning exercises, as are informal resources at museums and other institutions. There are many approaches to take in the design of an online earth science course, but at-home kits, simulations, remote labs, virtual and authentic field trips, and Google Earth applications are useful elements. An earth science pedagogical approach like KI that centers on big earth science themes with assignments that apply principles is a sound foundation for building online courses. Communication and interaction structures among students and between students and the instructor should be carefully designed, and assessment of student learning should be frequent and balanced among the diverse variety of activities that support a best practice array of learning structures.

References

Allen, I. E., & Seaman, J. (2013). *Changing course: Ten years of tracking online education in the United States*. Wellesley, MA: Babson College.

Anido-Rifón, L. E., Fernández-Iglesias, M. J., Caeiro-Rodríguez, M., Santos-Gago, J. M., Llamas-Nistal, M., Sabucedo, L. A., & Pérez, R. M. (2014). Standardization in computer-based education. *Computer Standards and Interfaces, 36*(3), 604–625.

Arasasingham, R. D., Martorell, I., & McIntire, T. M. (2011). Online homework and student achievement in a large enrollment introductory science course. *Journal of College Science Teaching, 40*(6), 70–79.

Arbaugh, J. B., Bangert, A., & Cleveland-Innes, M. (2010). Subject matter effects and the Community of Inquiry (CoI) framework: An exploratory study. *The Internet and Higher Education*, *13*(1–2), 37–44.

Bailey, J. E., Whitmeyer, S. J., & De Paor, D. G. (2012). Introduction: The application of Google Geo Tools to geoscience education and research. In S. J. Whitmeyer, J. E. Bailey, D. G. De Paor, & T. Ornduff (Eds.), *Google Earth and virtual visualizations in geoscience education and research* (GSA Special Papers 492) (pp. vii–xix). Denver, CO: Geological Society of America.

Balfour, S. P. (2013). Assessing writing in MOOCS: Automated essay scoring and Calibrated Peer Review. *Research and Practice in Assessment*, *8*(1), 40–48.

Barclay, E. J., Renshaw, C. E., Taylor, H. A., & Bilge, A. R. (2011). Improving decision making skill using an Online Volcanic Crisis Simulation: Impact of data presentation format. *Journal of Geoscience Education*, *59*(2), 85–92.

Blenkinsop, T. G. (2012). Visualizing structural geology: From Excel to Google Earth. *Computers and Geosciences*, *45*, 52–56.

Boling, E. C., Hough, M., Krinsky, H., Saleem, H., & Stevens, M. (2012). Cutting the distance in distance education: Perspectives on what promotes positive, online learning experiences. *The Internet and Higher Education*, *15*(2), 118–126.

Çaliskan, O. (2011). Virtual field trips in education of earth and environmental sciences. *Procedia: Social and Behavioral Sciences*, *15*, 3239–3243.

Cervato, C., Kerton, C., Peer, A., Hassall, L., & Schmidt, A. (2013). The big crunch: A hybrid solution to earth and space science instruction for elementary education majors. *Journal of Geoscience Education*, *61*(2), 73–186.

Clary, R. M., & Wandersee, J. H. (2014). Integration of inquiry fossil research approaches and students' local environments within online geoscience classrooms. In V. C. H. Tong (Ed.), *Geoscience research and education: Teaching at universities (Innovations in science education and technology)* (Vol. 20, pp. 111–148). Dordrecht, the Netherlands: Springer.

Cloutis, E. (2010). Laboratories in the earth sciences. In D. Kennepohl & L. Shaw (Eds.), *Accessible elements: Teaching science online and at a distance* (pp. 147–165). Edmonton, Canada: AU Press.

Collins, T., Gaved, M., & Lea, J. (2010, October). *Remote fieldwork: Using portable wireless networks and backhaul links to participate remotely in fieldwork*. Paper presented at the Ninth World Conference on Mobile and Contextual Learning (mlearn 2010), Valletta, Malta. Retrieved from oro.open.ac.uk/24711

Davis, M. G., & Chapman, D. S. (2012). A web-based resource for investigating environmental change: The Emigrant Pass Observatory. *Journal of Geoscience Education*, *60*(3), 241–248.

Davis, L. E. (2012). Another geoscience department "bites the dust." *The Compass: Earth Science Journal of Sigma Gamma Epsilon*, *84*(2), Article 2.

Day, T. (2012). Undergraduate teaching and learning in physical geography. *Progress in Physical Geography*, *36*(3), 305–332.

Dong, S., & Hubble, T. (2004). Making online learning more student-centered in the Department of Earth Sciences at the University of Nanjing. *CAL-laborate*, *11*, 27–32.

Dong, S., Xu, S., & Lu, X. (2009). Development of online instructional resources for earth system science education: An example of current practice from China. *Computers and Geosciences*, *35*(6), 1271–1279.

Downing, K. F., & Holtz, J. K. (2008). *Online science learning: Best practices and technologies*. Hershey, PA: IGI Global.

Downing, K. F., & Holtz, J. K. (2012). Best practices for online paleontology instruction. In M. M. Yacobucci & R. Lockwood (Eds.), *Teaching paleontology in the 21st century* (Vol. 12, pp. 109–122). Boulder, CO: The Paleontological Society.

Feig, A. D. (2010). An online introductory physical geology laboratory: From concept to outcome. *Geosphere*, *6*(6), 942–951.

Flowers, L. O., Moore, J. L., III, & Flowers, L. A. (2011). Effective use of the virtual laboratory in online science courses. *Online Classroom*, 2–3.

Gold, A. U., Ledley, T. S., Buhr, S. M., Fox, S., McCaffrey, M., Niepold, F., . . . Lynds, S. E. (2012). Peer-review of digital educational resources: A rigorous review process developed by the Climate Literacy and Energy Awareness Network (CLEAN). *Journal of Geoscience Education*, *60*(4), 295–308.

Gorsky, P., & Caspi, A. (2010). Learning science at a distance: Instructional dialogues and resources. In D. Kennepohl & L. Shaw (Eds.), *Accessible elements: Teaching science online and at a distance* (pp. 19–36). Edmonton, Canada: AU Press.

Granshaw, F., & Duggan-Haas, D. (2012). Virtual fieldwork in geoscience teacher education: Issues, techniques, and models. In S. J. Whitmeyer, J. E. Bailey, D. G. De Paor, & T. Ornduff (Eds.), *Google Earth and virtual visualizations in geoscience education and research* (GSA Special Papers 492) (pp. 285–303). Denver, CO: Geological Society of America.

Hariri, M. M. (2013). Effective use of LMS (learning management system) in teaching graduate geology course at KFUPM, Saudi Arabia. In *Proceedings of the Fourth International Conference on e-Learning Best Practices in Management, Design and Development of e-Courses: Standards of Excellence and Creativity* (pp. 342–347). Washington, DC: IEEE Computer Society.

Hart, C. (2012). Factors associated with student persistence in an online program of study. *Distance Education Report*, *16*(11), 4–8.

Holbrook, J., & Dupont, C. (2011). Making the decision to provide enhanced podcasts to post-secondary science students. *Journal of Science Education and Technology*, *20*(3), 233–245.

Jeschofnig, L., & Jeschofnig, P. (2011). *Teaching lab science courses online: Resources for best practices, tools, and technology.* San Francisco, CA: Jossey-Bass.

Jolley, A., Lane, E., Kennedy, B., & Frappé-Sénéclauze, T.-P. (2012). SPESS: A new instrument for measuring student perceptions in earth and ocean science. *Journal of Geoscience Education*, *60*(1), 83–91.

Jordan, K. (2014). Initial trends in enrolment and completion of massive open online courses. *The International Review of Research in Open and Distance Learning*, *15*(1), 133–160.

Kennepohl, D. (2010). Remote control teaching laboratories and practicals. In D. Kennepohl & L. Shaw (Eds.), *Accessible elements: Teaching science online and at a distance* (pp. 167–190). Edmonton, Canada: AU Press.

Kennepohl, D., & Shaw, L. (2010). *Accessible elements: Teaching science online and at a distance.* Edmonton, Canada: AU Press.

Kerton, C., & Cervato, C. (2014). Assessment in online learning: It's a matter of time. *Journal of College Science Teaching*, *43*(4), 20.

Kim, J. (2013). Influence of group size on students' participation in online discussion forums. *Computers and Education*, *62*(3), 123–129.

Kim, R., Olfman, L., Ryan, T., & Eryilmaz, E. (2014). Leveraging a personalized system to improve self-directed learning in online educational environments. *Computers and Education*, *70*(3), 150–160.

King, K. P., & Cox, T. D. (Eds.). (2011). *The professor's guide to taming technology: Leveraging digital media, Web 2.0, and more for learning.* Charlotte, NC: Information Age Publishing.

Kirkwood, A. (2008). Getting it from the web: Why and how online resources are used by independent undergraduate learners. *Journal of Computer Assisted Learning*, *24*(5), 372–382.

Lee, Y., & Choi, J. (2011). A review of online course dropout research: Implications for practice and future research. *Educational Technology Research and Development*, *59*(5), 593–618.

Lin, H., Hong, Z.-R., & Lawrenz, F. (2012). Promoting and scaffolding argumentation through reflective asynchronous discussions. *Computers and Education, 59*(2), 378–384.

Lorenzetti, J. P. (2013). What we can learn from students who leave online courses. *Recruitment and Retention, 27*(7), 8.

Lyall, R., & Patti, A. (2010). Taking the chemistry experience home: Home experiments or "kitchen chemistry." In D. Kennepohl & L. Shaw (Eds.), *Accessible elements: Teaching science online and at a distance* (pp. 83–108). Edmonton, Canada: AU Press.

Manduca, C. A., & Kastens, K. A. (2012a). Geoscience and geoscientists: Uniquely equipped to study Earth. *Geological Society of America Special Papers, 486*, 1–12.

Manduca, C. A., & Kastens, K. A. (2012b). Mapping the domain of spatial thinking in the geosciences. *Geological Society of America Special Papers, 486*, 45–49.

Mathers, N., Goktogen, A., Rankin, J., & Anderson, M. (2012). Robotic mission to Mars: Hands-on, minds-on, web-based learning. *Acta Astronautica, 80*, 124–131.

Mawn, M. V., Carrico, P., Charuk, K., Stote, K. S., & Lawrence, B. (2011). Hands-on and online: Scientific explorations through distance learning. *Open Learning, 26*(2), 135–146.

Missett, T. C., Reed, C. B., Scot, T. P., Callahan, C. M., & Slade, M. (2010). Describing learning in an advanced online case-based course in environmental science. *Journal of Advanced Academics, 22*(1), 10–50.

Moller, L., Robison, D., & Huett, J. B. (2012). Unconstrained learning: Principles for the next generation of distance education. In L. Moller & J. B. Huett (Eds.), *The next generation of distance education: Unconstrained learning* (pp. 1–20). New York, NY: Springer.

Monet, J., & Greene, T. (2012). Using Google Earth and satellite imagery to foster place-based teaching in an introductory physical geology course. *Journal of Geoscience Education, 60*(1), 10–20.

Morris, T. A. (2011). Exploring community college student perceptions of online learning. *International Journal of Instructional Technology and Distance Learning, 8*(6), 31–43.

Otter, R. R., Seipel, S., Graeff, T., Alexander, B., Boraiko, C., Gray, J., . . . Sadler, K. (2013). Comparing student and faculty perceptions of online and traditional courses. *The Internet and Higher Education, 19*, 27–35.

Palmer, R. E. (2013). Learning geomorphology using aerial photography in a web-facilitated class. *Review of International Geographical Education Online, 3*(2), 118–137.

Reddy, C. (2014). A new species of science education: Harnessing the power of interactive technology to teach laboratory science. *American Biology Teacher, 76*(1), 28–33.

Sellés-Martínez, J. (2013). Informal educational strategies in teaching geosciences when formal courses are unavailable: The experience of AulaGEA in Buenos Aires, Argentina. *Journal of Geoscience Education, 61*(1), 3–11.

Smith, C. H. (2013). *The nearly free university and the emerging economy: The revolution in higher education*. Berkeley, CA: CreateSpace Independent Publishing Platform.

Stillings, N. (2012). Complex systems in the geosciences and in geoscience learning. In K. A. Kastens & C. A. Manduca (Eds.), *Earth and mind II: A synthesis of research on thinking and learning in the geosciences* (GSA Special Papers 486) (pp. 97–111). Denver, CO: Geological Society of America.

Stott, T. A., Litherland, K., Carmichael, P., & Nuttall, A. M. (2013). Design, development and evolution of interactive virtual field guides for teaching geosciences. In V. C. H. Tong (Ed.), *Geoscience research and education: Teaching at universities (Innovations in science education and technology)* (Vol. 20, pp. 163–188). Dordrecht, the Netherlands: Springer.

Todd, C. E. D., & Goeke, E. R. (2012). Incorporating student-led field trips and learner-centered teaching in a capstone geology course. *Journal of Geoscience Education, 60*(3), 268–276.

Tong, V. C. H. (Ed.). (2014). *Geoscience research and education: Teaching at universities (Innovations in science education and technology)* (Vol. 20). Dordrecht, the Netherlands: Springer.

Traphagan, T., Kucsera, J. V., & Kishi, K. (2010). Impact of class lecture webcasting on attendance and learning. *Educational Technology Research and Development, 58*(1), 19–37.

Ucar, S., & Trundle, K. C. (2011). Conducting guided inquiry in science classes using authentic, archived, web-based data. *Computers and Education, 57*(2), 1571–1582.

van der Hoeven Kraft, K. J., Srogi, L., Husman, J., Semken, S., & Fuhrman, M. (2011). Engaging students to learn through the affective domain: A new framework for teaching in the geosciences. *Journal of Geoscience Education, 59*(2), 71–84.

Wallace, D. J., & Witus, A. E. (2013). Integrating iPad technology in earth science K–12 outreach courses: Field and classroom applications. *Journal of Geoscience Education, 61*(4), 385–395.

Weng, Y. H., Sun, F. S., & Grigsby, J. D. (2012). GeoTools: An Android phone application in geology. *Computers and Geosciences, 44*, 24–30.

Wenk, L., & Tronsky, L. (2011). First-year students benefit from reading primary research articles. *Journal of College Science Teaching, 40*(4), 60–67.

Werhner, M. J. (2010). A comparison of the performance of online versus traditional on-campus earth science students on identical exams. *Journal of Geoscience Education, 58*(5), 310–312.

Whalley, P., Kelley, S., & Tindle, A. (2011). The role of the virtual microscope in distance learning. *Open Learning, 26*(2), 127–134.

Wysession, M. E., LaDue, N., Budd, D. A., Campbell, K., Conklin, M., Kappel, E., . . . Tuddenham, P. (2012). Developing and applying a set of earth science literacy principles. *Journal of Geoscience Education, 60*(2), 95–99.

Xu, D., & Jaggars, S. S. (2013). *Adaptability to online learning: Differences across types of students and academic subject areas* (CCRC Working Paper No. 54). New York, NY: Community College Research Center, Columbia University.

Yang, D. (2013, December). Instructional strategies for teaching science online. *2013 IEEE Frontiers in Education Conference,* 1477–1479. Retrieved from dx.doi.org/10.1109/FIE.2013.6685081

4

PHYSICS TEACHING IN DISTANCE EDUCATION

Robert Lambourne and Nicholas Braithwaite
The Open University

Abstract

A broad introduction to the characteristics that distinguish the teaching of physics in distance education from its teaching in more conventional face-to-face contexts is presented. The coverage is designed to be of particular value to those who are starting to use the methods of distance education for the first time, irrespective of their institutional setting. The authors draw on their own experience at The Open University in the United Kingdom, and elsewhere, and pay particular attention to the motivations, challenges, and methodologies of providing students with the benefits of practical physics in the context of distance education.

In a large modern lecture theater, it would be easy to think that distance education in physics is concerned with ensuring that students in the back row can hear and see as much as those in the front row. The reality, of course, is that distance education is rarely about lecture theaters and almost never aimed at students sitting in rows. Sometimes defined as "the presentation of an educational curriculum through self-study materials, often supplemented by regular contact with an instructor," (Al-Shamali & Connors, 2010. p. 131) *distance education* has grown and changed with the development of communications technology.

It was the introduction of reliable postal services that gave distance education (by correspondence) its initial impetus. Its detailed practice was then modified by the successive introduction of telephones, radio and TV broadcasting, and home audio recording, leading to bodies such as the Australian "Schools of the Air"; the proposed "University of the Air"; and, in 1969, its fully realized successor, The Open University (OU) in the United Kingdom. The technology took another step forward with the introduction of home video recording. However, the development that has had the greatest impact on distance education in recent decades has undoubtedly been the widespread availability of powerful, low-cost, personal computers and the parallel developments of the World Wide Web and the Internet—the "nervous system" of planet Earth. So profound has been the impact of this latest communications revolution that it is easy to make the mistake of equating distance education with computer-based education. The truth, however, is that the center of distance education remains the act of communication between the teacher and the learner and the learner's internal response to that message—the teaching and learning nexus—irrespective of the technology used to deliver it.

The overall effect of these changes and developments, along with the move toward a more mobile and dynamic society in which jobs are rarely for life and lifelong learning is a requirement rather than an aspiration, has been to make distance education an increasingly central part of the general educational process. No longer is distance education primarily aimed at geographically isolated or physically handicapped students who cannot participate in conventional education. Nor is it the preserve of those who are unable to attend a conventional institution because of cost or lack of time. Rather, it has become part of the spectrum of available educational methodologies with well-appreciated characteristics. Distance education is unusually responsive to technical advances and can play a vital part in a conventional education and a crucial role in a nontraditional one. No longer the methodology of last resort, distance education has joined the mainstream and is increasingly deployed as simply another part of the modern educator's tool kit.

Physics, like the other sciences discussed in this book, has both influenced and been influenced by the development of distance education. The nature of that two-way interaction has naturally been shaped by the particular characteristics that distinguish physics from other parts of science. It is natural, therefore, to start with a characterization of physics, at least in its pedagogical aspect, and attempt to uncover those features of distance education that provide particular opportunities and challenges for distance education in physics.

Characteristics of Physics Courses

Physics is rightly viewed as a subject rooted in and validated by experiment. No matter how attractive or potentially valuable a physical theory, it requires continued and repeated experimental support. Many physicists would add that new experimental data are also needed to ensure that the extension and renewal of existing theories are headed in the right general direction.

Despite the vital importance of firm experimental foundations, the most widely recognized distinguishing feature of physics is its strong emphasis on mathematics. This runs through the whole subject and is as relevant to practical work as it is to theory. This is reflected in the fact that many physics teaching programs aim to equip students to be competent and flexible quantitative problem solvers or solution finders, valued at least as much for what they can do as for what they know.

The findings of physics, whether describing individual quantities or relationships between quantities, are often described in mathematical terms, typically involving scientific notation and units of measurement (now usually SI), as well as conventional indications of error ranges and uncertainties. Moreover, the arguments used are themselves likely to take a mathematical form and may depend on lengthy chains of deductive reasoning involving typographically complicated symbols such as derivatives, definite and indefinite integrals, and summation signs. A common adjunct to this is the extensive use of italic, Roman, and Greek fonts; lots of subscripts and superscripts; and the critical application of emboldening to distinguish multicomponent vectors, tensors, or matrices from single-component scalars. The widespread use of mathematical symbols and notation in physics teaching means that the preparation of texts—for study, support, or assessment—is likely to require careful consideration of the limitations of print and display equipment. Even introductory physics courses based on algebra rather than calculus are likely to require systems that can handle the entry of superscripts and subscripts. Of course, many powerful and versatile text-handling systems already exist, such as LaTeX, MathType, and Microsoft Word's Equation Editor. These are well able to meet any reasonable challenge in mathematical or scientific typography. However, all of them take time to master, and none of them offer anything like the speed and ease of conventional pencil and paper when it comes to setting out large amounts of mathematically based physics. In addition, these systems may involve additional costs or specific technical requirements that limit their suitability for student use in a given context. This can be a particular issue in the case of basic e-mail and social media systems, which are not primarily designed for the communication of technical messages.

Similar comments apply to the provision of graphs and diagrams. In a largely online world, it is generally very easy to ask a student to sketch a graph illustrating some specified relationship, but the challenge this poses may well have more to do with the tools available for graph plotting than the student's knowledge of the required relationship. The growing availability of tablet computing is going some way toward making the online production and sharing of mathematics, graphs, and diagrams easier in both conventional and distance teaching, but there is still some way to go before all of the presentational problems will be truly overcome.

Partly as a result of the increasing amount of mathematics encountered in upper division physics courses, physics is generally seen as a hierarchical subject. Classical mechanics naturally precedes quantum mechanics, and quantum field theory just as naturally follows quantum mechanics and classical field theory. Because of this inbuilt hierarchy, many physics degree programs have the following general structure in which the levels or stages are studied sequentially, and each might typically correspond to a year of full-time study:

- *Stage 1:* Basic applied math and the first part of a broad physics survey course
- *Stage 2:* More advanced math and the more advanced parts of a broad physics survey course
- *Stage 3:* Specialist courses applying principles taught earlier in particular contexts
- *Stage 4:* Specialist options and project work

Another of the distinguishing features of physics as an educational enterprise is the existence of an exceptionally strong community of discipline-based educational researchers, particularly in the United States. Few of the leading practitioners in the field have a specific interest in distance education, but the findings and resources they have generated are of value to all of those engaged in physics teaching and are a good indication of a potential area of growth in the future. A useful starting point for those seeking further information on this topic is the comprehensive review originally prepared as part of a

U.S. Board of Science Education study that included comparisons between the work relating specifically to physics and that being conducted in biology, chemistry, and earth science (Docktor & Mestre, 2014).

Course Elements

Anyone attempting to teach a physics course or module online will need to consider several different aspects of the provision. Even a minimal listing should probably include the following elements:

- A clear statement of expected learning outcomes
- Advertisement and student recruitment (including entry requirements if any)
- Student registration, provision of online access, and fee collection (if relevant)
- Provision of basic learning materials (textbooks, study notes, and/or online equivalents)
- Provision of additional learning materials (audiovisual materials, computer simulations, online activities, relevant websites, online library, etc.)
- Study support resources, including access to individual tutorial support (if provided), specialized math support if needed, and a student–tutor forum for message sharing
- Continuous assessment (and self-assessment) resources, including systems for distributing questions, collecting and marking the answers, and (where appropriate) returning feedback to the students so that they can learn from their mistakes and improve their performance
- Provision of a final exam or end-of-course assessment (the format and scale of this might be dictated by institutional policy, as might the need for any additional tests at midsession or other times)
- Systems for recording and conflating exam and assessment scores, determining final results, and reporting results to students and other relevant parties

At least half the items in the preceding list are standard aspects of conventional course provision. Those working in an established institution who are simply adding an element of distance teaching to their existing course or module will probably already have arrangements (or at least institutional requirements) in place for such subject-independent tasks. In many cases, an institutional virtual learning environment (VLE), based on a system such as Moodle or Blackboard, will provide the necessary framework. Even so, special arrangements may have to be put in place to enable off-campus students or tutors to have access to the VLE used by those on campus, and this may require the sending of a private text or some other kind of secure message that can provide the student with a personal identifier and a password.

Of course, for those starting completely from scratch, everything will have to be considered, including the acceptable range of student locations. In a globally offered course, for instance, just one or two students living in China or Australia can make the provision of real-time (i.e., synchronous) tutorial support very arduous for a tutor living in the United States or the United Kingdom. Even in cases where students are required to live "nearby," it must be remembered that many students may have to travel as an essential part of their work; this is certainly the case for students in the armed forces or embassy personnel who may be particularly encouraged to undertake distance education.

Study Materials

Much of the physics syllabus, particularly at the introductory level, has become highly conventionalized over the past few decades. Many colleges and universities now offer introductory physics in algebra-based and calculus-based varieties that use different versions of the same few "compendium" textbooks. These books often originate in the United States, though they may be specialized for specific overseas markets and are often intended primarily for those planning to major in engineering rather than physics. The increasing amount of common ground in these introductory physics courses has encouraged the publishers of the standard texts to create substantial resource banks (question banks, activity banks, multimedia banks, and banks of PowerPoint slides for use in lectures) that support, extend, and enhance the textbook. Many of the publishers also have in place well-developed arrangements for providing electronic access to a particular version and edition of their textbook, either in addition to the print version or in place of it.

For those institutions newly engaged in the provision of distance education in introductory physics, the adoption of one of these compendium texts, particularly through an online version, is an obvious way of meeting their students' need for basic study materials and perhaps for much else besides. However, despite publishers' natural confidence in their texts' suitability for distance learners, it is necessary to examine what is on offer with some caution. Conventional textbooks are generally designed to support a lecture course, not to replace it. They often show the terseness one would expect of a text designed to be studied after a lecture rather than the more supportive text that distance learners are likely to need. The economic argument in favor of adopting a resource-rich conventional compendium text may be undeniable, but those just starting to provide distance education should carefully consider providing additional materials such as study guides and glossaries that can give students extra targeted help with topics or issues that are well-known sources of difficulty or are soon shown to be in the light of experience. At the very least, distance learners are likely to need much more "signposting," because their more isolated way of working can easily leave them feeling uncertain about how long to spend getting to grips with a new concept. In physics, this is often longer than the time taken to simply read the words devoted to a particular topic. For this reason, a printable study calendar that sets the pace of study and lists all of the key dates and deadlines that students should meet is often one of the most essential aids to studying at a distance. Students should be encouraged to keep a copy where they can see it easily and refer to it often.

Whatever study materials are used, those planning a distance education course will need to have in mind a realistic estimate of just how much reading, writing, or online interacting students can be expected to do given the material and technology available. Such are the demands of learning from even a well-written physics text that relatively slow reading rates of 150 words per minute are generally thought to be realistic (Carver, 1992). The average reading rate is about 250 words per minute for adults. Those preparing to write scripts for audio or video presentations should probably be planning on the order of three words per second. A picture, it is often said, is worth a thousand words; for some particularly rich images (e.g., the color-magnitude diagram so beloved by stellar astronomers), this may be almost literally true. More generally, however, the distance educator must be aware of the time and encouragement that students will need to properly engage with a picture. In the specific case of physics, similar comments also apply to equations. For advanced students, equations make powerful shorthand; however, for the beginner, reading an equation or even an extended mathematical argument is a demanding task that will lengthen rather than shorten reading times.

Most educators will have their own preferences regarding which particular texts or styles they prefer. Some features, such as the consistent use of SI units, the highlighting of newly introduced terms, and the boxing of major equations, are now almost universal in introductory books, though they may be absent in the more advanced texts. However, some particularly useful general insights may be obtained from the work carried out by Norman Reid (2009) and other members of the Glasgow University Science Education group over a number of years. The group has paid particular attention to the role of short-term operational memory in learning, and a clear lesson is the difficulty that students encounter when they are required to carry more than about six items in their head simultaneously when trying to learn something new. The sense that a new subject is somehow "too big" to grasp will be familiar to many, though the source of that feeling may be less familiar, as may be the possibility of overcoming it by "rechunking" the study material in a different way.

Student Activity

Any kind of study is, of course, a form of activity. However, the term *student activity* is used here to denote some kind of purposeful activity that may have its own goals and outcomes and is sufficiently different from the general text-based mode of learning that it can be seen as "breaking up or rechunking" what might otherwise be a monolithic block of learning material. Student activities are therefore seen as a useful device for adding motivation, improving engagement, and avoiding tedium, as well as simply providing logical developments of the argument. Many designers of online teaching materials use more or less formal rules to determine the number and extent of student activities in a given period of study. Others claim a sense of what feels right in a given situation. In either case, it is important to avoid overloading students with additional tasks and never to waste the students' time by assigning a pointless or irrelevant task (Price, Carroll, O'Donovan, & Rust, 2011). Even telling students to take a coffee break is better than that!

Many conventional teachers of physics have at least some sympathy with the discovery dictum: "Tell me and I forget, show me and I remember, let me discover and I understand." However, most will also say that a crowded physics curriculum generally has too little time for the extensive use of discovery learning and, frequently, insufficient resources as well. Often the best that can be done is to teach clearly, provide plenty of relevant examples (possibly including experimental demonstrations), and then try to drive home the points with quantitative problems that the students must solve for themselves. Distance teaching can certainly offer counterparts to each of these pursuits but may also provide some specific advantages when it comes to student activity.

Quantitative problem-solving is one form of student activity that almost all physicists recognize as important, and many would deem it essential. Activities can range from simple "seek-and-substitute" exercises intended to illustrate a particular point to complicated multistep problems designed to improve problem-solving skills (Rebello, Cui, Bennett, Zollman, & Ozimek, 2007). Online access to solutions can be arranged in a number of ways (using hyperlinks, etc.) and may even be controlled or recorded for credit, though students generally dislike being unable to access different parts of an online text. One system that has worked well at OU allows students to make three attempts at answering online questions. If the first answer is wrong, the system provides the student with a hint. A second wrong answer to the same question prompts the system to return a detailed hint that will enable most serious students to find the right answer after a little work. A third wrong answer is met with a full solution. Naturally, the credit that students can earn for answering a question is reduced as more help is given. This automatic quiz system is useful both for basic teaching and for revision. Its value is boosted by ensuring that, where possible, students returning to a question they have answered some time before at least encounter different quantitative data, so they cannot simply remember the answer—the aim is memorizing the method.

Students working online might have a real advantage when it comes to quantitative problem solving, because, if resources and background permit, they may be given immediate access to an algebraic computing package (e.g., Mathematica) that can do much of the mathematical analysis for them. This can leave the students free to concentrate on the task of converting physical problems into well-formulated mathematical ones and then, having solved the mathematical problems using the algebra package, converting the answers back into physically meaningful terms.

Online assignments are not limited to mechanical problem-solving. Many student activities involve watching a video; listening to audio material; consulting relevant external websites; or interacting with some piece of software, such as one of the many so-called physlets available online (see Christian & Belloni, 2001, 2013; the resource site webphysics.davidson.edu/Applets/Applets.html; one of the excellent pieces of PhET software developed at the University of Colorado, Boulder [Wieman, Adams, & Perkins, 2008]; and the current PhET website [phet.colorado.edu]). Finding the appropriate resources can be a serious challenge, as anyone who has spent time looking through low-quality, poorly conceived, and badly explained YouTube videos can attest. However, there are some valuable items available, and the problem of finding them can sometimes be alleviated by going to a repository site, especially one that includes standardized reviews of "discovered" software. One well-known source of this kind can be found at the ComPADRE website (www.compadre.org), though there are several others. Another innovation to be aware of is the reusable learning object (RLO). What constitutes an RLO is still a matter of debate, but the basic concept is that of a small digital learning package designed in such a way that it can be incorporated into a wide range of online courses without any significant modification; hence, the term *reusable*. See, for example, Lambourne (2010) and links therein.

Student activity is certainly not limited to what a single student may achieve while using a computer. Collaborative activities may be arranged, and the activity itself may involve real-world observations, measurements, or actions. One possible form of student activity is the creation of new resource material, especially in the form of videos, posters, or PowerPoint presentations. If approached in the right way, each of these can be a valuable and engaging activity, though it is always necessary to be clear about the purpose of the activity. As the late Eric Rogers observed, physics is fun but fun is not necessarily physics.

Experimentation is also a form of student activity. Such student activities can be just short and simple experiments, sometimes supported by low-cost practical kits that can be loaned to the student or even given away as disposable items. However, despite the obvious challenges, experimental activities are not necessarily small scale, nor are supplmentary practical kits always low cost. Such is the importance of experimental work in distance education; so great are its challenges, and so rich the range of innovations it has inspired, that this is really a subject that deserves its own specialized and extended coverage, which is provided next.

The Nature of Practical Work

Before considering the challenges that practical work poses for distance educators, let us reflect on the nature, variety, and purpose of practical work. Practical work in science is an important means of engaging students with opportunities to learn. The aims are to impart science knowledge, to evolve conceptual understanding, and to develop the skills of inquiry. A relevant general report titled "Practical Work in Science," primarily concerning school science but containing many points of clear definition and general validity, is that of the Science Community Representing Education (2008) based in the United Kingdom.

In 1997, the American Association of Physics Teachers (www.aapt.org/Resources/policy/upload/Goal.pdf) proposed the following goals for introductory physics laboratories and for more advanced practical work up to, but perhaps not including, individual project work:

I. *The Art of Experimentation*: The introductory laboratory should engage each student in significant experiences with experimental processes, including some experience designing investigation.

II. *Experimental and Analytical Skills*: The laboratory should help the student develop a broad array of basic skills and tools of experimental physics and data analysis.

III. *Conceptual Learning*: The laboratory should help students master basic physics concepts.

IV. *Understanding the Basis of Knowledge in Physics*: The laboratory should help students understand the role of direct observation in physics and to distinguish between inferences based on theory and the outcomes of experiments.

V. *Developing Collaborative Learning Skills*: The laboratory should help students develop collaborative learning skills that are vital to success in many lifelong endeavors.

The spectrum of practical devices available to the educator ranges from well-choreographed, instructor-led demonstrations to subtly guided journeys of personal discovery. In the former, the students are shown phenomena that they are as yet insufficiently skilled and inadequately resourced to reveal for themselves. This encompasses the classic lecture demonstrations presented in lecture theaters by the likes of Michael Faraday and his modern successors, who now also use broadcast media to reach their audience. In the other extreme, students must be presumed to have acquired the basic techniques of inquiry. They must also have access to appropriate tools for the task. In practice, the availability and fidelity of measurement instruments often constrains what can be discovered, and then the guidance is less subtle.

Experimental apparatuses are designed to eliminate the confounding factors that mask the true relationship, thereby enabling specific effects to be observed. For example, sources of noise are subdued, uncertainties in positioning are minimized, leakage currents are taken into account, and the physical environment is stabilized. For these reasons, the concept of a laboratory emerges as a place that is equipped for measurements and that wholly contains the systems under study. The reductionist approach of traditional physics sits very comfortably in this scenario.

Another class of practical work space is the observatory. Here the data flow into the measurement space from outside, classically exemplified by an astronomical observatory. The key distinction between this and a laboratory is that the raw signals arrive without any opportunity to affect the source directly. The investigator designs measurements and analysis but not the primary events.

The Challenge of Practical Work at a Distance

To make good use of practical work, the distance educator needs to be able to bring students close enough to see the preparation of the environment, to read the instruments, to feel the heat, and to witness the effects. *Firsthand* and *hands-on* are two descriptive terms that are often used in making the case for so-called real practical work. So how can we provide opportunities for personal, tactile experiences of science in action?

Until the late twentieth century, the options for providing practical work in physics were the following: the students were sent "home experiment kits" supplemented by locally sourced materials or were required to attend a specific laboratory or observatory for specific periods of time. Of course, the latter undermines the notion of distance education; nevertheless, at OU, a combination of these two has been used for over 40 years. Interestingly, the use of home experiment kits was phased out a few years ago because of difficulties with shipping the kit to students outside the United Kingdom, advances in health and safety practice, statistics showing low student use, and concerns about expense.

The advent of desktop computers appeared to offer a third option, namely computer-based experiments, a somewhat disruptive technology. However, there is a major difference between contrived, algorithmic interactive graphics and investigations of an unknown world. Computer simulations have an important role to play in illustrating established relationships, but they are a poor substitute for education and skills training for practical science. There remains the opportunity to use computers to present real data through authentic interfaces, that is, a recreation of real events as opposed to a simulation of an artificial reality.

A far larger disruption is enabled when those desktop computers are connected over the Internet. As well as offering unprecedented access to instrumentation and data, this option most closely replicates the real world of practical-based research, where networked tools accessed through keyboards and screens are ubiquitous. By its very nature, physics is at the forefront of this revolution.

There is a further wave of revolution initiated by the personalization and democratization of communication technology. Tablets and mobile devices now provide multisensor, multimeter capability that is powered by the ingenuity of myriad application developers. Furthermore, social connectivity enables rapid data transfer and data pooling. Adapting teaching labs to the availability of social tools and social media will be an exhilarating exercise, one that will remain in a perpetual state of development as new capabilities emerge. Thus, the challenge for distance education has become one of discovering how to use the Internet, and things connected to it, to provide the personal, tactile experiences that we need for practical science in general.

Options and Opportunities for On-Screen Labs and Observatories

Campus-based institutions as well as online educators have something to gain from the development of on-screen options for practical work. For the more ethereal presence of the distance learning regime, on-screen devices are the major enabler for genuine practical activities at a distance, but for conventional laboratories and observatories, these tools increase efficiency when using space and apparatus. Indeed, the on-screen approach offers safe environments for unsupervised learning of practical skills and facilities for revisiting after hours. There is a clear pedagogic imperative for developing and evaluating on-screen labs and observatories to the benefit of both sectors.

In the next sections, we describe the following examples of on-screen practical engagement:

- Interactive screen experiments (ISEs) that represent archival data in a realistic version of the original setting
- Immersive environments that present realistic visual clues aimed at creating a three-dimensional (3D) virtual reality within which real data can be accessed
- Robotic instrumentation that can be operated by remote users

Many activities use a combination of these. To provide a general framework for comparison, we offer here a classification system that allows the comparison of different genera (courtesy of our researcher Marcus Brodeur). The parameters represent the key distinctions between the various possible classes of scientific investigations. The schema works as shown in Table 4.1.

TABLE 4.1
A Classification Scheme for Practical Activity

Attribute	*Characterization*
Fidelity	Real-world data: fully (5)—artificial (0)
Locus	Representational setting: natural (5)—artificial (0)
Control	Data acquisition: user control (5)—auto/none (0)
Instrumentation	Use of scientific instruments: authentic (5)—none (0)

TABLE 4.1 *(Continued)*

Attribute	Characterization
Agency	Navigation: user control (5)—auto/none (0)
Temporality	Data flow: real time (5)—from archive (0)
Depth	Number of experimental quantities: n
Outcome	Instructional design: open-ended (5)—closed (0)
Sociability	Collaborative learning: essential (5)—none (0)

There is no single experimental ideal, whether in a face-to-face situation or at a distance, but an activity that scores zero in all aspects of this schema is unlikely to be an effective device for engaging students or for stimulating their inquiry and learning.

Interactive Screen Experiments

The use of archival images to reconstruct the experience of experimentation was pioneered in Germany as *interaktive Bildschirmexperimente* (Kirstein, 1999; Kirstein & Nordmeier, 2007; Theyßen, von Aufschnaiter, & Schumacher, 2002). The concept has been further interpreted as the Reality Viewer (www.st-andrews.ac.uk/~bds2/ltsn/reality.htm) (Sinclair, Gillies, & Bacon, 2004) and directly translated into ISEs for distance learners by colleagues at OU (Lambourne, 2007) and The OpenScience Laboratory (learn5.open.ac.uk/course/view.php?id=2).

In its broadest sense, an *ISE* can be defined as a highly interactive sequence of images captured from an experimental arrangement. Images of the equipment may be taken simultaneously from a small number of fixed locations to follow the action. An ISE is recorded (using still-image and video cameras) as the experiment is being performed. A simple movie that can be moved forward or backward at different rates would present limited interactivity, which, though valuable, would restrict the range of possible interactions. The ISE instead allows users to select images and views on the basis of the experimental quantities (e.g., a voltage level, an angle, a position, a knob setting). The images may also capture the simultaneous instrument readings, the physical disposition of component parts, and the colors that would be seen by a local experimenter. Capturing the whole requires the recording of all "reasonable" combinations of the parameters. It then allows an experimenter at some later time to adopt one parameter as an independent variable, with any remaining controllable quantities as parameters, and to follow one or more of the outputs as dependent variables.

A single parameter is easily accommodated. For example, the strength of the axial magnetic field of a short solenoid carrying a given current can be detected with a Hall probe and recorded as a function of axial position for various levels of coil current. The archive needs to store digital images for each small increment of axial position, for each "choice" of the magnitude and direction of current in the coil current. For just the axial field, the data set is manageable, but why bother when there are simple algebraic formulas that relate the axial field (and even the off-axis field) to the current and spatial position? In these simple situations, the algebraic formulas are applicable only when all of the current flows at the coil radius and at $z = 0$, which is conveniently located on the axial midplane. Therein lies the answer to the question "Why do the experiment?" The real scenario is at odds with the model scenario. The coil has finite dimensions (in r and z) and is not exactly circular. The classification for this ISE is given as an example in Table 4.2.

Clearly, as more parameters are included in an ISE (e.g., if a second coil, carrying an independently controlled current, is introduced into the axial field ISE example previously discussed at an adjustable position on the same axis), the number of combinations increases drastically. To keep the archive of images within reasonable bounds, one has to be prepared to surrender resolution or else to adopt a whole new approach based on virtual reality rather than the real world.

TABLE 4.2
Evaluation of an Interactive Screen Experiment (ISE) on the Axial Magnetic Field of a Coil

Attribute	*Characterization*	*Score and Comments*	
Fidelity	Real-world data: fully (5)—artificial (0)	5	Real data
Locus	Representational setting: natural (5)—artificial (0)	3	Somewhat contrived (though realistic)
Control	Data acquisition: user control (5)—auto/none (0)	5	1D data sets for a few coil currents
Instrumentation	Use of scientific instruments: authentic (5)—none (0)	5	Hall probe and ammeter
Agency	Navigation: user control (5)—auto/none (0)	5	Yes
Temporality	Data flow: real time (5)—from archive (0)	0	Historic data
Depth	Number of experimental quantities: n	2	Axial position and current
Outcome	Instructional design: open-ended (5)—closed (0)	0	Closed, given restriction to axial field
Sociability	Collaborative learning: essential (5)—none (0)	0	Minimal; compatible with single user but could operate for pairs

Immersive Environments

A major limitation of on-screen representations of objects is inherent flatness of the screen representation of what is truly a 3D scene. There are aspects of authentic experimentation that benefit from a greater sense of space than can be gained from the two or three fixed points of observation that might be used in an ISE. For example, where an apparatus involves parts that can be displaced and rotated relative to each other, or where the interaction of parts can most easily be inferred by observation made from a succession of viewpoints, then the data capture and data storage for an ISE quickly become unmanageable. Though visually appealing for some, using ISEs with a 3D imaging technology only makes the data problem worse.

In this case, an alternative approach is to reconstruct the view seen from any particular point, using knowledge of what is present in the space and how it is lit. Nonvisual aspects such as the strength of electric and magnetic fields could also be calculated in the conceived space (though there is still scope to keep the nonvisual data real). This is the domain of computer gaming. Now there is a new incentive to interact, because the user or viewer can seek out vantage points from which to view whatever phenomena are involved. Table 4.3 sets out the objective score that might be claimed by an immersive representation of the experiment to measure the axial field of a short coil, using calculated measurement data. Now the experimenter can walk around the apparatus, physically set the coil in a suitable place for the experiment, come in close to the details of the windings, and stand back to see the whole setup before choosing the best vantage point for the main task.

In a 3D virtual world, one can develop and test the ability to set out and connect equipment. One can explore the interaction of the user with the experimental space, and that can be much more open ended than a purely 2D abstraction of the basic ISE described previously. One could also imagine combining an archive of real data with a virtual-world reconstruction.

TABLE 4.3
Evaluation of a 3D Immersive Experiment on the Axial Magnetic Field of a Coil

Attribute	Characterization		Score and Comments
Fidelity	Real-world data: fully (5)—artificial (0)	0	Computed data, based on simplifying assumptions
Locus	Representational setting: natural (5)—artificial (0)	2	Artificial (though realistic, the real thing may never have existed)
Control	Data acquisition: user control (5)—auto/none (0)	5	1D data sets for a few coil currents
Instrumentation	Use of scientific instruments: authentic (5)—none (0)	5	Hall probe and ammeter
Agency	Navigation: user control (5)—auto/none (0)	5	Yes
Temporality	Data flow: real time (5)—from archive (0)	3	Real time within the scope of the immersive environment
Depth	Number of experimental quantities: n	4	Axial/nonaxial positions of coils and sensor, coil current, field
Outcome	Instructional design: open-ended (5)—closed (0)	3	Constrained by equipment designed into the work space
Sociability	Collaborative learning: essential (5)—none (0)	3	Multiplayer mode feasible

Robotic Instrumentation

The goal of the distance educator with respect to opportunities for practical science is effectively to make the laboratory or observatory accessible to students. The Internet offers a way to reconstruct the visual and instrumental experience even without the continued existence and functioning of extant apparatuses and instruments. However, the Internet also facilitates access to real instruments in real places and in real time through

robotic control of remote apparatuses. This is an area in which our engineering colleagues have been active for many years, and it is now becoming a more established
option in physics teaching (Gröber, Eckert, & Jodl, 2014); for the distance learner, it is
more than just an option.

The astronomy end of the physics curriculum is especially well suited to remote observation. There are many robotically operated telescopes that are used as teaching tools. OU
has an optical instrument, PIRATE (pirate.open.ac.uk), and a radio telescope, ARROW
(learn5.open.ac.uk/course/format/sciencelab/section.php?name=radio_telescope), which
are both currently used in distance learning modules. Both are used for collaborative investigations in groups of four to five students, even though no two students are in the same
location; all activity is conducted over the Internet. OU also has a fully interactive online
Compton Scattering experiment. Indeed, there are several online labs around the world
featuring robotically controlled laboratory installations that are available on request. It
is easy to find on the Internet several labs offering authentic practical investigations of a
wide variety of physical phenomena aimed at undergraduate physics, such as radioactiv-
ity, simple harmonic motion, motion on low-friction tracks, microscopes, optical spectra,
diffraction, fluid mechanics, photoelectric effect, electricity (electronic circuits), and electromagnetism. The role of remote laboratories is discussed in more detail in chapter 9. A
useful snapshot of the functionality and availability of remote laboratory websites is also
given by Gröber and colleagues (2014).

The chief advantage offered by real-time access to a real instrument is the sense of
ownership that users feel about data they have collected for themselves "from the ether."
The classification for a robotic version of the axial field experiment would be as given in
Table 4.4.

TABLE 4.4
Evaluation of a Robotic Experiment on the Axial Magnetic Field of a Coil

Attribute	Characterization	Score and Comments	
Fidelity	Real-world data: fully (5)—artificial (0)	5	Real data
Locus	Representational setting: natural (5)—artificial (0)	5	Real kit
Control	Data acquisition: user control (5)—auto/none (0)	5	1D data sets for a few coil currents
Instrumentation	Use of scientific instruments: authentic (5)—none (0)	5	Hall probe and ammeter
Agency	Navigation: user control (5)—auto/none (0)	5	Yes
Temporality	Data flow: real time (5)—from archive (0)	5	Real time
Depth	Number of experimental quantities: n	4	Axial position of coil and senor, current and field
Outcome	Instructional design: open-ended (5)—closed (0)	0	Closed, given restriction to axial field
Sociability	Collaborative learning: essential (5)—none (0)	2	Potential operation by small group (in this case no special merit)

Student Support

In modern distance educations systems, students are rarely expected to work entirely alone. Traditional lectures may be eschewed in favor of prescribed readings, viewings, and other activities, but most distance education programs also provide some form of student support. The support will generally include an online forum in which students can discuss problems among themselves (usually subject to limitations on the extent to which assessment problems may be discussed, and possibly monitored by the tutor). However, most systems will also have a facility for tutor-led support in which the support provided may be synchronous or asynchronous.

Asynchronous support may be as simple as a student sending a message to a designated tutor or forum with an expectation that a reply will come within a designated time or by a designated date. The simplest forms of tutor-led synchronous student support are Skype meetings; telephone conferences; and, most conventional of all, face-to-face gatherings. Face-to-face tuition for those normally studying at a distance may involve a significant amount of travel. Organizing daylong schools helps to justify the time spent traveling.

An increasingly popular alternative to a face-to-face meeting (though still somewhat more pedagogically challenging) is the use of a virtual classroom of the kind provided by Blackboard Collaborate (www.blackboard.com/platforms/collaborate/products/black board-collaborate.aspx) and its competitors. In principle, such virtual classes can involve video and audio communication, allowing students to submit text questions at any time during the meeting or perform the electronic equivalent of raising a hand if they want the tutor to allow them to speak to the group or share an image or equation. At present, concerns about bandwidth often cause users of virtual rooms to opt for audio-only communication. Nonetheless, the increasing availability of fast broadband connections and tablet computing systems that allow equations, graphs, and diagrams to be handwritten and discussed in real time is helping to boost the popularity of virtual rooms in teaching physics at a distance. One of the greatest advantages of the virtual room is the fact that a synchronous session can be recorded and replayed as an asynchronous revision resource for all those with access, whether or not they were participants in the original meeting. In this way, the best online tutorial sessions can endure from year to year.

However it is accomplished, the provision of face-to-face study support in distance education is inevitably costly. In the case of OU, the production and distribution of physics learning materials has long been handled centrally from the university's national headquarters in the English Midlands. Tutorial support, on the other hand, was, until recently, a mainly "local" matter, with part-time physics tutors being recruited and trained on a regional basis. This was a complicated and expensive part of the university's operation, largely organized and overseen by a small number of dedicated full-time staff tutors based in The Open University's United Kingdom–wide network of regional offices, with the national regions of Scotland, Ireland, and Wales having their own office. Costly as it was, the provision of high-quality student support is generally seen as vital to ensuring reasonably high levels of student success and retention (Baxter & Haycock, 2014).

There is a continuing debate about the need to retain at least some measure of regional support, particularly for students who are completely new to distance education, even though the old regionally based study support model is being progressively dismantled. Extra fuel has been added to this debate by the very low success rates reported by some of the technically oriented massive open online courses that, irrespective of the quality of their study materials, generally do not have any face-to-face study support (Jordan, 2014).

Assignments, Assessments, Feedback, and Examinations

Assignments keep students on schedule and ensure an appropriate depth of study. They may be computer marked (if sufficiently simple in format) or tutor marked. They may also be used summatively (i.e., for credit, as part of an assessment of the student) or formatively (i.e., for self-assessment and learning). Of course, the two uses may be combined; this is commonly the case in physics teaching, where assignments are often marked for credit as part of an assessment activity. Marker comments are returned to students in the expectation that students will learn from their mistakes and thereby improve their understanding.

Computer-marked assignments require little effort at the marking stage but are costly in terms of setting time if they are properly constructed and truly probing. This is a key reason for the popularity of the online assessment banks provided by the publishers of many of the introductory physics texts that were mentioned earlier. Tutor-marked assignments, in contrast, are relatively easy to set but require much greater effort in marking. In the case of OU, the marking and tutoring functions are combined, and it is expected that markers will not only correct students' work but also provide detailed comments that will tell students exactly what they should do to improve their performance. OU, like a number of other distance teaching institutions, provides its tutor markers with a special form so that the general comments and developmental advice being fed back to students can be clearly distinguished from the purely script-focused comments that are returned at the same time. Whatever the balance between summative and formative, or computer marked and tutor marked, it is generally recognized that assignments play an important part in guiding student study, so time spent on developing good assignment questions is usually time well spent.

Traditional exams present a major challenge in distance education and may be dropped in favor of an online end-of-module assignment if regulations permit. If there is a final exam, it may be taken online if the technology is available or at local centers, in which case students must be informed well in advance of which items they may or may not take into the examination room (e.g., programmable calculators may be prohibited in some exams). It should be noted that this is an area in which institutional policies and requirements may take precedence over the desires and preferences of those designing distance education courses in physics or any other subject. In any case, steps must be taken to ensure that the person taking the exam really is the registered student; in distance education the students will often be unfamiliar to whoever invigilates their examination.

Future Trends

Predicting the future is always difficult. Nonetheless, as physics continues to advance, it seems clear that the need for effective, up-to-date physics education that makes full use of all the available educational technologies will also continue to expand. It might be that distance education, as a distinct mode of teaching and learning, will have no role in this future world. Not that its methods will be irrelevant, but rather that they will become so much a part of the mainstream that it will simply cease to be meaningful to draw a distinction between conventional and distance education. Already there are many examples of inverted classrooms where basic study is carried out individually, using the self-study methods of distance education, so that the precious resource of class time spent in the physical presence of an experienced teacher can be devoted to the hardest parts of the subject. It may even be, as suggested in the recent documentary *Ivory Tower* (Rossi, 2014), that the rising cost of conventional college education and the increasing indebtedness of its student consumers will lead to a complete reconsideration of the value of university education, as well as its methods. In any case, it seems certain that in a world where the Internet changes everything, the methods of distance education will continue to be of value and interest.

The existence of the Internet does not just allow us to perform traditional educational tasks in new ways. It also enables new kinds of interaction. For example, given that many professional scientists now end up working as experts in multidisciplinary teams, there is a need to foster employability skills and collaborative working in the full twenty-first-century context. Internet-connected student cohorts are ideally placed to develop, deploy, and refine the skills of distributed teamwork. This also offers new opportunities for assessment and evaluation of student learning and may eventually be viewed as a real legacy of *distance education*, whatever that term comes to mean in an increasingly connected world.

References

Al-Shamali, F., & Connors, M. (2010). Low cost physics home laboratory. In D. Kennepohl & L. Shaw (Eds.), *Accessible elements: Teaching science at a distance* (pp. 131–146). Edmonton, Canada: AU Press.

Baxter, J. A., & Haycock, J. (2014). Roles and student identities in online large course forums: Implications for practice. *The International Review of Research in Open and Distance Learning*, *15*(1), 20–40.

Carver, R. P. (1992). Reading rate: Theory, research, and practical implications. *Journal of Reading*, *36*(2), 84–95.

Christian, W., & Belloni, M. (2001). *Physlets: Teaching physics with interactive curricular material*. Upper Saddle River, NJ: Prentice Hall.

Christian, W., & Belloni, M. (2013). *Physlet physics: Interactive illustrations, explorations, and problems for introductory physics* (2nd ed.). Retrieved from www.compadre.org/Physlets

Docktor, J. L., & Mestre, J. P. (2014). Synthesis of discipline-based education research in physics. *Physical Review Special Topics: Physics Education Research*, *10*. doi:10.1103/PhysRevSTPER.10.020119.

Gröber, S., Eckert, B., & Jodl, H.-J. (2014). A new medium for physics teaching: Results of a worldwide study of remotely controlled laboratories (RCLs). *European Journal of Physics*, *35*(1), doi:10.1088/0143-0807/35/1/018001.

Jordan, K. (2014). *MOOC completion rates: The data*. Retrieved from www.katyjordan.com/MOOCproject.html

Kirstein, J. (1999). *Interaktive Bildschirmexperimente: Technik und Didaktik eines neuartigen Verfahrens zur multimedialen Abbildung physikalischer Experimente* (Unpublished doctoral dissertation). Technischen Universität Berlin, Berlin.

Kirstein, J., & Nordmeier, V. (2007). Multimedia representation of experiments in physics. *European Journal of Physics*, *28*(3), S115–S126.

Lambourne, R. (2007). Laboratory-based teaching and the Physics Innovations Centre for Excellence in Teaching and Learning. *European Journal of Physics*, *28*(3), S29–S36.

Lambourne, R. (2010). *E-learning in physical science through sport (ELPSS)*. Retrieved from elpss.open.ac.uk

Price, M., Carroll, J., O'Donovan, B., & Rust, C. (2011). If I was going there I wouldn't start from here: A critical commentary on current assessment practice. *Assessment and Evaluation in Higher Education*, *36*(4), 479–492.

Rebello, N. S., Cui, L., Bennett, A. G., Zollman, D. A., & Ozimek, D. J. (2007). Transfer of learning in problem solving in the context of mathematics and physics. In D. H. Jonassen (Ed.), *Learning to solve complex, scientific problems* (pp. 223–246). Mahwah, NJ: Lawrence Erlbaum.

Reid, N. (2009). Working memory and science education: Conclusions and implications. *Research in Science and Technological Education*, *27*(2), 245–250.

Rossi, A. (Producer & Director). (2014). *Ivory tower* [Motion picture]. United States: CNN Films.

Science Community Representing Education. (2008). *Practical work in science: A report and proposal for a strategic framework*. Retrieved from www.score-education.org/media/3668/report.pdf

Sinclair, B., Gillies, A., & Bacon, R. (2004). Simulations for physics and astronomy. *LTSN Physical Science News*, *5*(1), 10.

Theyßen, H., von Aufschnaiter, S., & Schumacher, D. (2002). Development and evaluation of a laboratory course in physics for medical students. In D. Psillos & H. Niedderer (Eds.), *Teaching and learning in the science laboratory* (pp. 91–104). Dordrecht, the Netherlands: Springer.

Wieman, C. E., Adams, W. K., & Perkins, K. K. (2008). PhET: Simulations that enhance learning. *Science*, *322*(5902), 682–683.

PART TWO

Applications: Case Studies and Special Topics

5

SCIENCE ONLINE

Bringing the Laboratory Home

Mary V. Mawn
SUNY Empire State College

Abstract

Laboratories are an essential component of science courses. Experimentation provides students with real-world contexts to apply scientific concepts, develop critical thinking skills, and engage in scientific processes. For the online educator, designing laboratories can be challenging, but lab kits, field experiences, simulations, and remote instrumentation can enable students to investigate fundamental concepts from their locations. This chapter will discuss the goals and objectives of laboratories in general, summarize research findings that describe several successes in online environments, present a case study highlighting processes and considerations for online science course development, and propose a model for designing laboratories for online environments.

Laboratory experiments are a defining characteristic of science courses. Such experiences provide students with opportunities to apply technical knowledge and skills, extend their learning of scientific concepts, strengthen critical thinking skills, engage in scientific processes, and further their interest in science (Hofstein & Lunetta, 2004; Hofstein & Mamlok-Naaman, 2007; Ma & Nickerson, 2006; Ottander & Grelsson, 2006). Given their importance, science courses generally include required laboratory components (Reid & Shah, 2007), which are taught in facilities located on campus or in specified field locations.

In recent years, there has been an increase in online course offerings. Allen and Seaman (2014) estimated that at least 7.1 million students in the United States are taking at least one online course. This represents an all-time high of 33.5% of higher education students. In addition, academic leaders believe it is *likely* or *very likely* that in five years, a majority of students will be taking at least one online course (Allen & Seaman, 2014). As the number of online courses increases, there will be a growing demand to develop online science courses that incorporate laboratory experiences. These courses will need to integrate scientific content and processes, promote the development of key laboratory skills, apply best practices for laboratory design, and positively impact students' learning and retention.

Questions are often raised regarding whether science can be taught online. However, learning science through distance learning is not a new phenomenon. For example, founded in 1969 as the United Kingdom's first distance teaching university, The Open University (OU) mailed lab kits to its science students, which included "microscopes, circuit boards, chemistry sets, fish tanks, and even lasers" (Waldrop, 2013, p. 268; see also MacQueen & Thomas, 2009). In addition, television broadcasts were used to reach these distance learning students (The Open University, n.d.). With the growth of the Internet in the 1990s, lab work is now available online through The OpenScience Laboratory at OU. Students can collect real-time data from remote instruments and use simulated instruments such as a virtual microscope (Waldrop, 2013). Like OU, numerous colleges and universities use lab kits, simulations, and remote instrumentation to engage their online students in laboratory science.

The challenge, then, is to consider ways to "bring the laboratory home" and provide students with authentic and rigorous laboratory experiences that address relevant learning goals. This chapter begins by exploring the approaches and objectives for laboratories in general. The next section discusses laboratory options currently being used in online science courses. This is followed by a discussion of several research studies that serve as examples of successes in the field. Then, a case study highlights considerations and approaches for developing online science courses. Finally, a design model and working definition for the *online science laboratory* is considered.

Science Laboratories: Approaches and Objectives

Although there are a wide variety of science disciplines which students can pursue—from astronomy to zoology—a common feature of science course work is the laboratory. Over the years, laboratory instruction has been included in varying degrees in science courses. As noted earlier, such experiences provide students with opportunities to explore scientific phenomena, apply theoretical concepts, develop technical skills, and extend their understanding of the natural world.

Domin (1999) described four teaching approaches used in laboratory settings: expository, inquiry, discovery, and problem based. In the expository approach, the instructor determines the experiment, the procedures are well stated, and a predetermined outcome results. This is often referred to as the cookbook laboratory, because students follow defined procedures and collect specific data to confirm known results. This generally results in an emphasis on basic technical skills such as attention to protocols, observation, measurement, and data collection, with less focus on planning an investigation or interpreting results (Domin, 1999).

In the inquiry and discovery (guided-inquiry) modes of instruction, students have greater control over the experimental question and design. For an inquiry-based experiment, the outcome is unknown to the instructor and student; during a discovery lab, the instructor guides students to the desired outcome. These modes of laboratory instruction emphasize more advanced technical skills, such as experimental design, problem-solving, and data analysis. Students also engage in higher order thinking processes as they hypothesize, investigate, analyze, and evaluate evidence (Domin, 1999).

Finally, for problem-based instruction, the students are presented with a problem, and they determine the experimental methods needed to find a solution. Similar to the inquiry and discovery modes, students engage in higher order cognitive skills as they analyze problems, formulate testable hypotheses, devise approaches, and conduct investigations. In addition, students must apply their understanding of relevant concepts as they design solutions to a problem (Domin, 1999).

These instructional approaches can impact students' engagement levels, technical and cognitive processes, and learning outcomes. Is the goal to strengthen students' manipulation skills, to confirm known concepts, or to discover new phenomena? What are the benefits and limitations of each approach for meeting such educational needs? Although the mode of laboratory instruction is a key factor to consider, an equally important, and perhaps a higher priority, factor is clearly pinpointing learning objectives and outcomes. For example, an objective might be to "properly prepare and view specimens for examination using microscopy," and one outcome might be to "explain how magnification and resolution are controlled in a microscope" (American Society for Microbiology, 2012, p. 6, and 2014, p. 6). Such objectives and outcomes should serve as the basis for selecting curriculum and teaching strategies and for assessing student work and laboratory programs (Bretz, Fay, Bruck, & Towns, 2013; Hofstein & Lunetta, 2004).

Often, the writing of learning objectives for laboratories is not done, which makes the evaluation of such experiences difficult to measure and assess (Feisel & Rosa, 2005). In addition, it is important for students to understand the goals and aims of their investigations. They often fail to understand the relationship between the purpose of their experiments, which at times can feel rather procedural, and the underlying scientific concepts and phenomena being explored (Feisel & Rosa, 2005; Hofstein & Lunetta, 2004).

To clarify the role of the laboratory, several groups have recommended learning goals, objectives, and outcomes. Hofstein and Lunetta (2004) proposed five learning goals: understanding of scientific concepts, interest and motivation, scientific practical skills and problem-solving abilities, scientific habits of mind, and understanding of the nature of science (Hofstein & Lunetta, 2004). In engineering, a committee of educators from across the country identified 13 fundamental objectives for instructional laboratories: instrumentation, models, experiment, data analysis, design, learning from failure, creativity, psychomotor, safety, communication, teamwork, ethics in the laboratory, and sensory awareness (Feisel & Rosa, 2005). In chemistry, Reid and Shah (2007) described four general aims: skills relating to learning, practical skills, scientific skills, and general skills. Finally, a national survey of chemistry faculty identified seven undergraduate laboratory themes: research experience; group work and broader communication skills; error analysis, data collection, and analysis; connection between lab and lecture; transferable skills (lab specific); transferable skills (not lab specific); and laboratory writing (Bruck & Towns, 2013).

Although these goals and objectives come from different disciplines and perspectives, they share many features in common. In particular, each group identified learning goals and objectives that go beyond reinforcing technical skills. These categories can be classified according to the three domains of knowledge: cognitive, psychomotor, and affective (Bretz et al., 2013; Feisel & Rosa, 2005). Although greater emphasis is often placed on the cognitive and psychomotor areas, goals in the affective domain can promote meaningful learning experiences and lead to gains in areas such as behavior, attitudes, creativity, safety, communication, teamwork, and ethics (Bretz et al., 2013; Feisel & Rosa, 2005). Overall, each domain plays an important role in developing students' understanding of the concepts, methodologies, and nature of science and should be considered when designing coherent learning experiences for the laboratory (Feisel & Rosa, 2005).

Online Science Laboratories: Possibilities and Options

In addition to identifying laboratory approaches (i.e., expository, inquiry, discovery, and problem-based experiments) and defining goals and objectives in the knowledge domains (i.e., cognitive, psychomotor, and affective), delivering the lab components must be considered. In the on-campus setting, cost and space considerations aside, students generally have ready access to instrumentation, equipment, reagents, and materials. This is not the case for online students, who are often unable to travel to campus because of time limitations, distance, or both.

Cancilla and Albon (2008) described several approaches for engaging online students in laboratory experiences. In the hybrid model, students view lectures and participate in other activities online (e.g., discussions, virtual labs) but are required to travel to campus for in-person laboratory experiences. Sessions might be scheduled throughout the semester (i.e., weekly) or held during focused, intense periods of time (i.e., over a weekend). Another option is through partnerships with regional centers or campuses that provide face-to-face, mentored laboratory experiences for online students. Again, this requires students to travel to specific locations to fulfill their laboratory requirement.

Additional options include the use of lab kits, field-based experiments, computer simulations, and remote instrumentation (Hallyburton & Lunsford, 2013; Kennepohl, 2009; Mawn, Carrico, Charuk, Stote, & Lawrence, 2011; Waldrop, 2013). Similar to on-campus laboratory settings, each approach challenges educators to design learning experiences that address appropriate objectives and outcomes and ensure that the desired skills and concepts are being taught. Benefits and limitations of various options are outlined in the following:

- *Lab kits*, in combination with household items, provide the means to conduct experiments at home on a smaller scale and without the need for expensive equipment (Casanova, Civelli, Kimbrough, Heath, & Reeves, 2006; Jeschofnig, 2009; Reeves & Kimbrough, 2004). This engages online students in authentic, hands-on experiences that promote technical skills development and conceptual understanding, with the small quantities being used reducing hazards and risks. Many science vendors offer commercially available prepackaged lab kits. Faculty can also design customized lab kits based on their online courses. However, kit-based investigations can be limited in scope because of the cost and availability of specialized equipment and materials; the inability to repeat experiments because of limited reagents, which requires greater dexterity when conducting experiments that can be done only once; and concerns related to material disposal and lab safety (Crippen, Archambault, & Kern, 2013).

- *Field-based experiments* provide students with real-world opportunities to collect and analyze data from their locations (Reuter, 2009; Waldrop, 2013). Nature centers, zoos, parks, and even backyards can serve as field stations for experimentation. This eliminates the costs associated with setting up comparable sites on campus, and the cost to the student is often minimal. In addition, the online setting provides an ideal forum for students to share, discuss, and compare data collected from a variety of locations. For example, citizen science projects such as Cornell University's Lab of Ornithology connects scientists, conservationists, engineers, educators, and students as they engage in scientific discovery and collect data on wildlife in their local communities (birds.cornell .edu). A downside to field-based experimentation is that opportunities may be limited in some locations and may be dependent on particular climates or seasons. In addition, topics can be discipline specific and may not be an option for many courses.

- *Computer simulations* provide alternatives to complex experiments that might be too large, expensive, or dangerous for physical manipulation or not feasible for a large number of students (Feisel & Rosa, 2005). When properly designed with options for variation, such programs can allow students to adjust parameters and experiment in ways that might not be possible in a traditional lab (Carnevale, 2003; Feisel & Rosa, 2005; Pyatt & Sims, 2012; Schwab, 2012). In addition, simulations can provide students with prelab experiences prior to conducting hands-on experiments (Feisel & Rosa, 2005). For example, the University of Colorado Boulder offers free interactive, research-based simulations that actively engage students through inquiry (see About PhET: Free online physics, biology, earth science, and math simulations at phet.colorado.edu/en/about). Unfortunately, authentic simulations can be costly and time-consuming to create (Casanova et al., 2006) and are not readily available in all topic areas and disciplines. In addition, although simulations can provide students with opportunities to design experiments, make observations, and collect data, tactile learning and technical skills development can be limited (e.g., learning how to handle equipment, apply sterile techniques).

- *Remote instrumentation* gives students online access to scientific apparatus for manipulation, data collection, and analysis (Baran, Currie, & Kennepohl, 2004; Crippen et al., 2013; Hallyburton & Lunsford, 2013). This provides students with concrete and authentic lab experiences complete with the possibility of error and potential for generating unexpected results (Baran et al., 2004; Petre, 2011). For example, the North American Network of Science Labs Online (www .wiche.edu/nanslo) and the British Columbia Integrated Laboratory Network (truchemonline.wix.com/bciln) offer remote access to scientific instrumentation for analyzing provided and student-collected samples. One downside to this approach is that it can be costly to maintain instrumentation, facilities, and remote access (Hallyburton & Lunsford, 2013). In addition, students' experiences with manipulating equipment and materials using remote instruments will differ from those gained through on-campus experiences.

Although there may be limitations to these approaches, there are numerous possibilities as well. The challenge is not to simply recreate campus-based experiments in online settings. Rather, a key component is to specify the goals and objectives for each laboratory experience and then design experiments using the tools, methods, concepts, and technical skills that will enable students to achieve the desired learning outcomes.

Learning Outcomes in Online Science Courses

A number of studies have explored ways that science can be taught online, with a specific focus on the laboratories. This work provides the necessary data and evidence to show what is and is not possible. These findings also provide much-needed insights and examples, which will help online science educators define best practices for course design and instruction. Three examples of such studies are summarized in this section.

In the first study, students enrolled in on-campus and online versions of general chemistry were compared to determine the effectiveness of alternative approaches to instruction (Casanova et al., 2006). The face-to-face students completed experiments on campus, whereas online students conducted "kitchen chemistry" experiments. To compare these groups, the researchers collected qualitative and quantitative data, the latter in the form of final exam and laboratory practical scores. Overall, the online students were satisfied with their experiences and appreciated the flexibility but found the course more difficult than a conventional course. Regardless of this perception, the online students scored significantly higher on the final exam and achieved greater scores in every category of the on-campus lab practical (procedure, data presentation, and data analysis). This indicated that the online students had little difficulty using glassware and equipment during the practical, despite the fact that they used common household items during the semester (Casanova et al., 2006).

In the second study, online students of a junior-level fluid mechanics laboratory engaged in video-based, "hands-off" experiments by watching recordings of an instructor and student conducting experiments, and the face-to-face students conducted identical experiments on campus (Abdel-Salam, Kauffman, & Crossman, 2006). The effectiveness of these approaches was measured by comparing achievement on eight laboratory reports and a final exam. Although the two groups performed similarly on the final exam, the online students achieved higher averages on the laboratory reports. Comparing responses on the final exam, the researchers found both groups scored similarly on their overall writing performance, although the distance learning students outperformed their counterparts in technical comprehension. These results show that the lack of a hands-on experience did not negatively affect the performance of the online students (Abdel-Salam et al., 2006).

In the third study, online and on-campus students in a general education soil science course were compared to determine if online students could effectively learn laboratory skills in a field-based course using lab kits (Reuter, 2009). Similar lab experiments were conducted by the two groups, with several of the field experiments being identical. Lab assignment and final course averages between the groups were similar. However, pre- and postassessment results revealed differences. The online students showed greater gains and scored higher on the postassessment, with an average score increase of 42% (online) versus 21% (on campus). In addition, when researchers compared postassessment student essays and a skills test for hand-texturing soils, they found both groups scored similarly. These findings show no significant difference between the online and on-campus formats in achieving learning outcomes, with the online students showing greater gains in the postassessment (Reuter, 2009).

Scientific Inquiry in Online Science Courses

As these studies demonstrate, online students are able to successfully engage in laboratory experiences as evidenced by exam scores, lab grades, course assessments, and lab practicals. To build on these findings, researchers have investigated to what extent online students engage in scientific inquiry. To address this, the following studies characterized the scientific process skills used by online students.

Harlen and Doubler (2004) compared on-campus and online students enrolled in a course called Try Science. This course is designed to further elementary and middle school teachers' understanding of science content and teaching science through inquiry. During the first six weeks, students used scientific inquiry as they investigated the properties of ice and water. Starting in week seven, the focus shifted to teaching approaches and considering ways to involve students in inquiry. The majority of online students engaged in scientific inquiry as they raised questions, reported observations, made and tested predictions, proposed explanations and hypotheses, and extended their investigations. In comparison to the on-campus students, the online students reflected more frequently on their learning and the process of inquiry, reported significantly greater changes in their understanding of science content, and expressed greater confidence in their abilities to teach science through inquiry. Several advantages of the online environment were identified as a result of this study. Asynchronous discussions provided the time and space for greater precision in choosing words, clarifying points, reviewing and engaging in multiple exchanges, and reflecting on ideas. The online environment also allowed for greater flexibility for when to study, when to conduct investigations, how long to experiment, and whether to explore follow-up questions (Harlen & Doubler, 2004).

Mawn and colleagues (2011) characterized inquiry skills used by online students enrolled in one of three nonmajor undergraduate science courses: Contemporary Environmental Issues, Invention by Design, and Energy: The Issues and the Science. These courses each included five to six hands-on experiments, field-based activities, and/or simulations. One experiment per course was selected for analysis. Written work was evaluated for the presence of 16 elements of scientific inquiry (Mawn et al., 2011). Findings show that these online students engaged in scientific inquiry as they tested questions, made predictions and observations, collected and analyzed data, identified variables, formulated explanations, and extended their investigations. Several recommendations resulted from this work. Because investigations are not bound by the time and space limitations of on-campus laboratories, there can be options to design more open-ended experiments for online students when appropriate, taking into account factors such as resource availability and lab safety. In addition, online discussions can provide students with opportunities to share experimental findings, explore alternate explanations, and extend their learning. Finally, learning objectives for online science courses should include a focus on inquiry skills (Mawn et al., 2011).

Field Notes for Designing Online Science Courses

Given the evidence in the literature and prior experience designing online science courses, a team of faculty at SUNY Empire State College set out to develop six online science courses in Biology I and II, Chemistry I and II, and Physics I and II that included a rigorous lab component comparable to the on-campus experience. The Motorola Solutions Foundation funded this project, and the author of this chapter served as co-principal investigator (PI). The development team consisted of two co-PIs (one served as a faculty member and one as an instructional designer), two additional faculty members, and three content experts in biology, chemistry, and physics.

At the start of the project, the team explored questions such as the following: Who is the target student population? What are the key learning goals and objectives? Which experiments will students perform? What equipment and techniques are important? Will each course use lab kits, simulations, field-based experiments, and/or remote instrumentation? How might these materials affect costs to the student? Are there safety and disposal considerations? Will students interact as they conduct these experiments? How will students submit their findings and results?

On the basis of these discussions, the co-PIs proposed a set of guiding principles related to the laboratories (see Box 5.1). After we drafted this list, it became clear that these principles can be applied in both online and on-campus settings. This list is by no means exhaustive, but it provided the development team with a common understanding of laboratory experiences. These principles highlight how laboratories can bridge theory and practice; engage students as they explore natural phenomena, connect to real-world experiences, and develop key skills; and expose students to the nature of science.

BOX 5.1
Guiding Principles for a Laboratory Course

Laboratories are considered a key component of the science curriculum. Lab experiments allow students to make connections between theory and practice and offer additional ways to learn beyond a text-based approach.

Laboratory experiences provide students with opportunities to use the tools and techniques of scientists, develop key skills, interact with natural phenomena, and extend their understanding of scientific concepts and processes.

Laboratories can take place beyond the confines of the lab bench. Conducting experiments in familiar settings helps students make connections between science and their lives and can also remove the time and space limitations placed on experiments in traditional lab settings.

Laboratory experiences require clear expectations, meaningful experiments, and ongoing engagement.

The co-PIs also developed a set of recommendations related to the instructional design of online laboratories (see Box 5.2). Similar to the principles found in Box 5.1, these guidelines can be extended to on-campus environments. These recommendations describe the importance of specifying content and process learning goals, actively involving students in scientific investigations, allowing flexibility to adjust variables and extend investigations, building on previous knowledge and process skills, and providing opportunities for discussion and reflection.

BOX 5.2
Instructional Design of Laboratory Experiments

Laboratory learning objectives should consider goals related to scientific content, skills building, and relevance (i.e., conceptual, procedural, and affective learning outcomes) and specify measureable levels of achievement for meeting these goals and objectives.

Laboratory experiments should clearly connect to course content, and these connections should be made explicit to students.

Laboratory activities should encourage active exploration, experimentation, and inquiry and allow students to adjust parameters and repeat experiments.

Laboratory exercises should include progression by building on conceptual and procedural learning within individual labs and over the course of the semester.

Laboratory experiences should allow for not only individual experimentation but also opportunities for reflection and discussion of experimental designs, findings, conclusions, and relevance.

Development of the six online courses was done between fall 2011 and summer 2012. For the lab component, the team opted to use commercially available lab kits for each course. The experiments in each kit mirrored the types of lessons typically seen in comparable on-campus courses. In some cases, similar materials and methods were used, whereas alternative hands-on and virtual options were used for those experiments requiring specialized equipment or materials. In the interest of lab safety, materials and reagents were provided in small quantities to limit reactions. In addition, safety and disposal guidelines, material safety data sheets, and appropriate safety equipment (i.e., lab apron, safety glasses, and gloves) were provided.

Pilot courses were offered to online students starting in spring 2012. Each online course was then revised and regularly offered to students starting in fall 2012. In addition to textbook readings and written lectures, these online students engaged in four types of graded learning activities: written assignments, quizzes, laboratories, and discussions. The written assignments included problem sets where students applied science content and connected these concepts to real-world applications. Weekly quizzes consisted of conceptual questions that challenged and enhanced students' understanding of the material. The laboratories included hands-on and virtual experiments designed to complement each module's material and solidify students' understanding of key concepts. Online class discussions provided students with opportunities to articulate their views and ideas on a variety of topics and discuss their experimental designs and findings with their classmates.

End-of-term survey data were collected from a subgroup of students ($n = 14$) to determine the impact of these learning activities. When asked to rate the extent to which these activities supported their learning, all students *strongly agreed* or *agreed* that the written assignments (100%) and laboratories (100%) were important factors, whereas the quizzes (85%) and discussions (57%) rated somewhat lower. It was interesting, but not surprising, to note the lower rating given to discussions, because many students prefer not to engage in discussions for a variety of reasons, both online and on campus. However, this aspect is worth further exploration and consideration.

Related to course experiences, students ($n = 43$) in a closing discussion were asked to reflect and comment on their overall experiences. Their postings highlighted a number of features of these courses. One student commented,

> The rigor of the problem sets and the quality of the labs were superior to that of other sciences courses I have taken as a distance learning student. I felt I had to work a good deal to earn a grade and learned a lot in the process.

A second student noted, "[The] topics were well formulated, and I was happy with the level of respectful argumentation. It allowed me to relate my personal experience and opinions to the science, and to observe the experiences and opinions of other[s]." A number of students commented specifically about their laboratory experiences. One stated,

> The labs best supported my learning. I've always felt that hands-on learning is the best way to teach someone something. Another aspect of the labs that helped was to work with different variables, and see how they affected the results. They're a solid method to exercise critical thinking.

Another student commented that the labs provided opportunities to apply course concepts:

> My views about the lab exercises [are] that they are awesome. They were my favorite part of the course. I am a "hands on" type of learner. Every time I did a lab, that is when the readings and the material began to make more sense to me. I enjoyed being able to apply my knowledge I had gain[ed] in the labs and in the lab reports.

Similarly, another student stated, "I found the labs to be very useful. It can be hard to really imagine the concepts and see them applied to real life, and I found that the labs did this very well." Finally, this student commented on the flexibility of this approach: "[I] liked the labs, [they] made learning the content more interesting, and [I] liked being able to perform somewhat real labs from home."

While commenting about the usefulness of the labs (e.g., "The lab component definitely brought some of the points discussed in the chapters to life"), one student noted early concerns: "Initially I felt nervous about safely completing a lab without the input of others in the same room." This highlights the importance of providing students with clear instructions and lab supports. In these online courses, lab manuals were included with the lab kits, and this information was supplemented with written instructor commentaries. In addition, informal discussion areas were available where students could post lab questions (e.g., related to experimental setup, materials, techniques).

Additional options include posting images or video demonstrations, assigning prelab questions or simulations, and sharing supplemental web resources. In addition, it is important to include clear information regarding lab safety and disposal guidelines for each experiment.

Overall, these findings show that students can successfully study and engage in science from a distance. Students commented on the value of each learning activity, particularly the written assignments and laboratory exercises. They also recognized the importance of conducting hands-on experiments and how they supported learning science content.

Recommendations for Online Science Course Design and Defining *the Online Science Laboratory*

On the basis of the principles and practices for incorporating laboratories in science courses, the findings presented in the literature, and firsthand experiences designing and teaching online science courses, I propose the 3E model for science laboratory design. This model focuses on three aspects: defining lab expectations, engaging students in experimentation, and fostering student engagement:

- *Expectations:* Laboratory learning objectives should made explicit and include measureable learning outcomes. These objectives and outcomes should be made clear to students. These should also take into consideration the three domains of knowledge (i.e., cognitive, psychomotor, and affective), for example, by strengthening student understanding of scientific concepts and processes, engaging students in a variety of investigations, and relating experiments to their everyday lives.
- *Experimentation:* Laboratories should actively engage students in scientific investigations. Such experiences can support the development of specific technical skills, provide opportunities to adjust and test variables, build on and extend critical thinking skills, and allow for student-directed explorations when appropriate. Opportunities for student collaboration and experimental data sharing are also options to explore.
- *Engagement:* Asynchronous and synchronous tools (e.g., discussion forums, chat spaces, wikis, surveys, and image- and video-sharing tools) can be used to engage learners in relevant topics, allow for the comparison and debate of experimental findings, provide opportunities to link observations with theory and practice, and challenge and strengthen students' conceptual understanding. In addition, opportunities for sharing and reflection can help students become more aware of their learning and also make this learning more visible to the instructor and others.

Overall, the 3E model for science laboratory design provides a comprehensive approach for designing lab-based experiences, regardless of mode of delivery. This model takes into consideration the "why" (*expectations*) and "how" (*experimentation*) and completes the experience by providing a venue for data sharing and interpretation and connecting students with their peers (*engagement*), similar to how scientists engage with their colleagues in the scientific community.

Given the information presented in this chapter, what might be a working definition for the *online science laboratory*? This is not an easy question to address, and there is likely more than one answer. What is clear, however, is that there should not be a need to distinguish between on-campus and online settings. Both learning environments can address scientific content and process learning goals. Well-designed investigations can actively engage students in experimentation even if they are not in a physical laboratory setting. Student-directed explorations can allow learners to engage in scientific inquiry, experiment with fundamental concepts, and experience the nature of science.

The challenge for online science educators is to design laboratories that overcome many of the perceived limitations of the distance learning setting, such as the lack of specialized equipment and limited access to specific materials. What are the best approaches for designing engaging laboratory experiences that help students gain technical skills, develop conceptual understanding, and extend their interest in science? Can this be done in a coherent and measurable fashion using a combination of lab kits, simulations, and remote experiments? To this end, it is important to define learning objectives and measureable outcomes that bridge cognitive, psychomotor, and affective domains and then design appropriate and relevant learning activities that promote experimentation and engage students with the content and their peers. This will provide students with rich laboratory experiences that go beyond the mechanics of "cookbook" experiments and actively engage them in scientific processes, regardless of whether the experimentation is done at home, on campus, or elsewhere.

Acknowledgments

Funding was provided by Motorola Solutions Foundation's 2011–2012 Innovation Generation Grant. Sincere thanks are extended to the following individuals for their work on this project: Ken Charuk, co-PI and instructional designer; Pauline Carrico and Diane Shichtman, project faculty; and Cinzia Cera, Catherine Gleason, and John Herman, content experts and instructors.

References

Abdel-Salam, T., Kauffman, P. J., & Crossman, G. (2006). Does the lack of hands-on experience in a remotely delivered laboratory course affect student learning? *European Journal of Engineering Education, 31*(6), 747–756.

Allen, I. E., & Seaman, J. (2014). *Grade change: Tracking online education in the United States.* United States: Babson Survey Research Group and Quahog Research Group, LLC. Retrieved from www.onlinelearningsurvey.com/reports/gradechange.pdf

American Society for Microbiology. (2012). *Recommended curriculum guidelines for undergraduate microbiology education.* Retrieved from www.asm.org/images/Education/FINAL_Curriculum_Guidelines_w_title_page.pdf

American Society for Microbiology. (2014). *General microbiology learning outcome examples.* Retrieved from www.asm.org/images/Education/FINAL_Learning_Outcomes_w_title_page .pdf

Baran, J., Currie, R., & Kennepohl, D. (2004). Remote instrumentation for the teaching laboratory. *Journal of Chemical Education, 81*(12), 1814–1816.

Bretz, S. L., Fay, M., Bruck, L. B., & Towns, M. H. (2013). What faculty interviews reveal about meaningful learning in the undergraduate chemistry laboratory. *Journal of Chemical Education, 90*(3), 281–288.

Bruck, A. D., & Towns, M. (2013). Development, implementation, and analysis of a national survey of faculty goals for undergraduate chemistry laboratory. *Journal of Chemical Education, 90*(6), 685–693.

Cancilla, D. A., & Albon, S. P. (2008). Reflections from the moving the laboratory online workshops: Emerging themes. *Journal of Asynchronous Learning Networks, 12*(3–4), 53–59.

Carnevale, D. (2003). The virtual lab experiment. *The Chronicle of Higher Education, 49*(21), A30.

Casanova, R. S., Civelli, J. L., Kimbrough, D. R., Heath, B. P., & Reeves, J. H. (2006). Distance learning: A viable alternative to the conventional lecture-lab format in general chemistry. *Journal of Chemical Education, 83*(3), 501–507.

Crippen, K. J., Archambault, L. M., & Kern, C. L. (2013). The nature of laboratory learning experiences in secondary science online. *Research in Science Education, 43*(3), 1029–1050.

Domin, D. S. (1999). A review of laboratory instruction styles. *Journal of Chemical Education, 76*(4), 543–547.

Feisel, L. D., & Rosa, A. J. (2005). The role of the laboratory in undergraduate engineering education. *Journal of Engineering Education, 94*(1), 121–130.

Hallyburton, C. L., & Lunsford, E. (2013). Challenges and opportunities for learning biology in distance-based settings. *Bioscene: Journal of College Biology Teaching, 39*(1), 27–33.

Harlen, W., & Doubler, S. J. (2004). Can teachers learn through enquiry on-line? Studying professional development in science delivered on-line and on-campus. *International Journal of Science Education, 26*(10), 1247–1267.

Hofstein, A., & Lunetta, V. N. (2004). The laboratory in science education: Foundations for the twenty-first century. *Science Education, 88*(1), 28–54.

Hofstein, A., & Mamlok-Naaman, R. (2007). The laboratory in science education: The state of the art. *Chemistry Education Research and Practice, 8*(2), 105–107.

Jeschofnig, L. (2009, Fall). Lab science courses can now be fully online. *Community College Week,* Technology Update, 16.

Kennepohl, D. (2009). Science online and at a distance. *American Journal of Distance Education, 23*(3), 122–124.

Ma, J., & Nickerson, J. V. (2006). Hands-on, simulated, and remote laboratories: A comparative literature review. *ACM Computing Surveys, 38*(3), Article 7, 1–24.

MacQueen, H., & Thomas, J. (2009). Teaching biology at a distance: Pleasures, pitfalls, and possibilities. *American Journal of Distance Education, 23*(3), 139–150.

Mawn, M. V., Carrico, P., Charuk, K., Stote, K. S., & Lawrence, B. (2011). Hands-on and online: Scientific explorations through distance learning. *Open Learning, 26*(2), 135–146.

Ottander, C., & Grelsson, G. (2006). Laboratory work: The teachers' perspective. *Journal of Biological Education, 40*(3), 113–118.

The Open University. (n.d.). *The OU story.* Retrieved from www.open.ac.uk/about/main/strategy/ou-story

Petre, M. (2011). Online experimentation. *ACM Inroads, 2*(1), 18–19.

Pyatt, K., & Sims, R. (2012). Virtual and physical experimentation in inquiry-based science labs: Attitudes, performance and access. *Journal of Science Education and Technology, 21*(1), 133–147.

Reeves, J., & Kimbrough, D. (2004). Solving the laboratory dilemma in distance learning general chemistry. *Journal of Asynchronous Learning Networks, 8*(3), 47–51.

Reid, N., & Shah, I. (2007). The role of laboratory work in university chemistry. *Chemistry Education Research and Practice, 8*(2), 172–185.

Reuter, R. (2009). Online versus in the classroom: Student success in a hands-on lab class. *American Journal of Distance Education, 23*(3), 151–162.

Schwab, Z. (2012). Growing STEM students: How Late Nite Labs' online platform is spreading science and saving schools' resources. *Journal of Educational Technology Systems, 41*(4), 333–345.

Waldrop, M. M. (2013). Education online: The virtual lab. *Nature, 499*(7458), 268–270.

6

PRACTICAL BIOLOGY AT A DISTANCE

How Far Can We Go With Online Distance Learning?

Mark C. Hirst and Hilary A. MacQueen
The Open University

Abstract

This chapter describes some examples of cutting-edge tools for teaching practical biology at a distance from The OpenScience Laboratory of The Open University. Various means of assessing student performance are discussed, and data relating to students' perceptions and achievements are presented. Students approach the use of the tools in a skeptical way, but their experiences convert many of them into advocates of online practical teaching methods. Both qualitatively and quantitatively, the online tools can be judged as successful in teaching practical skills to undergraduates. Participation and feedback on these tools from other education deliverers are encouraged.

As a science, biology has practical work at its core; it is inconceivable to teach biology without acknowledging this fact. However, times change; access to science learning is widening across the world, and new technologies can enhance students' learning experiences. Biology has a history of innovative use of technology in teaching, applied to both face-to-face teaching and teaching at a distance. Unsurprisingly, the development of such teaching methodologies has not been trouble free (MacQueen & Thomas, 2009), and both teachers and students have reported problems in using new teaching packages (Rolfe, Alcocer, Bentley, Milne, & Meyer-Sahling, 2008; Wolter, Lundeberg, & Bergland, 2013). Nevertheless, the use of information technology and online teaching resources has grown rapidly, and here we review progress and explore the effectiveness of many options available for distance teaching of practical biology. In this chapter, we describe some recent developments in online practical biology teaching, focusing on experiences gained over many years at The Open University (OU) in the United Kingdom, and present evidence demonstrating that students can learn effectively in this way. Before doing so, however, we need to explore some fundamental concepts.

What Are We Trying to Teach?

In the United Kingdom, it is generally recognized that degree-level graduates, in addition to having knowledge and understanding in their subject area, should have key subject-specific skills and more generic transferable skills (The Quality Assurance Agency for Higher Education, 2007). Table 6.1 lists a number of these skills. Both skill sets can be addressed by online distance learning (ODL). For those unfamiliar with OU, an online-delivered module typically consists of a blend of text, animation, video, and audio interspersed with interactive formative and summative assessments. Much of the text is also accessible via screen reader devices for off-line study. A typical 30-credit module would require 300 hours of study, studied at the pace of the individual student.

Our experience is that students are keen to learn the skills relating explicitly to their chosen subject area, but they are often less interested in learning generic skills in isolation, as they are perceived as dry and boring. At OU (as elsewhere), our strategy has been to embed teaching generic skills into a topic-relevant context, such that students gain a better understanding of why they have to learn material that is less appealing at first sight. In addition, constructing activities where generic skills are recognized from these contextualized examples and then articulated is also key. Thus, the two skill sets can be combined when ODL material is being designed and the tools are provided to allow students to record and articulate these skill sets.

Some of the subject-specific skills listed in Table 6.1 imply an element of manual dexterity that can best be learned in a hands-on environment. In developing ways to teach practical skills, OU has sought to examine each of the subject-specific skills and break them down to identify particular components that can be developed through ODL. In this chapter, we describe examples of ODL tools that have been developed and used in this way.

TABLE 6.1
Some Skills Expected of a Typical Biology Graduate

Subject-Specific Skills	Generic Skills
Observation and classification of living organisms	Literacy and numeracy
Hypothesis generation and testing	Working as a team
Experimental designs	Information gathering and analysis from diverse sources (including digital online materials)
Collection and preservation of biological samples	Critical analysis and reflective practice
Data analysis	Oral, visual, and written communication
Basic core techniques (e.g., microscopy, sampling, micropipetting, concentrations and molarity)	Creative thinking and problem-solving
Advanced techniques involving specialist protocols or equipment	Business and commercial awareness
	Time management

How Should We Teach It?

Successful learning depends not only on the teaching style adopted but also on the receptiveness and engagement of the student. The key to learning is to get students to physically and mentally do something to further their own learning rather than passively listen to a lecture or watch video materials. This so-called active learning is achieved by a number of pedagogic approaches, such as problem-based learning.

The concept of active learning has had a mixed reception over the years (Michael, 2006; Prince, 2004), but more recently it has found strong advocates (Freeman et al., 2014; Haidet, Morgan, Wristers, Moran, & Richards, 2004; Jeffries, Huggett, & Szarek, 2014). We contend that the active learning approach is key to teaching practical biology by ODL, and we discuss some successful examples later. They can be summarized as the provision of (usually) online tools that allow students to make decisions about key aspects of experimental design; to collect their own data and make judgments about their quality, the sources of variability, and the reliability of measurements; and then to report and reflect on this experience.

An ODL approach provides some distinct advantages over hands-on laboratory or fieldwork in traditional educational settings, which are often limited in resources (equipment, consumables, etc.), time, and facilities. However, ODL also presents additional challenges both in the creation and maintenance of ODL tools and in supporting students. We discuss later how these issues are addressed, but we start by looking at the types of tools typically used in ODL for practical skills.

The Range and Types of Practical Work Taught at a Distance

The range of teaching packages currently available through the Internet is very wide and includes material suitable for students at all levels from primary to postgraduate, as well as a plethora of citizen science projects and activities. A number of open-access repositories of online teaching materials now exist. One example is the Royal Society of Biology's higher education teaching (heteaching.societyofbiology.org/index.php/heteaching-home) in the United Kingdom, which features open educational resources that support practical biology and research-led teaching in bioscience. The examples we describe in this chapter are available through an online repository called The Open-Science Laboratory (OSL), which can be viewed online (learn5.open.ac.uk/course/view .php?id=2). OSL is an initiative funded by The Wolfson Foundation to make OU-developed practical science teaching tools available for educators worldwide. Table 6.2 lists a number of current OSL assets.

One common type of tool is data and field observation repositories, where individuals post data about particular organisms (including images and geo-locations). These build to create large data sets and act as focal points for communities of experts to help in species identification. OU has run this type of activity for many years, and current projects include iSpot, Evolution MegaLab, and Treezilla. One observational survey that was carried out by OU students in the 1970s provided data sets on the coloration in peppered moths (*Biston betularia*) that were used in a research paper published in *Science* (Cook, Mani, & Varley, 1986) and provided important data contributing to the story of industrial melanism.

Examples of ODL Tools

We now expand on three examples from Table 6.2, all of which are web-based software programs that present students with experimental tools with which to collect data.

TABLE 6.2
Examples of Some Online Distance Learning Tools Used at OU

Area or Technique	ODL Tools	Target Groups
Observational	iSpot: field observations and species identification	Citizen science
		Informed public
	Treezilla: tree records	Specialist biologists
	Virtual field trip	Undergraduate
Digital microscopy	Animal physiology: cold adaptation changes in WAT and BAT	Senior school student
		Undergraduate
	Plant stomata	Postgraduate
	Histopathology: slide sets of basic histology techniques and normal and pathological tissues	Undergraduate
		Postgraduate
Animal work	Cold adaptation in rats	Undergraduate
	Rat training (operant training)	
Spectroscopy	DNA quantitation	Undergraduate
	Lipid and protein quantitation	
	Nitrate detection	
	Pesticide detection	
Analytical	Polymerase chain reaction	Undergraduate
	Technipedia: a repository of techniques	Postgraduate
	qHPLC	
Data analysis	*t* test	Senior school student
	Graph plotting	Undergraduate
Experimental tools	RVP task	Undergraduate

Note. Many of these assets are available from the OpenScience Laboratory repository. ODL = online distance learning; WAT = white adipose tissue; BAT = brown adipose tissue; qHPLC = quantitative high-performance liquid chromatography; RVP = rapid visual processing.

Virtual Animal Work

In some areas, the effectiveness of ODL teaching is well evidenced. For example, online teaching tools modeling animal studies have been successfully used in pharmacology teaching (John, 2013). Such animal-based tools are effective ways to replace work using real animals and provide an opportunity to practice the 3Rs approach—replacement, reduction, refinement (Russell & Burch, 1959)—and to give students opportunities to experience animal work, something they are unlikely to have in most undergraduate

Figure 6.1 Rat training laboratory.

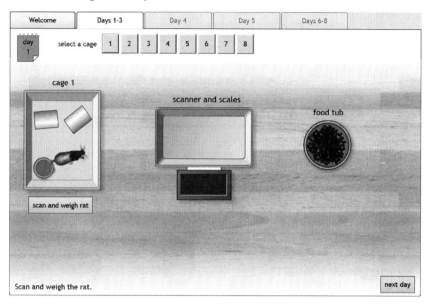

Note. In the rat training laboratory, students are required to collect data on animal body weight and to weigh out food for eight virtual rats over a simulated period of eight days, choosing food levels that maintain a healthy weight in animals and also drive appropriate behavior in several operant training laboratories. The level of food provided determines the animals' responses in the operant tests. This laboratory replicates training required to prepare rats to carry out a sustained attention task but also requires attention to good animal husbandry.

teaching environments. Although such tools cannot replace the tactile and sensory aspects of handling animals, they do allow students to experience some key aspects of working with experimental organisms.

As an example, OU's rat training laboratory (Figure 6.1) asks students to apply their understanding of good animal husbandry, taught in online text, to the maintenance of virtual rats at a healthy weight yet sufficiently diet restricted to shape their behavior in a simple food-rewarded task. Students operating this tool recognize the benefit of using a virtual approach for teaching in this sensitive subject area. A survey of OU students who used the rat training laboratory within the context of an investigation of sustained attention found that 79% (141/180) felt that their experience had given them a new perspective on the ethics of experimenting with test animals. When this group was asked about the benefits of the online tool, 90% (162/180) felt that the online laboratory reduced animal usage for teaching purposes, and 80% (143/180) felt it provided an opportunity to carry out work that would not normally be available to undergraduates.

Digital Microscopy

A digital microscope (DM) used to explore biological samples is one of the most versatile of the online tools. Creation of an online interactive screen that replicates some of the important features of a microscope shell allows any number of digitally captured tissue

sections to be used in a flexible manner. OU used to send its undergraduates real microscopes, at considerable expense. We now use a DM to deliver to students sets of images
that have been captured on a real microscope from actual tissue sections. Image sets
have been created, often from reference slide sets, and are available for teaching human
histopathology to undergraduates and postgraduates (through a project funded by the
Joint Information Systems Committee [JISC]) and for teaching exam-led curriculum to
groups of students from 16 to 18 years old. Many OU modules use the DM, often as part
of larger investigations, including a project studying the physiology of cold adaptation in
mammals (Figure 6.2). In this case, slide sets were created from sections of adipose tissue
samples originally generated at an OU on-site teaching class that is no longer active.

The generation of new slide sets requires specialized imaging systems, but the images
are easy to collect (as an image set at each magnification) and load into the DM software.
Students develop basic microscopy skills and then progress to detailed analyses of the
materials on the slides. The background techniques of sample isolation, preparation, and
sectioning to generate the slides are taught using video and online text. These reference
materials are housed in a central online techniques repository accessible to all students as
a reference resource, such as OU Technipedia.

Figure 6.2 Histological analysis of brown adipose tissue using a DM.

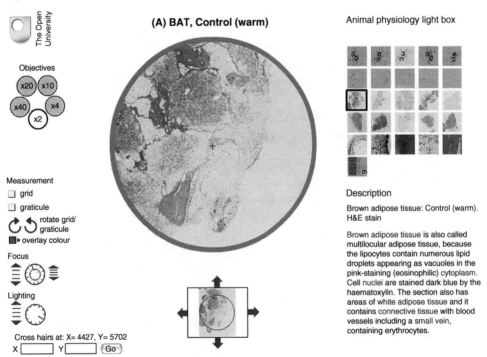

Note. Students are taught the use of a microscope, including magnification controls, basic sampling, and
the use of calibration slides and a grid to collect data on cell numbers in BAT and WAT samples taken
from control and cold-adapted rats. BAT = brown adipose tissue; WAT = white adipose tissue.

Spectrophotometry

An example of a core laboratory technique is spectrophotometry, commonly used in many areas of biology. As an analytical tool, therefore, it lends itself well to sit at the center of different student investigations. In current OU curricula, spectrophotometer-based assays are used to investigate nitrate and pesticide pollution of water supplies, assess levels of protein and lipid in control and cold-adapted brown and white adipose tissue in rats, and quantitate genomic DNA samples. Such interactive tools provide opportunities to teach the basic principles of instrumentation, including the use of positive and negative controls to check and zero the machines, and to develop systematic working practices. Student exercises include generating calibration curves and using them to quantitate the level of a substance in a relevant biological sample, such as the quantitation of DNA using ultraviolet (UV) spectroscopy (Figure 6.3). Students using this instrument have first studied background information describing the principles underlying the technique.

In the interactive instrument shown in Figure 6.3, students have access to various functions through buttons operated via their mouse, a touch screen, or accessibility "hot

Figure 6.3 DNA quantitation spectrophometer.

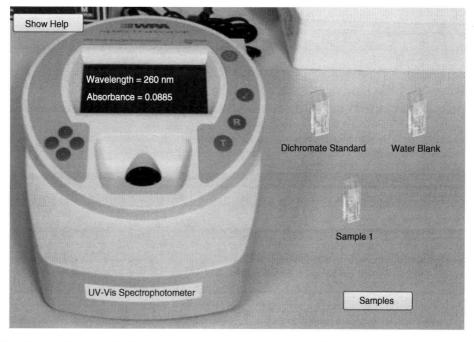

Note. Students interact with the various on-screen buttons to switch on the spectrophotometer and adjust the wavelengths. Using this online interactive interface, students are asked to determine whether any samples have protein contamination by calculating the $A_{260nm}:A_{280nm}$ ratio. They are asked to determine the concentration of DNA and then calculate a dilution factor to prepare a solution with a concentration of 50 ng/µl, suitable for a subsequent polymerase chain reaction–based assay.

keys" for individuals with limited use of the mouse or screen. To switch the machine on and to set and change wavelengths, students use the mouse or touch screen to "push" the relevant buttons on the instrument, exactly as would be done with the real machine. The software is programmed with the full absorbance spectrum for both DNA and protein across the UV spectrum and does not prevent students from collecting data at the wrong wavelength. The program generates a small amount of random error, as is expected for this type of instrument, making the values reported back for any sample similar to those obtained with an actual instrument. To obtain accurate values for their DNA samples, students must obtain multiple readings from several independent samples, determine the A_{260nm} value, and then calculate the DNA concentration using the known relationship between A_{260nm} and DNA concentration. We use this next example to assess how effectively students complete this exercise.

Interactive instruments such as the spectrophotometer and the DM illustrate just how far on-screen interactive interfaces that simulate instruments and can be used in ODL have advanced in terms of usability and realism. Nevertheless, it could be argued that even with the sophistication of packages such as these, ODL cannot replicate the hands-on aspects of practical biology, and therefore true practical biology can only ever be taught in a face-to-face laboratory or field context. Although there is some strength to this argument, we contend that ODL goes some way toward accustoming students to hands-on research. First, we can support them to carry out their own (risk-assessed) experiments at home. An example is the Rapid Visual Processing task tool that allows students to carry out a study on human attention at home. Second, through highlighting the skills that are developed with ODL, we provide the knowledge and understanding for the hands-on skills to be developed in an on-site context. This incidentally offers a useful, complementary avenue for many teachers with limited resources to deliver face-to-face laboratory or field-based teaching.

Putting Tools Together Into a Learning Journey

We have described the types of online tools that can be used; equally important is to contextualize their use. In each case, tools such as the DM or spectrophotometer are presented to students within the context of an investigation that is delivered using online text, videos, and animations that provide details of sample preparation and the biological and experimental context. One advantage of having a suite of ODL practical tools is that they can be put together into larger investigations with a logical story or context. Thus, students learn about different applications of various techniques and are engaged with the origin and processing of samples and data interpretation. Two examples of how several different ODL tools are woven together into a student investigation are shown in Figure 6.4 and involve several of the assets discussed previously. Each investigation requires students to study background materials and then perform their practical work. Each activity is expected to take students approximately 50 hours, of which over half would be working in the relevant virtual laboratory and analyzing their data.

Figure 6.4 Two examples of how online distance learning tools can be integrated into a contextualizing narrative to enhance students' learning.

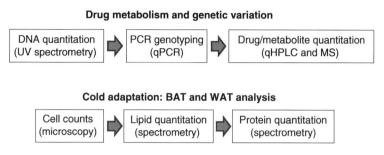

Drug metabolism and genetic variation

DNA quantitation (UV spectrometry) → PCR genotyping (qPCR) → Drug/metabolite quantitation (qHPLC and MS)

Cold adaptation: BAT and WAT analysis

Cell counts (microscopy) → Lipid quantitation (spectrometry) → Protein quantitation (spectrometry)

Note. PCR = polymerase chain reaction; qPCR = quantitative polymerase chain reaction; qHPLC = quantitative high-performance liquid chromatography; MS = mass spectrometry.

Supporting Students Through Practical ODL

One challenge that assembling ODL tools into pathways brings is that for students to succeed, they must be well supported in their learning journey. The primary requisite for successful support is to devise an online environment in which students feel secure and can explore and that delivers the underlying pedagogy of the materials.

Design of the Tools

Straightforward navigation within ODL tools is essential, and students should be made to feel part of the process; teaching should be "with students," not "at students" (Muirhead, 2007). Giving students some control over their interactions with the package has a positive effect on their learning (Means, Toyama, Murphy, Bakia, & Jones, 2010). It is also helpful to tell students at the outset how long the exercise should take them. One acknowledged disadvantage of ODL is that it is easy to spend far more time than necessary exploring the site, repeating steps needlessly, and working ineffectively (Means et al., 2010). It is also worth emphasizing that the information technology must be robust and fully functional on all common platforms. The advent of HTML5-based programming has enabled the use of tablets and mobile devices for delivery of ODL, but some features of many teaching packages are currently incompatible with such devices. A recent survey of 71 OU students studying practical biology ODL revealed information technology issues to be a major cause of noncompletion. In feedback, 99% (70/71) of these students said they enjoyed learning through printed text and 90% (64/71) through audiovisual materials; however, only 83% (59/71) enjoyed learning through online materials. This remains a challenge for distance educators.

Instructor Support

Another essential for good student support is the personal touch, specifically a dedicated tutor who can answer questions or provide additional guidance. Interestingly, it appears that a tutor does not need to be a real person: Yu, Brown, and Billett (2007) showed that an avatar tutor increased student success in a virtual learning environment teaching package. However, in all OU assets, the tutor is a real person, accessible by e-mail or on a forum. In contrast to many of the standard OU modules students have previously studied, the more active style of learning on the practical ODL packages is often one of the major challenges the students face. This is managed by offering students a two-tier level of support, with specialist topic advisers available for forum support (the equivalent of teaching assistants or demonstrators who might be present in a "wet" lab). Interestingly, the educators who fulfill these roles report that many responsibilities are very similar to supporting students in face-to-face situations in terms of where students make mistakes or need support and reassurance but that it is harder to spot when that help is required. We discuss later how instructor interventions may change in the future. OU students are also supported by their personal tutors, who lead online tutorials using Blackboard tools around core skills, data analysis, and interpretation of results, besides providing more general academic and personal support and marking the experimental write-ups.

Teamwork and Collaborative Interactions

Many of the individual ODL tools described here are part of an undergraduate second-level, 30-credit module that teaches all the subject-specific and generic skills listed in Table 6.1. Most students have reported that they have had very little exposure to practical activities before starting the module. They often have a negative view of online practical science before they start, but their attitude changes with experience, and they are much more positive at the end of the module (Nicholas, Robinson, & Swithenby, 2014). Although students study this module individually, some aspects of collaborative work are built into it. Students are set tasks to work on together, ranging from setting experimental parameters in the planning phase to doing data-pooling exercises. These requirements promote peer-group interactions and help with the development of support networks and science communication skills. Forums, wikis, and Blackboard rooms are available for students to use at various stages of their work to help with these aspects. A U.S. Department of Education report (Means et al., 2010) confirms that instructor-driven or collaborative learning produces significantly better results than independent learning in an ODL context.

As an example, in the study on genetic variation and drug metabolism shown in Figure 6.4, students are tasked with analyzing a population of individuals by qHPLC. In their background work, they established a relationship between specific gene variants and drug metabolizer status. The qHPLC analysis requires the students to identify the correct peaks for drug and metabolite by comparing MS spectra and then to quantitate each using a graphic tool to integrate the area under a curve. These values are read against a calibration curve for drug and metabolite that they have drawn up using the same tools. To determine the metabolizer status of the entire study population, students work in teams, each assigned to a subgroup of individuals with a specific genotype. Team interactions are achieved through forum postings and a wiki, where students discuss their own and others' data, the sources of uncertainty in the values, and a consensus drug–metabolite ratio for their subgroup. The results are then pooled to form a data set for the population. This team-working aspect of the investigation allows students to discuss the origins of variation in their data in terms of random variations from instrumentation and the systematic errors from slightly differing data collection methodologies. In a survey of

70 respondents, 49 (70%) agreed that this collaborative work helped them to learn, with only a single student definitely disagreeing.

Online forums can also be exploited to facilitate peer assessment and support. Indeed, we find that as students' confidence increases, they are more likely to participate actively in forums, helping their peers informally and in formal tasks. Linton, Farmer, and Peterson (2014) showed that students working collaboratively in peer groups outperformed students working individually, and our observations support this finding.

Assessment: Evidencing Skills and Learning

One advantage of having ODL tools that generate random errors within data sets is that it is virtually impossible for any two students to obtain the same data if they have worked independently, providing obvious advantages for detecting cases of collusion. This means that assessment can be remarkably robust even without the use of plagiarism software.

There is current enthusiasm for embedding formative assessment with feedback into ODL packages, yet so far there is scant evidence that students find this useful; indeed, meta-analysis failed to reveal any improvement in students' learning when videos and quizzes are embedded in the material (Means et al., 2010). Such assessment can, however, be used effectively by instructors to check student progress, especially when data analysis is involved. We will return to this shortly, but we first will mention several other routes for assessing students using ODL practical tools.

Reporting Practical Work

As with face-to-face practical teaching, arguably the best way to assess whether students have understood and learned is by means of a written report of an investigation, with data presented and discussed, at the end of the practical session. This has the merit of being standard currency in higher education and means that students can be judged academically by the same criteria as their peers studying in face-to-face mode. Although such assessment can reveal much about achievement of the subject-specific skills, many students do not appreciate that they have demonstrated the generic skills as well. Inclusion of an additional requirement to produce a written article for a nonscientific audience (e.g., an information leaflet for children or a press release) about their investigation is one way that students can be challenged into practicing and demonstrating their generic communication skills, both written and graphical. Out of 68 respondents to a survey, 60 (88.2%) agreed that this form of assessment helped to consolidate their learning.

Skills Portfolios

Perhaps a more transparent way for students to evidence their development of generic skills is by portfolio, where they can match specific pieces of work to particular learning outcomes. Examples include submitting a screenshot of their response to a forum posting from a fellow student or editing a wiki to demonstrate their participation in a team project. Portfolio use has been found to improve student knowledge and understanding, self-awareness and reflection, and independent learning abilities (Buckley et al., 2009).

Analytics

From the perspective of educators, success can be measured both quantitatively, by key performance indicators such as pass rates, and qualitatively, by student feedback via questionnaires. In terms of a quantitative evaluation of the practical module described here, 96% of 126 students in the first cohort passed. Qualitative feedback revealed some discontent with information technology systems (see previous discussion), but other students were more enthusiastic. One said,

> The course for me was a total success. I am not too academic, so much preferred the interactive practical approach, and the easy-to-read topic material. With an excellent group and tutor, this has been my favorite course and I really wish there were more like it (please!).

Interestingly, it is possible to use data derived from tracking student activity on each web page, as well as by monitoring students' responses to embedded quizzes. This form of analysis is in its early days but has already revealed that students of practical biology ODL have the same issues as their peers who are receiving face-to-face instruction: Sixteen percent of students made numerical errors, such as with units, decimal places, and concentrations. Embedded quizzes may not add to the student experience, but they do provide a useful tool for educators to judge the success of their teaching materials. In our examples, quiz results are based on three attempts, with feedback to prompt correction of units, concentrations, and so on. For example, students carrying out the DNA quantitation exercise using the interactive spectrophotometer are required to test and report on five genomic DNA samples using a quiz that the instructor can access. Table 6.3 shows the outcomes for a typical cohort of students on one such quiz. Just fewer than 65% of the students correctly used the instrument to determine the concentration of DNA, with the majority doing so on their first attempt. Of

TABLE 6.3
Analysis of Student Quiz Answers (*N* = 294) for a DNA Quantitation Exercise

Outcome	*Number of Responses*	*Notes*
Correct first attempt	164	64.97% accurate DNA quantitation achieved
Correct second attempt	16	
Correct third attempt	11	
Incorrect answers (at all stages)	47	Raw A_{260nm} value entered; order of magnitude, dilution factors, or unit errors; and answers outside the question tolerances (indicating no replicates)
	56	Previously entered values, random numbers, blank entries

Note. Students use the DNA quantitation online interactive tool to determine the concentration of five genomic DNAs based on samples of differing dilution. Students can attempt each question up to three times.

the incorrect attempts, a number of common errors were identified that are expected in this type of exercise. Anticipation of the expected errors can be built into the feedback provided after unsuccessful attempts at the quiz. Such analyses allow us to review and amend the teaching materials.

The Future of Practical Biology ODL

It has taken quite some time for ODL to become established as a credible method of teaching, but it is now a fundamental part of most educators' repertoires (Scanlon, 2011). This cannot yet be said for practical ODL.

Are We Limiting Students' Future Prospects?

The concern remains that students who have never worked in a real-life lab or field setting cannot be said to be practically competent. It is clear that the majority of the elements of practical work—in fact all of them apart from real biological sample collection and preparation—can be achieved equally well in an ODL scenario. If students can be adequately supported to carry out the sampling activities for themselves, in any experimental context, then they will be able to claim competence in most aspects of practical biology at a certain level. Clearly, graduates who are going to work in a lab or field setting will need to improve their dexterity and familiarity with the specific techniques and equipment used in that location, but as anybody who has taught postgraduate students will know, this needs to happen in almost every case, regardless of students' educational background. If that proviso becomes widely accepted, then we can truly claim that ODL is an equally valid route for delivery of the learning outcomes required of a biology graduate.

Changing Technologies: Challenges and Benefits

Without a doubt, one of the major challenges ahead with all ODL tools, such as the interactive experimental interfaces discussed here, lies with the operating and software systems on which the tools are designed to run. Even—or especially—within a web environment, changes are inevitable: A move away from Flash-based programming to HTML5 requires ongoing reprogramming. Nevertheless, there are benefits of delivering in more accessible formats, and live streaming from webcams now allows real-time viewing of experiments running in laboratories. This opens up a whole new area of experimentation.

Another challenge for ODL delivery is language. This applies to the delivery of assets produced in English to students for whom this is not their primary language and also to differences in the way operating systems and keyboards are tailored. ODL tools may not always work on all systems, and keyboards may be set to country-specific features: a keyboard programmed to use a comma as a decimal point can cause problems if these are critical values in an input table.

The development of more sophisticated analytics is likely to bring new insights into how our ODL tools are used. Although using quizzes to assess how well an instrument performs within a teaching environment can be helpful, it would be more helpful still to gain an insight into how students interact with the instrument and whether their technique improves with experience. In innovative research, eye-tracking technology is being used to design better interactive instruments that will eventually be used and delivered online. A major goal for analytics is to be able to identify a student who is struggling (perhaps through detecting a random or nonsystematic use of buttons on screen) such that a suitable intervention can be made. Such items remain, as yet, an aspiration.

Final Reflections on OU's ODL Practical Skills

OU has always provided practical biology education to its students. In the past, this was provided by face-to-face residential courses and home-based experimental kits, but requirements for global delivery have meant finding new approaches to teach key practical skills. Devising novel and innovative ways to teach them has always been, and will remain, a challenge. However, in creating teaching tools and making them available to other educators, OU is fulfilling one important aspect of its mission: to be open. We encourage you to try the various tools that are available through OSL and work with us to help refine them for the greater benefit of the community of biology students and instructors.

References

Buckley, S., Coleman, J., Davison, I., Khan, K. S., Zamora, J., Malick, S., . . . Sayers, J. (2009). The educational effects of portfolios on undergraduate student learning: A best evidence medical education (BEME) systematic review. BEME Guide No. 11. *Medical Teacher, 31*(4), 282–298.

Cook, L. M., Mani, G. S., & Varley, M. E. (1986). Postindustrial melanism in the peppered moth. *Science, 231*(4738), 611–613.

Freeman, S., Eddy, S. L., McDonough, M., Smith, M. K., Okoroafor, N., Jordt, H., & Wenderoth, M. P. (2014). Active learning increases student performance in science, engineering and mathematics. *Proceedings of the National Academy of Sciences (USA), 111*(23), 8410–8415.

Haidet, P., Morgan, R. O., Wristers, K., Moran, B. J., & Richards, B. (2004). A controlled trial of active versus passive learning strategies in a large group setting. *Advances in Health Science Education, 9*(1), 15–27.

Jeffries, W. B., Huggett, K. N., & Szarek, J. (2014). *Adapting classroom assessment and other technologies to a flipped classroom.* Retrieved from www.iamse.org/development/2014/was_013014/was_013014_resource.pdf

John, L. J. (2013). A review of computer assisted learning in medical undergraduates. *Journal of Pharmacology and Pharmacotherapeutics, 4*(2), 86–90.

Linton, D. L., Farmer, J. K., & Peterson, E. (2014). Is peer interaction necessary for optimal active learning? *CBE—Life Sciences Education, 13*(2), 243–252.

MacQueen, H., & Thomas, J. (2009). Teaching biology at a distance: Pleasures, pitfalls and possibilities. *American Journal of Distance Education, 23*(3), 139–150.

Means, B., Toyama, Y., Murphy, R., Bakia, M., & Jones, K. (2010). *Evaluation of evidence-based practices in online learning: A meta-analysis and review of online learning studies.* Washington, DC: U.S. Department of Education, Office of Planning, Evaluation and Policy Development. Retrieved from www2.ed.gov/rschstat/eval/tech/evidence-based-practices/finalreport.pdf

Michael, J. (2006). Where's the evidence that active learning works? *Advances in Physiological Education, 30*(4), 159–167.

Muirhead, R. J. (2007). E-learning: Is this teaching at students or teaching with students? *Nursing Forum, 42*(4), 178–184.

Nicholas, V., Robinson, D., & Swithenby, S. (2014, April). *Student perceptions of online practical science.* Paper presented at the HEA STEM Annual Learning and Teaching Conference, Edinburgh, UK.

Prince, M. (2004). Does active learning work? A review of the research. *Journal of Engineering Education, 93*(3), 223–231.

The Quality Assurance Agency for Higher Education. (2007). *Biosciences benchmarking statement.* London, UK: Author.

Rolfe, V., Alcocer, M., Bentley, E., Milne, D., & Meyer-Sahling, J. (2008). Academic staff attitudes towards electronic learning in arts and sciences. *European Journal of Open, Distance and e-Learning.* Retrieved from www.eurodl.org/?p=archives&year=2008&halfyear=1&article=313

Russell, W. M. S., & Burch, R. (1959). *The principles of humane experimental technique.* London, UK: Methuen.

Scanlon, E. (2011). Open science: Trends in the development of science learning. *Open Learning, 26*(2), 97–112.

Wolter, B. H. K., Lundeberg, M. A., & Bergland, M. (2013). What makes science relevant? Student perceptions of multimedia case learning in ecology and health. *Journal of STEM Education: Innovations and Research, 14*(1), 26–35.

Yu, J. Q., Brown, D. J., & Billett, E. (2007). Design of virtual tutoring agents for a virtual biology experiment. *European Journal of Open, Distance and e-Learning.* Retrieved from www.eurodl.org/materials/cotrib/2007/Yu_Brown_Billett.htm

7

ASSESSMENT IN PHYSICS DISTANCE EDUCATION

Practical Lessons at Athabasca University

Farook Al-Shamali and Martin Connors
Athabasca University

Abstract

Meaningful and valid assessment of students' learning is at the heart of credit-granting institutions, especially for courses delivered at a distance. At Athabasca University, we have extensive experience in teaching online first-year physics courses, most of which include home lab components. Practical experiences and data-driven conclusions demonstrate that online assessment can be conducted effectively in the distance education environment. The turnaround time and quality of feedback on marked assignments and lab reports can be comparable to (if not exceed) that in conventional classrooms. The blended exam format (multiple-choice and long-answer questions) appears suitable for introductory physics courses, because it balances exam validity and course administration efficiency. A comprehensive final exam that carries more weight than the midterm appears to be a justified practice.

Educational institutions develop and offer for-credit courses largely so that registered students can achieve specific learning outcomes. Many students, however, enroll in a course and aim to achieve "a satisfactory grade with the least possible effort" (Redish, Saul, & Steinberg, 1998, p. 213). To them, it seems that what appears in the transcript is what matters at the end of the day. Science courses are no exception in this regard. An alarming gap between instructional goals and actual student learning in introductory physics courses was realized a few decades ago and incited pertinent research activity in physics education (McDermott, 1990).

Meaningful and valid assessment of students' learning is, therefore, at the heart of credit-granting institutions and "is a core component for effective learning" (Gikandi, Morrow, & Davis, 2011, p. 2334). This is particularly important in the distance education model, which strives to position itself alongside the conventional face-to-face system. It was noted by Dominguez and Ridley (1999) that "distance education programs

116

. . . must demonstrate equivalency of learning outcomes in order to gain a more permanent position on campus, and evidence is typically gathered through assessment" (p. 70).

The impressive evolution of distance education into online learning, during the past 20 years, added another dimension in this regard. It was acknowledged early on that "as online learning environments for higher education expand, assessment is increasingly being recognized as a critical issue" (Reeves, 2000, p. 105). It was also eloquently phrased by Carnevale (2001) that "assessment is taking center stage as online educators experiment with new ways of teaching and proving that they're teaching effectively" (p. A43). This is particularly crucial with the "increased demand for accountability, growth, and excellence in educational institutions" (Gaytan & McEwen, 2007, p. 130). Therefore, it is important that all components of student assessment be a reflection of the desired learning outcomes, regardless of delivery format (Robles & Braathen, 2002).

Course Delivery: Guidance and Expectations

Before we discuss assessment in distance education and our experience in this regard, it is important to talk about course delivery. It is clear that a positive experience and fruitful interaction with the course material are vital for stimulating student learning through independent study. There is mounting evidence in the literature that online environments can be as effective as conventional classrooms, provided that a high quality of online instruction is ensured (Tallent-Runnels et al., 2006). The convenience of online courses comes with added responsibility for the student's own learning. At the same time, the instructor's duty shifts more toward the authorship and development of high-quality (text and/or multimedia) course material to improve the study experience of students.

The textbook is a very (if not the most) important educational resource in a typical physics course. However, it is usually written with the traditional classroom in mind and may not be sufficient as stand-alone course material suitable for independent learning. The face-to-face lecture and the textbook have been the traditional combination, presenting the necessary teaching material to students. In this case, the instructor acts as a guide and provides the learners with a road map to progress in the course. This is accomplished by communicating the expected learning outcomes, guiding the students through the main concepts and relevant textbook material, and demonstrating the detailed solutions of a suitable number of relevant questions and problems. In most cases, demonstrations and laboratory exercises make the link between theory and the real world that characterizes physics. From an assessment point of view, the instructor sets the course requirements and standards. Thus, in this prevalent model of education, the instructor and the textbook complement each other to provide students with an efficient and effective learning experience.

In a course offered fully through distance education, there is no instructor in the traditional sense. Students, in this educational model, are expected to progress in the course more independently but without compromising standard learning outcomes. The "study guide" in this case becomes an essential component, which is expected to complement the textbook and substitute for the instructor and his or her lecture notes. Therefore, an effective study guide is designed to be compatible with the textbook and suitable for self-study. Most important, the study guide should include the specific learning outcomes for each unit and provide example solutions and answers to a sufficient number of questions related to the subject matter. Students in an introductory physics course, in particular, appreciate well-laid-out solutions of end-of-chapter problems, which they perceive to have a direct impact on their performance in assignments and (most important) in examinations.

Athabasca University (AU) is an open university located in Alberta, Canada, with over 40 years of experience in distance education. Most courses offered by AU are non-paced and follow the continuous enrollment model. This means that a student can start a course at the beginning of any month of the year and progress at his or her own rate (although with an overall deadline), as opposed to "paced" courses in which a time syllabus is set.

Limited tutor service is available for registered students, where assigned tutors respond to students' questions, by e-mail or over the phone, and mark submitted assignments. The university standard in this regard is that a student's question is answered within two business days, and submitted course work is marked within five business days. Students can also interact with their tutors through the internal mail of the learning management system (in this example, Moodle). The chat feature of Moodle, however, is currently disabled for the physics courses. Despite our belief, in general, in the benefits of student–student interaction, it may not be suitable for our course delivery model at this time. This is because students do not advance in the course in parallel and do not share deadlines for assignments and exams. Student–student interaction in such an environment will most probably be counterproductive and compromises academic integrity. In the following sections, we present our practical experience in students' assessment in two nonpaced physics courses at AU.

Introductory Physics (PHYS 200)

PHYS 200 is a standard algebra-based physics course that provides an introduction to Newtonian mechanics. When combined with a follow-up course (either PHYS 201 or PHYS 202, which have different second-term, freshman-level content), it fulfills the equivalent of one year in introductory physics, which can be matched to offerings at other institutions (Connors, 2004). PHYS 200 is one of the highest enrollment courses at AU, with nearly 500 students registering annually from different parts of the country, as well as some international students. Besides the textbook (Giancoli, 2005), the course material includes a carefully written study guide. In addition to learning objectives and extended explanations of certain concepts, the bulk of the study guide consists of detailed solutions to a significant number of end-of-chapter problems.

The course also includes a hands-on lab component, where students perform seven experiments in the convenience of their home. The lab experiments are of high quality and use modern devices and up-to-date software for data collection and analysis. Material and equipment necessary for the experimental setup are prepared in the science lab and packaged in the lab kit, which can be borrowed from the AU library. The science lab personnel are remotely accessible and can provide technical support related to the lab equipment. Students in PHYS 200 are expected to submit two assignments and seven lab reports and write a midterm and a final examination.

Assignments

The assignment is not just a summative assessment tool; it is actually part of the learning process. As concluded by Cheng, Thacker, Cardenas, and Crouch (2004), "graded homework is a significant factor in increasing students' understanding of physics concepts" (p. 1453). Students in PHYS 200 are expected to submit two relatively long assignments covering each half of the course. Each assignment consists of 18 problems, which require detailed solutions and contribute 10% to the overall course grade. Even though the assignment questions vary in complexity and difficulty, they all have the same weight in marking. Students are encouraged to have the first assignment submitted and marked before taking the midterm exam. Similarly, the second assignment should be marked before the students take the final exam. We believe that the effort students make while struggling with physics homework problems, combined with the help they may receive in the process, contributes significantly to improved learning.

In preparing the set of assignment questions, we made an effort to include a healthy balance of simple (level I), normal (level II), and complex (level III) questions. We believe that a good assignment should be composed of 20% level I, 60% level II, and 20% level III questions. An assignment that is mostly composed of level I problems could be deceiving by giving the student a false impression of mastery of the subject. On the other hand, an assignment that consists mostly of level III problems may cause frustration and raises concerns of unfair evaluation.

One may argue that giving students difficult assignments should make them overprepared for the exam, in which they would then excel, achieving a higher overall mark in the course. We disagree with this argument, because unrealistically high expectations can have a negative effect on one's self-confidence. It is important to maintain sufficient motivation for students to complete the course, especially in distance education. As stated by Scouller (1998), "The quality of student learning and students' pursuit of higher grades are enhanced by the careful selection of an assessment method that firstly, encourages students' development of higher order intellectual skills and the employment of deeper learning approaches; and secondly, allows students to demonstrate their development" (p. 470). We also do not have excessive reservations on giving students some hints on difficult assignment problems. Research has indicated that "the most effective feedback is that which is given at the time the learning is constructed" (Wolsey, 2008, p. 323).

Because most of the solutions to assignment problems consist of calculations and algebraic manipulations, submitting typed solutions becomes a challenge. In the absence of a convenient equation editor, students find that preparing handwritten solutions is by far the most practical choice. Some students make the extra effort of producing a "typed" document using the formula-editing tools on a word processor. In practice, we noticed that handwritten solutions are easier to mark than typed documents. Most students are not experts in formula-editing tools and, many times, produce formulas that are not easy to read. Also, because of the extra effort required, students tend to be more conservative when it comes to showing detailed calculation steps. Therefore, students are encouraged to scan handwritten solutions and save them as portable document format (PDF) files. We noticed that some students simply take pictures of their assignment pages, using high-definition cameras of modern smartphones, and merge them into a single file. Each electronic assignment's file is then uploaded to the corresponding online drop box in the learning management system (Moodle).

Assignments are marked using Acrobat Professional and then uploaded again to Moodle for students to view. In addition to *X*s and check marks, the software allows written comments and feedback. Acrobat Professional, however, does not have an equation editor, which makes it difficult to write nonsimple equations. One way around this difficulty is that correct solution steps are inserted as pictures taken from the solution key. It is also possible to insert a new page in the PDF file if a long solution of a certain problem is required. The electronic submission to online drop boxes is a step forward compared to postal methods, helping reduce turnaround time and saving postage costs for both parties. A further major advantage is the centralized tracking and archiving of all student course work. This is very helpful in monitoring marking activities to ensure compliance with the university's standards in this regard. In addition, original assignment submission can be turned to in case of a student's appeal or the suspicion of academic misconduct.

An evaluation survey is sent to each student to solicit feedback on tutor performance and satisfaction with course material. Of particular interest are students' responses to the following three questions:

1. How satisfied were you with the time your tutor took to mark and return your assignments?
2. How useful was the assignment feedback you received from your tutor?
3. Do you feel the marks you have received from your tutor accurately reflect the quality of your work?

Despite the relatively low return of these surveys, they communicate important comments and views, which are used to enhance the quality of course content and improve the students' experience. Table 7.1 displays the responses of 45 students who returned the survey from July 2012 to June 2014. Overall, there is clear student satisfaction in the process and validity of assessment in the PHYS 200 course. It should be noted here that relatively lower satisfaction ratings concerning feedback on returned assignments (Question 2) were mostly from the students of one of the seven tutors of this course.

TABLE 7.1
Students' (*N* = 45) Responses to the Three Evaluation Survey Questions Returned From July 2012 to June 2014

Survey Question	Fully Satisfied	Reasonably Satisfied	No Response	Somewhat Satisfied	Dissatisfied
Question 1	30 (67%)	13 (29%)	0 (0%)	2 (4%)	0 (0%)
Question 2	22 (49%)	11 (24%)	1 (2%)	5 (11%)	6 (13%)
Question 3	30 (67%)	8 (18%)	2 (4%)	5 (11%)	0 (0%)

Lab Reports

The concept of physics home labs and AU's experience in this regard is discussed in greater detail in previous publications (Al-Shamali & Connors, 2010; Connors, 2004). Unlike lab experiments performed in traditional facilities, the home lab model is relatively more demanding and places a heavier load on students. In some experiments, it is a challenge to construct a working setup on the first attempt, especially in the absence of an on-site lab technician or lab partner. Therefore, the independent preparation of a working experimental setup is considered an important outcome of the home lab component. The next step, of course, is the collection of meaningful data, followed by appropriate analysis and writing the lab report.

In the lab component of PHYS 200, students are required to submit seven lab reports, which contribute 20% to the overall course grade. Furthermore, passing the lab is a requirement for passing the course. For marking purposes, the report is divided into eight components carrying different weights. Following is an excerpt from the introduction section of the PHYS 200 lab manual explaining mark distribution in the lab report:

> The lab report serves several purposes and gives an organized framework for recording your procedures and results. Although some students may have encountered laboratory reports before and may feel that there is a standard format for reports, this is not entirely true. However, make sure to include the following sections:
>
> *Cover Page:* On this page you write the course's name and number, lab manual version, experiment's title, your name, student ID, and date completed.
> *Introduction:* (10%) Provide theoretical background including all formulas required in the analysis.
> *Procedure:* (10%) Give a clear and detailed description of your steps in performing the experiment. If there is more than one part to the lab, it is usually best to describe the actions and observations separately for each part.
> *Pictures:* (10%) Include clear pictures of your setup.
> *Data:* (10%) Organize and present the data collected in the experiment and provide a description of the trend and behavior of collected data. No calculations or analysis should be included in this section of the report.
> *Analysis and Discussion:* (40%) This is a very important section of the lab report. In here you are expected to give clear and detailed analysis of your data, as described in the manual. Make sure to include sample calculations, especially for new calculated columns in data tables. You may also need to produce graphs and perform appropriate fits using the Logger Pro software. Errors in the observations may have a bearing on your analysis, and you should discuss their role here.
> *Conclusion:* (10%) Present a brief summary of your findings in this experiment, including the final numerical results.
> *Questions:* (10%) At the end of each lab, you will find a number of questions related to the experiment. Provide detailed answers to these questions.

Note that students are required to provide clear pictures of the experimental setup. Drawings and sketches cannot be accepted as substitutes for actual photographs. During the past few years, we have noticed that students rarely submitted a lab report without including at least one picture of the setup, so it was made mandatory. The convenience of digital photography, especially with the widespread use of smartphones, turned this into a simple task.

Unlike with assignments, most students choose to type their lab report, usually using Word, and insert pictures and diagrams into the same document. Some students find it convenient to include scanned (or actual) pictures of mathematical derivations and sample calculations done by hand on a sheet of paper. Normally, this would constitute a relatively small portion of the lab report. The report is then saved as a PDF file, which is marked electronically using Acrobat Professional, similar to the assignment.

Examinations

In PHYS 200, students are required to write midterm and final examinations. The midterm exam covers the first half of the course and contributes 20% to the overall course grade. The final exam is more comprehensive and carries 40% of the total grade. In addition, passing the final exam is a requirement for passing the course. Unlike assignments and labs, the two closed-book examinations must be properly invigilated, for obvious reasons. An AU student can write an exam at one of the many university-approved invigilation centers available Canada-wide. If the student lives more than 100 kilometers or 60 miles away from an invigilation center, he or she may arrange for an AU-approved invigilator. A hard copy of the exam is communicated, prior to the exam date, to the invigilator, who is responsible for sending it back after completion.

In an earlier version of the course, both examinations consisted of long-answer questions (seven in the midterm and nine in the final). In a subsequent course revision, a new format was adopted, in which the midterm has 8 multiple-choice questions and 4 long-answer problems, and the final has 12 multiple-choice questions and 6 long-answer problems. An effort was made to ensure balanced coverage of the learning outcomes by the two exams. The midterm covers the first half of the course, whereas the final is skewed (about 70%–80%) toward the second half of the course. Exam duration is based on students' requiring an average of 5 minutes for each multiple-choice question and 20 minutes for each long-answer problem. This results in a 2-hour midterm and a 3-hour final, which are the time limits allowed.

The new (mixed) examination format requires longer to prepare. The five answers listed for each multiple-choice question take into consideration common misconceptions and possible incorrect approaches by students. The advantages of the new exam format, however, are many. By nearly doubling the number of exam questions, as compared to the older format, we ensured better coverage of the various learning outcomes in each unit. In addition, the increased number of questions helped to enhance exam security, especially when combined with a larger pool of different exam versions sent randomly to students. This is particularly important in the continuous enrollment system at AU, with no minimum completion time. There are students writing either exam almost every day. Another important advantage of the new format is a reduction in marking time, which dropped by about 40%. Considering that the course coordinator is responsible for marking exams written by all students in the course, the new format constitutes a significant improvement of course management efficiency.

Statistical Comparison: Multiple-Choice Questions Versus Long-Answer Questions

To observe students' performance in the different components of mixed exams, we collected examination data over a period of nearly two years (2009 through 2010). Table 7.2 displays a summary of collected data for three versions of each exam. Note that the second column in the table shows the sample size, whereas the third and fourth columns display the average grades for the multiple-choice and long-answer sections, respectively. The last column shows the average exam grade for each of the three versions included in the study. The multiple-choice section, in each exam, contributes 40% to that total exam mark, whereas the long-answer section contributes 60%.

All 781 exams included in the study were graded by the same person (one of the coauthors), thus eliminating variances due to marking style. An overall observation of the numbers in Table 7.2 shows little indication of a significant difference between the average marks in the multiple-choice section compared to those in the long-answer section. This is especially the case for the more frequently written versions (Midterm A and Final A). So, on the basis of our data, we do not see a reason to differentiate between the two question formats in terms of validity of assessment.

Another interesting observation is the relatively greater variance in students' averages among the multiple-choice sections in different versions of the exam. This can be attributed to the nature of multiple-choice questions, for which no partial credit is given. Because there are only eight multiple-choice questions in the midterm, a single question that is too easy or too difficult can shift the mark in this section by more than 12%. In the final exam, the shift is about 8%. The long-answer sections in different versions show more conformity in average students performance. Here, partial marks are given for correct calculation steps.

The correlation between students' grades in both sections of the exam can be inspected more closely using scatter plots. For this purpose, we selected exam versions with the highest statistical validity. Figure 7.1 shows a scatter plot of the 212 points corresponding to the students who wrote Midterm A. The horizontal axis, in the diagram, corresponds to the mark in the multiple-choice section, whereas the vertical axis

TABLE 7.2
Average Scores (%) and Standard Deviations (*SDs*) for Different Exam Versions and Different Question Formats in the PHYS 200 Course

Exam Version	Number of Students	Multiple Choice % (SD)	Long Answer % (SD)	Total Mark % (SD)
Midterm A	212	62.4 (23)	63.4 (24)	63.0 (22)
Midterm B	102	55.8 (20)	63.6 (26)	60.4 (21)
Midterm C	88	73.2 (20)	65.1 (23)	68.4 (19)
Final A	177	62.3 (23)	60.7 (20)	61.2 (20)
Final B	110	78.2 (19)	66.6 (21)	71.2 (19)
Final C	92	67.7 (22)	68.7 (25)	68.3 (23)

Figure 7.1 Scatter plot showing correlation between marks in the long-answer and multiple-choice sections of Midterm A of the PHYS 200 midterm exam.

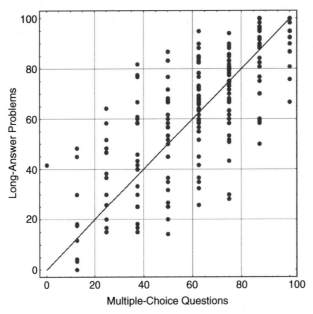

corresponds to the mark in the long-answer section. The identity (diagonal) line passes through the points that correspond to equal marks in both sections. Therefore, points below the identity line represent students who performed better on the multiple-choice part, whereas points above the identity line represent better achievement in the long-answer section of the exam.

In Figure 7.1, we clearly see a positive correlation between marks in the long-answer and multiple-choice sections of Midterm A. We also see that for each possible grade in the multiple-choice section, there is significant scatter in the marks in the long-answer section. Many students seem to do better in the multiple-choice questions, whereas many others appear to score higher in the long-answer questions. The significant spread of the points, on both sides of the identity line, suggests that the blended format produces a healthier and more properly balanced tool of assessment. The data show many students who would have achieved low marks in the exam if it weren't for the multiple-choice part and vice versa.

The scatter plot corresponding to Final A is shown in Figure 7.2. Here, one can also see a positive correlation between marks in the long-answer and multiple-choice sections. An interesting observation, however, is the relatively reduced scattering and spread of the points on both sides of the identity line. This is possibly because students generally benefit from their experience in the midterm exam and are better prepared for the final. This is in addition to some filtration that occurs when a number of students decide not to complete the course after poor performance on the midterm exam.

Figure 7.2 Scatter plot showing correlation between marks in long-answer and multiple-choice sections of Final A of the PHYS 200 final exam.

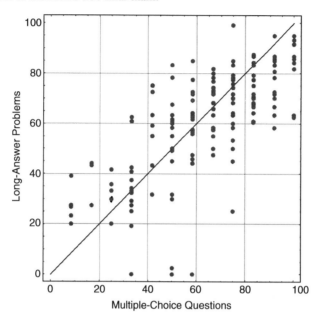

This study enhanced our belief that well-thought-out multiple-choice questions constitute a valid assessment tool in introductory physics courses. This style of exam is especially convenient for asking conceptual questions that explore higher order thinking and is supported by physics education research (Hake, 2007; McDermott, 1990) and by the wide adoption of the Force Concept Inventory tests (Hestenes, Wells, & Swackhamer, 1992). Exams that consist solely of long-answer problems involving arithmetic calculations and algebraic manipulations may not constitute a well-rounded form of summative assessment. As stated by McDermott (1990), "The ability to follow certain prescribed procedures for solving standard problems does not indicate development of scientific reasoning skills" (p. 303). Pollock, Pepper, Chasteen, and Perkins (2012) also expressed a similar opinion.

Statistical Comparison: Midterm Exam Versus Final Exam

Using a different group of students, we compiled examination marks for a sample of 138 students who completed the PHYS 200 course during the year 2013. Figure 7.3 displays the corresponding scatter plot between midterm and final examination marks for the students in this sample. Each data point represents one student writing both exams. Students who did not write the final exam are not included. Note that only the total mark is considered here regardless of exam version. In this sample, students averaged 67% on the midterm exam and 67.9% on the final. Because passing the final exam is a requirement for passing the course, no students below the 50% horizontal dashed line completed the course successfully.

Figure 7.3 Scatter plot showing correlation between midterm and final exam marks for a sample of PHYS 200 students.

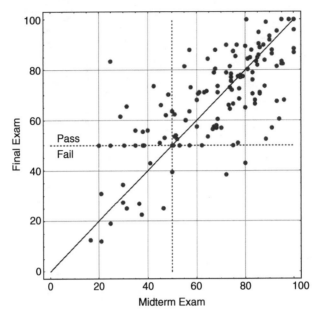

As expected, students who achieved relatively high marks in the midterm exam were most likely to excel in the final and vice versa. Another interesting observation from Figure 7.3 is the near absence of students who passed the midterm exam but failed the final. The reverse, however, is not true. Some students who did poorly on the midterm were able to make it up in the final. Apparently, the midterm exam result was a wake-up call, which helped these students change their study habits and put more effort into the course. Therefore, a comprehensive final exam that carries more weight than the midterm seems to be a good practice, leading to increased learning and improved overall performance.

Conceptual Physics (PHYS 210)

PHYS 210 is an introductory physics course. It follows a nonmathematical approach and focuses on central concepts in mechanics, properties of matter, and heat. The course does not have a lab component and can be taken by students in liberal arts, education, business, medical services, and other disciplines in which a basic understanding of physics principles is required. It can also be used as a bridge course for science and engineering students without high school physics.

Assessment in PHYS 210 is based on two online assignments (15% each), three short assignments that require descriptive answers (5% each), an essay (15%), and a final examination (40%). Students must achieve a minimum of 50% on the final examination and an overall grade of at least 50% to pass the course.

Assignments

The multiple-choice style of assessment seems to go well with a course of this nature. In particular, the learning outcomes can be probed more thoroughly with the relatively large number of questions that can be asked using the multiple-choice format. In this regard, students are expected to answer a total of 50 questions in both online assignments. Also, the administration and marking of these assignments are conveniently automated through the quiz module on Moodle.

An essay (800–1,200 words) that falls under one of the following topics is also required:

- Evolution of basic physics principles in the course of human civilization
- Applications or implications of basic physics concepts
- Explanation of observed physical phenomena using fundamentals of physics

As communicated to students, the marking of the essay is based on the following components:

Introduction

- Appropriate title page (5 marks)
- Overall essay objective and how it is related to the course and to the three main topics (10 marks)

Main body

- Originality and innovation (10 marks)
- Clarity and organization (10 marks)
- Conciseness (5 marks)
- Accuracy (10 marks)
- Reasoning and depth of analysis (25 marks)

Conclusion

- Summary, implications, and lessons learned (10 marks)

References

- Proper citation and complete bibliography (15 marks)

Because of the more descriptive approach of this course, students do not have the same challenges as in PHYS 200 in terms of preparation and submission of typed assignments. Unlike PHYS 200, the PHYS 210 course is available for a "challenge-for-credit" option. Students who believe they already have the knowledge of the course material can request to challenge the course. In this case, they will be required to write a four-hour examination that consists of 16 essay questions and 60 multiple-choice questions.

Statistical Comparison: Assignments Versus Final Exam

The two online assignments consist of exam-style questions and, therefore, can be regarded as a sample final examination. The main difference, of course, is that the final exam is written under invigilation with a closed book and a time limit of two and a half hours, whereas assignments are completed without restrictions on time or instructional resources. It is interesting to compare students' performance in the online assignments to what they achieved in the final examination. Because PHYS 210 is a relatively new course, we can use data only for the 31 students who completed the course up to the time of writing this chapter. The distribution of marks for the online assignments and the final examinations is displayed in a bar chart in Figure 7.4. Apparently, the restrictive exam conditions produced a more normal distribution of students' marks. Students in this limited sample averaged 86.0% on the online assignments and 73.7% on the final examination. This result basically means that breaking the exam into two halves and allowing the students unlimited time and resources caused a mark increase of about 12%.

In Figure 7.5, we see the corresponding scatter plot between the marks of the final examination and online assignments, where each data point represents one of the 31 students in the sample. Most students, understandably, achieved better marks on the online assignments than on the exam. However, it is interesting to note that a good number (nearly 40%) of students scored equal or better marks on the final exam compared to the assignments. Apparently, these students benefited from their experience in the online assignments to improve their learning.

Figure 7.4 Bar chart distribution of marks in online assignments and the final exam of 31 students in PHYS210.

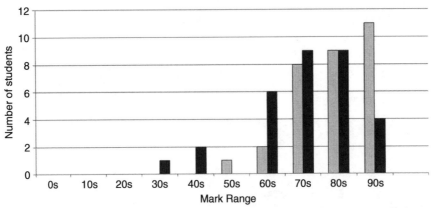

Note. Lighter columns represent online assignment score distribution and darker columns represent final exam score distributions.

Figure 7.5 Scatter plot showing correlation between final exam marks and online assignments for 31 students in PHYS 210.

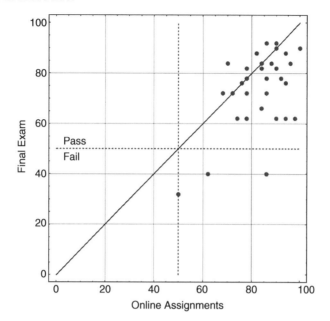

Conclusion

The distance education environment is undergoing rapid change caused by the accelerated advancement in technology and connectivity. We have entered the information age, where students are becoming more independent learners, and instructors are increasingly taking the role of facilitators of learning. In this respect, assessment becomes a vital tool of validation and certification. Massive open online courses (MOOCs) provide an interesting point of discussion, because they are at the forefront of distance education yet have not emphasized assessment. We foresee a transition in which allocation of credentials for this type of open study may depend on credible summative assessment, perhaps done by institutions other than those offering the original MOOC.

At AU, we now have extensive experience in teaching online first-year physics courses, most of which include home lab components. Our observations and assessment data collected over the past decade allow us to contribute to the advancement of physics education, especially in the distance education setting. The goal, of course, is to maximize student learning and demonstrate it through valid assessment.

Assignments and lab experiments are important components of an introductory physics course, and we have demonstrated that they can be conducted effectively in the distance education or online environment. The turnaround time and quality of feedback on marked assignments and lab reports can be comparable to (if not exceed) that in face-to-face classrooms. We also believe that the blended exam format works very well for an introductory physics course, because it balances exam validity and course administration efficiency. The two question styles (multiple choice and long answer) appear to complement each other and provide an assessment tool that adjusts better to the diversity of students' styles and provides a better probe of the different learning outcomes, especially higher order reasoning skills. A comprehensive final exam that carries more weight than the midterm exam (and that is mandatory to pass) appears to be a well-justified practice.

In conclusion, we would like to stress that quality assessment can have overreaching effects beyond accurate student grades. We quote here Gaytan and McEwen (2007) that "the main purposes of assessment are to monitor student learning, improve academic programs, and enhance teaching and learning" (p. 118).

References

Al-Shamali, F., & Connors, M. (2010). Low cost physics home laboratory. In D. Kennepohl & L. Shaw (Eds.), *Accessible elements: Teaching science at a distance* (pp. 131–146). Edmonton, Canada: AU Press.

Carnevale, D. (2001). Assessment takes center stage in online learning. *The Chronicle of Higher Education, 47*(31), A43–A45.

Cheng, K. K., Thacker, B. A., Cardenas, R. L., & Crouch, C. (2004). Using an online homework system enhances students' learning of physics concepts in an introductory physics course. *American Journal of Physics, 72*(11), 1447–1453.

Connors, M. (2004). A decade of success in physics distance education at Athabasca University. *Physics in Canada, 60*(1), 49–54.

Dominguez, P. S., & Ridley, D. (1999). Reassessing the assessment of distance education courses. *THE Journal, 27*(2), 70–76.

Gaytan, J., & McEwen, B. C. (2007). Effective online instructional and assessment strategies. *The American Journal of Distance Education, 21*(3), 117–132.

Giancoli, D. C. (2005). *Physics: Principles with applications* (6th ed.). Upper Saddle River, NJ: Pearson/Prentice Hall.

Gikandi, J. W., Morrow, D., & Davis, N. E. (2011). Online formative assessment in higher education: A review of the literature. *Computers and Education, 57*(4), 2333–2351.

Hake, R. R. (2007). Six lessons from the physics education reform effort. *Latin American Journal of Physics Education, 1*(1), 24–31.

Hestenes, D., Wells, M., & Swackhamer, G. (1992). Force Concept Inventory. *The Physics Teacher, 30*(3), 141–158.

McDermott, L. C. (1990). Millikan Lecture 1990: What we teach and what is learned—Closing the gap. *American Journal of Physics, 59*(4), 301–315.

Pollock, S., Pepper, R., Chasteen, S., & Perkins, K. (2012). Multiple roles of assessment in upper-division physics course reforms. In N. S. Rebello, P. V. Engelhardt, & C. Singh (Eds.), *AIP Conference Proceedings of 2011 Physics Education Research Conference* (Vol. 1413, pp. 307–310). Omaha, NE: AIP.

Redish, E. F., Saul, J. M., & Steinberg, R. N. (1998). Student expectations in introductory physics. *American Journal of Physics, 66*(3), 212–224.

Reeves, T. C. (2000). Alternative assessment approaches for online learning environments in higher education. *Journal of Educational Computing Research, 23*(1), 101–111.

Robles, M., & Braathen, S. (2002). Online assessment techniques. *The Delta Pi Epsilon Journal, 44*(1), 39–49.

Scouller, K. (1998). The influence of assessment method on students' learning approaches: Multiple choice question examination versus assignment essay. *Higher Education, 35*(4), 453–472.

Tallent-Runnels, M. K., Thomas, J. A., Lan, W. Y., Cooper, S., Ahern, T. C., Shaw, S. M., & Liu, X. (2006). Teaching courses online: A review of the research. *Review of Educational Research, 76*(1), 93–135.

Wolsey, T. D. (2008). Efficacy of instructor feedback on written work in an online program. *International Journal on E-Learning, 7*(2), 311–329.

8

COMPUTER-BASED LABORATORY SIMULATIONS FOR THE NEW DIGITAL LEARNING ENVIRONMENTS

Jessie Webb, Richard Swan, and Brian F. Woodfield
Brigham Young University

Abstract

Several studies show computer-based laboratory experiments are as effective in teaching conceptual knowledge as real laboratory experiments and are reviewed here. Other studies also provide evidence that these computer-simulated laboratories offer additional learning experiences that can be difficult to provide in real laboratory settings because of time, resources, complexity, safety, and abstract concepts. Three computer-based laboratory environments are highlighted: Late Nite Labs, Pearson's suite of virtual laboratories, and Physics Education Technology Interactive Simulations. A general description of each product's features, strengths, weaknesses, and supporting research is given.

Most science educators would agree students should have laboratory experiences to fully understand and appreciate scientific principles and processes. However, the same level of agreement does not exist for computer-simulated laboratory experiences. Some educators and researchers feel that computer simulations are not as effective as real experiences; the other end of the spectrum argues that simulated laboratories not only are just as effective but also provide opportunities and experiences not available in the real lab. This chapter will examine the research on computer-based laboratory simulations in chemistry, physics, and biology. We will look specifically at whether computer-based simulations are as effective as real labs and whether simulated labs can provide learning experiences beyond what is available in real labs. In addition, we will review a few specific products that are currently available for use or purchase.

Effectiveness of Computer-Based Laboratories

For specific learning outcomes, computer-based laboratory experiments are as effective as experiments in real labs. For instance, Supasorn, Suits, Jones, and Vibuljan (2008) showed the value of their Organic Extraction Simulation in teaching conceptual knowledge about extractions. Hawkins and Phelps (2013) compared computer-based electrochemistry exercises with real electrochemistry lab exercises and found that their computer-based lab taught concepts, facts, and cell setup just as well as a real laboratory. In physics, Chini, Madsen, Gire, Rebello, and Puntambekar (2012) tested the effect of a computer-simulated pulley experiment versus a real experiment. Their college students scored similarly on test questions regarding force and mechanical advantage regardless of the type of experiment performed. Furthermore, performing real experiments then computer-simulated experiments versus performing computer-simulated experiments then real experiments showed no statistical difference in students' conceptual understanding. Thus, the real pulley laboratory had no advantages over the computer-simulated pulley laboratory as far as developing students' conceptual knowledge. In an interesting twist, students who used the computer-based simulation scored higher on questions about work immediately after the experiment, but one week later, there was no statistically significant difference between the two groups' understanding of work.

Zacharia and Constantinou (2008) compared real and computer-simulated laboratory exercises on heat and temperature. They found that both types of laboratories were equally effective in helping students understand these concepts. Zacharia and Olympiou (2011) later performed a similar study and obtained similar results. They had five groups of students: real manipulation, computer-based manipulation, two sequential combinations of both real and computer-based manipulations, and traditional instruction without any experimentation. All experimental groups were equally effective in helping students understand heat and temperature conceptually, and they were all more effective than the control group that lacked experimentation.

Martinez, Naranjo, Pérez, Suero, and Pardo (2011) also sought to compare computer-based and real laboratories, but they compared what they called a hyperrealistic computer-simulated laboratory, a schematic simulated laboratory, and a traditional laboratory. The hyperrealistic simulated environment goes beyond a basic schematic simulation by including photorealistic visual output, similar to a real laboratory. Analysis showed that students using the hyper-realistic laboratory simulation scored 6.1 percentage points higher on a posttest than the students with the basic schematic simulated laboratory and 9.5 percentage points higher than the students in the traditional laboratory. Again, this study supports the idea that computer-simulated laboratories are equally, if not more, effective at teaching certain concepts.

Teaching What Real Laboratories Cannot

Analyzing mutant phenotypes is an important part of the study of genetics, but a genetics class often cannot perform genetic experiments for students to gain firsthand experience with mutagenesis screens because of time constraints (Breakey, Levin, Miller, & Hentges, 2008). Scenario-based-learning interactive software created by Shegog and colleagues

(2012) makes virtual transgenic experiments possible. (Transgenic technology allows for a gene suspected of causing a disorder to be engineered and implanted into a mouse.) Students who performed this computer-simulated laboratory showed a larger increase in both conceptual and procedural knowledge, compared to the control group, and that knowledge increased with more time spent in the computer-simulated laboratory. These simplified, safe transgenic simulations require less time and fewer resources than a real laboratory and thus are more accessible to high school students.

McGrath, Wegener, McIntyre, Savage, and Williamson (2010) developed a computer-simulated environment to teach special relativity, called Real Time Relativity. Students can explore the effects of traveling close to the speed of light using this program. During this study, students reported a positive experience using the simulation, and they found it made the subject less abstract. Real Time Relativity led to students being more able to answer questions about the concept of special relativity and having slightly better final exam scores, compared to those who did not use the simulation.

In another instance, high school students used a computer-based virtual environment, PartSims, as a support platform to help them engage with the topic of epidemiology (Fies & Langman, 2011). This simulated environment helped students make connections to the course material, such as learning how diseases spread, the definition of a *disease vector*, and the consequences of vaccinations. These are just a few of the examples of how computer-simulated laboratories can provide learning experiences that would be difficult to carry out in a real laboratory. Additional quality reviews and studies demonstrate the usability, versatility, and effectiveness of computer-based laboratories in the classroom, including publications by Ma and Nickerson (2006); de Jong, Linn, and Zacharia (2013); Zhou and colleagues (2011); Evans, Yaron, and Leinhardt (2008); Ketelhut and Nelson (2010); Ketelhut, Nelson, Clarke, and Dede (2010); Stone (2007); Cunningham, McNear, Pearlman, and Kern (2006); Lazonder and Ehrenhard (2014); Tatli and Ayas (2013); Chuang, Hwang, and Tsai (2008); Guan, Tsai, and Hwang (2006); Jara and colleagues (2009); Hatherly, Jordan, and Cayless (2009); Swan and O'Donnell (2009); and Crippen, Archambault, and Kern (2013).

Review of Available Products

In this section, we review three products that are available for instructors to use or purchase: Late Nite Labs, Pearson's suite of virtual laboratories, and Physics Education Technology (PhET) Interactive Simulations.

Late Nite Labs

Macmillan's Late Nite Labs provides online laboratories designed for introductory and intermediate undergraduate courses, but some high school classes also benefit from the experiments. Currently, 21 biology, 46 chemistry, 11 microbiology, and 11 physics computer-based experiments are available for free to instructors and for purchase to students at their website (www.latenitelabs.com). A screenshot of the photosynthesis experiment is provided in Figure 8.1. The laboratories are available for PC and Mac, and tech support is provided. Each experiment is front-loaded, so after the initial

Figure 8.1 Screenshot of the Late Nite Labs photosynthesis experiment.

loading wait time, the experiment should run smoothly. There is nothing to download or install.

One demo experiment is available in each of the four disciplines, and there are three video procedural tutorials and four microbiology tutorials for students. Starting manuals for both teachers and students also are available. Laboratories cover topics in (a) general chemistry, including properties of matter, chemistry of solutions, stoichiometry, gas laws, thermochemistry, acids and bases, redox, spectrophotometric analysis, and qualitative analysis; (b) biology, including cell structure and function, enzymes, diffusion, photosynthesis, mitosis, DNA, fungi, protists, plant reproduction, evolution, and ecology; (c) microbiology, including cultivation of microorganisms, microscopy, staining, bacterial growth and transformation, and polymerase chain reaction; and (d) physics, including conservation of energy and momentum, error analysis, centripetal force, free-falling bodies, kinematics, Newton's second law, Hooke's law, torque, waves, and buoyancy. A major goal of the creators of Late Nite Labs is to engage the students in experimentation that is not typical of a real laboratory in introductory college courses. For instance, Late Nite Labs' alcohol content of vodka by dichromate titration engages students by letting them explore real-world applications of chemistry (H. Goodman, personal communication, September 22, 2014).

Students are provided with a laboratory manual for each experiment that includes background information, procedures, space to type in a laboratory notebook, and an option to print this material (www.latenitelabs.com). A shelf hangs above the workbench and holds labeled containers, materials, and instruments. Other features include a zoom feature, an unlimited amount of supplies, an option to clear one object at a time or the whole workbench, a media player, an unlimited number of timers, and a laboratory log that details every step a student has taken. Teachers cannot see what students are doing in the laboratory in real time, but they can look over an individual student's laboratory log to know exactly what was done in the past. In addition to laboratory assignments, instructors can include multiple-choice and/or short-answer assessments. Currently, multiple-choice assessments cannot be edited, but the goal is to make every aspect of Late Nite Labs customizable by teachers (H. Goodman, personal communication, September 22, 2014). A grade book allows instructors to grade laboratory assignments and assessments on Late Nite Labs. Thus, it is conducive to distance learning or entirely online classes especially through its complete learning management system.

Late Nite Labs provides students with the psychology of presence; the interactive workbench makes students feel like they are in a laboratory. One advantage to this computer-based environment is that all the information students need is available on the screen. Premade laboratories are guided and prescriptive experiments, but teachers can edit them to include different chemicals, supplies, media support, procedures, and background information. They can customize laboratories to provide as much or as little structure as desired. Students are able to explore and be creative but only using the limited chemicals and supplies that the teacher makes available. Unknowns in experiments are set for each section as a whole; different students in a class cannot solve for different unknowns (H. Goodman, personal communication, September 22, 2014). Also, students are unable to perform practice runs to check their work before submitting final answers. Another downside is that students have access to these experiments only for the length of their class, but printable laboratory reports are automatically generated with each experiment to function as a consolidation of everything students performed.

Research

Pyatt and Sims (2012) studied student performance and attitudes using real chemistry laboratories versus Late Nite Labs. They found no statistically significant difference in student performance on a laboratory assessment between the two treatments, but students expressed a preference for the computer laboratories because of their usability and openendedness. Students found Late Nite Labs in chemistry to be effective and realistic. Additional research is performed within Late Nite Labs on their efficacy and usability, but results from these focus groups and formative assessments are shared only within the company.

Pearson's Suite of Virtual Laboratories

Virtual ChemLab, Virtual Physics, Virtual BioLab, Virtual Earth Science, and Virtual Physical Science are sold separately through both Pearson Education's School and Higher Education divisions. Virtual ChemLab is now also available for students via download. Virtual BioLab is the only program available online, and for the Higher Education products, it is available only through Pearson's MasteringBiology product. The laboratories are available for PC and Mac, and tech support is provided.

Virtual ChemLab for Higher Education offers 77 worksheet-guided experiments covering the topics of atomic theory, reactions and stoichiometry, thermodynamics, colligative properties, gas properties, acid-base chemistry, electrochemistry, and descriptive chemistry. A similar set of 33 worksheets is also available in the high school version. The laboratory settings include calorimetry, titrations, inorganic, gases, and quantum. A screenshot of the descriptive chemistry experiment is shown in Figure 8.2. Virtual Physics provides 34 worksheet-guided experiments in seven laboratory settings: mechanics, calorimetry, optics, circuits, density, gases, and quantum. Finally, Virtual BioLab for the

Figure 8.2 Screenshot of the descriptive chemistry experiment in Pearson's Virtual ChemLab.

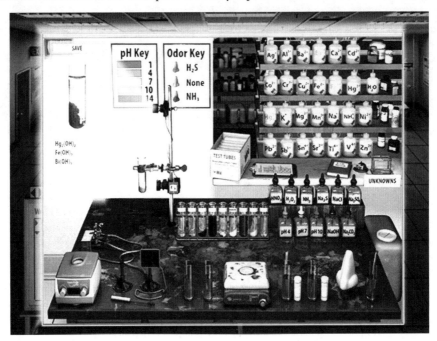

School division includes 27 worksheet-guided experiments on organisms and natural history, DNA, heredity, and biomes and populations. These experiments are performed in five laboratories: microscopy, genetics, ecology, systematics, and molecular biology. As mentioned previously, the Higher Education version of Virtual BioLab is available only through MasteringBiology, which has its own set of activities delivered through the MasteringBiology platform version. Virtual Physical Science is a combination of the chemistry and physics laboratories, and Virtual Earth Science covers appropriate topics in earth science using the same laboratories as found in Virtual Physical Science. Worksheets are available for each product at an appropriate middle school, high school, or higher education level.

In this system, a help option is provided with an overview of the simulated environment for students getting started. Students can enter notes and save experimental data into an electronic laboratory notebook provided, which can be saved and opened by instructors for grading. The CD-ROM comes with a workbook containing level-specific worksheets; for example, there is both a seventh-grade and a ninth-grade workbook for the Virtual Physics version. In addition to experiments using worksheets, there are clipboards in the laboratories with additional preset options, but instructors are welcome to write their own worksheets and activities. The laboratories are designed to be completely open-ended environments with a nearly unlimited array of experiments and outcomes. Because there are no detailed procedures built into the program, teachers are also able to give less structured assignments by not providing worksheets at all. Laboratories are provided with stockrooms of reagents to be used as part of preset experiments or in creative exploration. Students can create knowns and unknowns to analyze and practice with before working on an assignment, and some experiments offer students instant feedback.

These computer-based laboratories do not provide a grade book, because the overall design of the laboratories is to mimic an actual open-ended laboratory environment with its inherent flexibility, except with the advantages of a simulated environment. If students are more structured learners, they could find the open-ended environment overwhelming and prefer a structured setting where each experiment is given its own environment; however, this is mitigated using the structured worksheets and preset experiments available in each laboratory. There is some inconvenience in that most of the programs cannot be accessed online, but students are able to keep their program even after the course is over.

Research

A study found that students thought the inorganic qualitative analysis in Virtual Chem-Lab helped them apply principles from the classroom to solve problems (Woodfield et al., 2004). Most students liked the simulation because it let them explore freely, focus on the chemistry principles, repeat procedures, and/or navigate easily, but less than half of the students agreed that the simulation made them more confident in their abilities to think like chemists. Instructors liked the simulation because of its ability to integrate into existing curriculum. A major finding of this study was the discovery of a relationship between student performance and opinion and cerebral and limbic scores, as determined by the Herrmann Brain Dominance Instrument. A high cerebral score correlates to creative learners, whereas a high limbic score correlates to structured learners. The researchers concluded that creative learners felt they needed less guidance in the simulation, whereas structured learners wanted more help. Also, structured learners reported that they spent a smaller amount of time performing "what if?" experiments in the simulations than creative learners. Thus, this study provided researchers with an understanding of why students and instructors like the computer-based inorganic simulations.

Another study was performed to examine student responses to the organic synthesis and organic qualitative analysis simulations in Virtual ChemLab (Woodfield et al., 2005). Some of the features of these simulations include synthesizing products; mixing reactions; performing extractions; analyzing characterizations with nuclear magnetic resonance, infrared spectroscopy, thin-layer chromatography, and melting-point analysis; purifying products with distillation and recrystallization; and identifying unknowns using different functional group tests shown with real video footage. Students who found the organic simulation valuable and easy to use earned higher course grades (Woodfield et al., 2005). Also, students who were flexible and able to substitute equivalent reagents for reagents unavailable in the simulated laboratory received higher course grades. Creative learners were more likely to know what to substitute for unavailable reagents. Last, test scores showed that adding Virtual ChemLab assignments significantly increased the class performance as a whole. Overall, the computer-simulated laboratories increased student learning, as shown through observations, higher test scores, and student responses.

Physics Education Technology Interactive Simulations

The PhET Interactive Simulations project is a source of 128 simulations on physics, chemistry, biology, math, and earth science topics. These simulations are available for no cost online (phet.colorado.edu) and have been useful for elementary school, middle school, high school, and university students. They are developed at University of Colorado Boulder and evaluated for usability and effectiveness using feedback from teachers, student interviews, classroom testing, and educational research (Wieman, Adams, & Perkins, 2008). Researchers provide a rating system to inform educators of each simulation's level of testing. PhET simulations are actively being converted to HTML5 to be accessed on browsers and tablets. To date, 22 simulations have been updated. All the source code is also freely available. Students can access simulations by using the PhET website while online or downloading either the whole website or individual simulations to a computer, USB, or CD, although there is no off-line access for HTML5 simulations.

Of the 128 simulations, 126 are classified as physics, including motion; sound and waves; work, energy, and power; heat and thermodynamics; quantum phenomena; light and radiation; and electricity, magnets, and circuits. A screenshot of the balloons and static electricity simulation is provided in Figure 8.3. The PhET team classified 23 as biology, 39 as general chemistry, 13 as quantum chemistry, 17 as earth science, 15 as mathematical tools, 15 as mathematical applications, and 6 as cutting-edge research. These cutting-edge research experiments include optical tweezers, molecular motors, stretching DNA, optical quantum control, lasers, and self-driven particle model. All the PhET simulations are designed to easily be translated into other languages, with at least one simulation in 78 languages. Simulations are published alongside tips, activities, learning goals, and main topics as a reference for teachers, and users can also add their own ideas. PhET Sims on YouTube has a collection of 18 videos helping teachers to implement these simulations in their classrooms, lectures, homework, or laboratories. In addition, the PhET team is raising money to create Teach With PhET, a collaborative

Figure 8.3 Screenshot of the PhET balloons and static electricity simulation (HTML5).

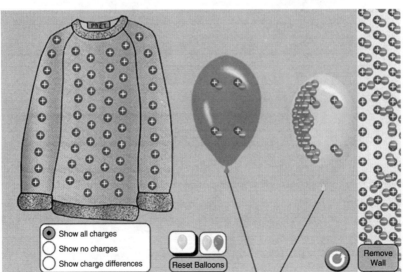

website for teachers to help each other choose simulations and incorporate them into lessons and activities.

PhET simulations emphasize conceptual learning and sacrifice a psychology of presence to achieve such learning. For example, the Circuit Construction Kit simulation allows students to see electrons traveling through circuits, which is not realistic but is effective in helping students visualize scientific concepts. These simulations show students things they cannot see in a real laboratory, such as diving inside an atom, slowing down or pausing time to see a ball's velocity at its peak, changing planets or gravitational fields, and adding in force arrows. The invisible is made visible; PhET simulations are highly interactive with different variables to adjust, and this teaches students which variables are important. Often simulations are supplemented with graphical representations or pictures of phenomena, providing another immediate visualization.

Another advantage of PhET simulations is their simplicity. Students can open up a simulation and simply start playing around with the variables and settings to figure things out intuitively. No instructions are needed, and students can focus on science rather than the usability of the program. Developers attempted to provide enough structure that students feel not lost but, rather, curious. They use implicit guidance and productive constraints to give students freedom to make productive inquiries. Improvements to PhET could include increasing tools for customization, data gathering for creating graded assignments, and integrating with educational products for teachers.

Research

Finkelstein and colleagues (2005) compared students using the PhET simulations to students using real lightbulbs, meters, and wires in a circuit construction laboratory. They found that students did more spontaneous experiments with the computer simulation than with real equipment. Students were also tested on understanding physics concepts and how to use real equipment. Students using the computer simulations performed better on both tasks than those who used the real equipment.

McKagan and colleagues (2008) studied a PhET simulation on the photoelectric effect. The simulations include visual representation of unobservable phenomena, including abstract ideas and microscopic behaviors, interactive environments, daily life connections, and assistance with calculations. Their study showed that 80% of students mastered the material, whereas with traditional lessons, only 20% of students mastered the material.

In addition, a PhET simulation for a wave on a string provided students with more conceptual learning than a normal demonstration did (Wieman et al., 2008). Using qualitative think-aloud protocols, researchers determined that students find the PhET simulations fun and engaging because of dynamic user-controlled visual environments, the right level of difficulty, and sufficient visual complexity to invoke curiosity but not discouragement. These researchers showed that when students used simulations to supplement real laboratory work, they preferred the simulations. Students commented that they could see what was happening better in the simulations and that the simulations were more engaging. When things went wrong in real laboratories, human or instrument error were blamed, effectively ending exploration.

Conclusion

Computer-simulated laboratories such as Late Nite Labs, Pearson's suite of virtual laboratories, and PhET Interactive Simulations can supplement the teaching of chemistry, physics, and biology as prelaboratories or as blended laboratories. They are a powerful tool in distance education and can function as stand-alone laboratories in distance learning situations where students do not have access to real laboratories. New collaborative opportunities between students and teachers are improving distance learning. Many studies support the claim that computer-simulated science laboratories are as effective as real laboratories and traditional homework at teaching conceptual knowledge. Another advantage of simulated experiments is their ability to optimize time and resources in the classroom. They require less time than real laboratories, and consequently, there is more time in computer-simulated laboratories for spontaneous, out-of-the-box experimentation contributing to learning, engagement, and excitement about science. As a result, computer-based laboratories can teach what real laboratories cannot by allowing for creative experimentation, providing visualization for abstract concepts, and immersing students in multiuser virtual environments. Learning occurs as students ask themselves questions and perform self-driven exploration. Wieman and colleagues (2008) noted that students must view simulations as scientists view their research. Students must be able to explore and challenge scientific ideas in risk-free computer simulations, without regard to time, amount of supplies, pressure from others, or the fear of making a mistake, which are common stressors in a real laboratory. In short, computer-based laboratory simulations can be used as an effective means to teach scientific principles.

References

Breakey, K. M., Levin, D., Miller, I., & Hentges, K. E. (2008). The use of scenario-based-learning interactive software to create custom virtual laboratory scenarios for teaching genetics. *Genetics*, *179*(3), 1151–1155.

Chini, J. J., Madsen, A., Gire, E., Rebello, N. S., & Puntambekar, S. (2012). Exploration of factors that affect the comparative effectiveness of physical and virtual manipulatives in an undergraduate laboratory. *Physical Review Special Topics–Physics Education Research*, *8*(1), 1–12.

Chuang, S.-C., Hwang, F.-K., & Tsai, C.-C. (2008). Students' perceptions of constructivist Internet learning environments by a physics virtual laboratory: The gap between ideal and reality and gender differences. *CyberPsychology and Behavior*, *11*(2), 150–156. Retrieved from www.liebertpub.com/overview/cyberpsychology-behavior-brand-social-networking/10/

Crippen, K. J., Archambault, L. M., & Kern, C. L. (2013). The nature of laboratory learning experiences in secondary science online. *Research in Science Education*, *43*(3), 1029–1050.

Cunningham, S. C., McNear, B., Pearlman, R. S., & Kern, S. E. (2006). Beverage-agarose gel electrophoresis: An inquiry-based laboratory exercise with virtual adaptation. *CBE—Life Sciences Education*, *5*(3), 281–286. Retrieved from www.lifescied.org/

de Jong, T., Linn, M. C., & Zacharia, Z. C. (2013). Physical and virtual laboratories in science and engineering education. *Science*, *340*(6130), 305–308.

Evans, K. L., Yaron, D., & Leinhardt, G. (2008). Learning stoichiometry: A comparison of text and multimedia formats. *Chemistry Education Research and Practice*, *9*(3), 208–218.

Fies, C., & Langman, J. (2011). Bridging worlds: Measuring learners' discursive practice in a PartSim supported biology lesson. *International Journal of Science and Mathematics Education, 9*(6), 1415–1438.

Finkelstein, N. D., Adams, W. K., Keller, C. J., Kohl, P. B., Perkins, K. K., Podolefsky, N. S., . . . LeMaster, R. (2005). When learning about the real world is better done virtually: A study of substituting computer simulations for laboratory equipment. *Physical Review Special Topics–Physics Education Research, 1*(1), 1–8.

Guan, Y.-H., Tsai, C.-C., & Hwang, F.-K. (2006). Content analysis of online discussion on a senior-high-school discussion forum of a virtual physics laboratory. *Instructional Science, 34*(4), 279–311.

Hatherly, P. A., Jordan, S. E., & Cayless, A. (2009). Interactive screen experiments: Innovative virtual laboratories for distance learners. *European Journal of Physics, 30*(4), 751–762.

Hawkins, I., & Phelps, A. J. (2013). Virtual laboratory vs. traditional laboratory: Which is more effective for teaching electrochemistry? *Chemistry Education Research and Practice, 14*(4), 516–523.

Jara, C. A., Candelas, F. A., Torres, F., Dormido, S., Esquembre, F., & Reinoso, O. (2009). Real-time collaboration of virtual laboratories through the Internet. *Computers and Education, 52*(1), 126–140.

Ketelhut, D. J., & Nelson, B. C. (2010). Designing for real-world scientific inquiry in virtual environments. *Educational Research, 52*(2), 151–167.

Ketelhut, D. J., Nelson, B. C., Clarke, J., & Dede, C. (2010). A multi-user virtual environment for building and assessing higher order inquiry skills in science. *British Journal of Educational Technology, 41*(1), 56–68.

Lazonder, A. W., & Ehrenhard, S. (2014). Relative effectiveness of physical and virtual manipulatives for conceptual change in science: How falling objects fall. *Journal of Computer Assisted Learning, 30*(2), 110–120.

Ma, J., & Nickerson, J. V. (2006). Hands-on, simulated, and remote laboratories: A comparative literature review. *ACM Computing Surveys, 38*(3), Article 7, 1–24.

Martinez, G., Naranjo, F. L., Pérez, A. L., Suero, M. I., & Pardo, P. J. (2011). Comparative study of the effectiveness of three learning environments: Hyper-realistic virtual simulations, traditional schematic simulations and traditional laboratory. *Physical Review Special Topics–Physics Education Research, 7*(2), 1–12.

McGrath, D., Wegener, M., McIntyre, T. J., Savage, C., & Williamson, M. (2010). Student experiences of virtual reality: A case study in learning special relativity. *American Journal of Physics, 78*(8), 862–868.

McKagan, S. B., Perkins, K. K., Dubson, M., Malley, C., Reid, S., LeMaster, R., & Wieman, C. E. (2008). Developing and researching PhET simulations for teaching quantum mechanics. *American Journal of Physics, 76*(4–5), 406–417.

Pyatt, K., & Sims, R. (2012). Virtual and physical experimentation in inquiry-based science labs: Attitudes, performance and access. *Journal of Science Education and Technology, 21*(1), 133–147.

Shegog, R., Lazarus, M. M., Murray, N. G., Diamond, P. M., Sessions, N., & Zsigmond, E. (2012). Virtual transgenics: Using a molecular biology simulation to impact student academic achievement and attitudes. *Research in Science Education, 42*(5), 875–890.

Stone, D. C. (2007). Teaching chromatography using virtual laboratory exercises. *Journal of Chemical Education, 84*(9), 1488–1496.

Supasorn, S., Suits, J. P., Jones, L. L., & Vibuljan, S. (2008). Impact of a pre-laboratory organic-extraction simulation on comprehension and attitudes of undergraduate chemistry students. *Chemistry Education Research and Practice, 9*(2), 169–181.

Swan, A. E., & O'Donnell, A. M. (2009). The contribution of a virtual biology laboratory to college students' learning. *Innovations in Education and Teaching International, 46*(4), 405–419.

Tatli, Z., & Ayas, A. (2013). Effect of a virtual chemistry laboratory on students' achievement. *Journal of Educational Technology and Society, 16*(1), 159–170. Retrieved from www.ifets.info

Wieman, C. E., Adams, W. K., & Perkins, K. K. (2008). PhET: Simulations that enhance learning. *Science, 322*(5902), 682–683.

Woodfield, B. F., Andrus, M. B., Andersen, T., Miller, J., Simmons, B., Stanger, R., . . . Bodily, G. (2005). The Virtual ChemLab project: A realistic and sophisticated simulation of organic synthesis and organic qualitative analysis. *Journal of Chemical Education, 82*(11), 1728–1735. Retrieved from pubs.acs.org/journal/jceda8

Woodfield, B. F., Catlin, H. R., Waddoups, G. L., Moore, M. S., Swan, R., Allen, R., & Bodily, G. (2004). The Virtual Chemlab project: A realistic and sophisticated simulation of inorganic qualitative analysis. *Journal of Chemical Education, 81*(11), 1672–1678. Retrieved from pubs.acs.org/journal/jceda8

Zacharia, Z. C., & Constantinou, C. P. (2008). Comparing the influence of physical and virtual manipulatives in the context of the Physics by Inquiry curriculum: The case of undergraduate students' conceptual understanding of heat and temperature. *American Journal of Physics, 76*(4–5), 425–430.

Zacharia, Z. C., & Olympiou, G. (2011). Physical versus virtual manipulative experimentation in physics learning. *Learning and Instruction, 21*(3), 317–331.

Zhou, S. N., Han, J., Pelz, N., Wang, X. J., Peng, L. Y., Xiao, H., & Bao, L. (2011). Inquiry style interactive virtual experiments: A case on circular motion. *European Journal of Physics, 32*(6), 1597–1606.

9

REMOTE ACCESS LABORATORY EQUIPMENT FOR UNDERGRADUATE SCIENCE EDUCATION

Daniel M. Branan and Paul Bennett
Colorado Community College System
Nicholas Braithwaite
The Open University

Abstract

Using the Internet to break down barriers to laboratory access is a powerful idea and one that may be of great benefit to online students. This chapter relates the experiences and lessons learned from two successful large-scale remotely accessible science laboratories, which have been used for undergraduate college science education. It then summarizes this practical firsthand knowledge, together with accounts from the literature, to present seven guiding principles that need to be considered when providing remote science laboratory access for teaching purposes.

What if we could give students access to laboratory equipment 24 hours a day from anywhere in the world? Educators and scientists have been thinking about the potential for remote science and engineering teaching laboratories since the early days of the World Wide Web in the mid-1990s (Aktan, Bohus, Crowl, & Shor 1996; Lustigova & Zelenda, 1997; Potter et al., 1996; Trevelyan, 2004). Using the Internet to break down barriers to laboratory access is a powerful idea and one that may be of great benefit to online students.

To start, we need to make an important distinction. When we talk about remote labs, we are specifically referring to the hands-on computer control of real laboratory equipment over the Internet (Chen, Song, & Zhang, 2010, p. 3844). This can be either in real time or by batch submission of parameters to an instrument. We point this out to distinguish our discussion from simulated or modeled lab environments or equipment.

History of and Need for Remote Access Science Labs

Is there truly a need for remote laboratories in science education? Well, there is certainly a need to meet the demand for online science courses. We wouldn't teach science face-to-face without practical work, so we should not omit it when teaching online. There are six ways to present the science laboratory curriculum for online students:

1. Students travel to a traditional laboratory.
2. Laboratory travels to the students.
3. Students receive at-home science kits.
4. Students participate in simulations.
5. Students use remote access laboratories.
6. Students participate in interactive screen experiments (ISEs), a blend of options 4 and 5.

Options 1 and 2 are impractical for many students and many institutions, but they certainly have a place in the spectrum of solutions. Options 3, 4, and 5 are each too limited to be a complete solution on their own, but we believe that they can be used together to offer a complete online science curriculum. At-home kits usually suffer from a lack of precision instrumentation because the required equipment would be prohibitively expensive. This often limits experimental results and makes it difficult or impossible for students to draw valid scientific conclusions. For example, a student attempting to determine the value of the gravitational acceleration constant, g, by rolling a ball down an inclined plane and timing it with a stopwatch will be lucky to get within a factor of five of the accepted value. We note with interest, however, the remarkable opportunities that smartphones offer the home experimenter. Nevertheless, even with a bolt-on camera adapter, a student attempting to understand the microscopic intricacies of intercellular structures will be unable to resolve details without professionally prepared specimens and professional apparatuses. These types of details can be elucidated clearly in a simulation, but simulations then suffer from a perceived lack of authenticity (Lindsay & Good, 2005; Ma & Nickerson, 2006; Sauter, Uttal, Rapp, Downing, & Jona, 2013). In addition, they may not adequately model all of the uncertainties, interferences, and mistakes that are part of real-world instrumental analysis. Simulations are suited to illustrating phenomena that cannot be visualized except with extremely high-cost or unique instrumentation, if at all. For example, quantum effects or the behavior of subatomic particles can be easily simulated but are very difficult to actually observe. Properly implemented, remotely accessed laboratory equipment can fill the voids left by kits and simulations. They can provide the kind of precision measurement that at-home kits lack, while allowing students to experience the vagaries of real-world data collection. By allowing precise and accurate measurement, the students learn more about the nature of the world around them and how scientific principles can be investigated and verified. ISEs blend simulations and remote labs to give a more scalable method of allowing students to obtain real-world data (Kirstein, 1999; Kirstein & Nordmeier, 2007; Theyßen, Schumacher, & von Aufschnaiter, 2002). We describe ISEs in more detail in a later section. Like any online resource, simulations, remote laboratories, and ISEs can all allow for synchronous collaboration, with several students accessing a resource simultaneously and working together to perform a scientific experiment.

With these advantages, why have we not seen a proliferation of remote science laboratory facilities in undergraduate education over the past couple of decades? It isn't for lack of attempts, as there were several large-scale (multimillion dollar) efforts to develop this capacity in the early to mid-2000s, such as the venerable Practical Experimentation by Accessible Remote Learning (PEARL) project (Cooper & Ferreira, 2009) and the Remote Laboratory Experience (ReLAX) trial (Eikaas, Schmid, Foss, & Gillet, 2003). As indicated by Cooper (2005); Salzmann and Gillet (2007); and Kara, Ozbek, Cagiltay, and Aydin (2011), three major factors have interfered with the ability to make remote science and engineering laboratories widespread: (a) lack of a sustainable economic model, (b) lack of easily useable and scalable hardware and software applications, and (c) resistance by students and instructors to the use of remote equipment for education.

In fact, there has been a proliferation of remote engineering laboratories in undergraduate education. Because of the remote nature of many engineering applications (process monitoring and control, etc.), engineering teaching labs were more easily adapted to the remote environment. According to recently published articles, the use of remote lab facilities is considered a standard approach in electrical engineering (Pradyumna, Tarun, & Bhanot, 2012), robotics (Prieto & Mendoza, 2013), and automation and control (Santana, Ferre, Izaguirre, Aracil, & Hernandez, 2013). The three obstacles listed previously are less of a problem in engineering education for several reasons. First, the types of equipment and resources necessary for enabling remote access engineering laboratories are generally not as expensive or complex as those needed for science laboratories. Second, the nature of the types of equipment being used in engineering education makes it much easier to create reusable and scalable systems. Third, because of the use of remote access and control in many real-world engineering applications, there is much less resistance to the idea of teaching engineering subjects remotely.

The idea of remotely interacting with laboratory equipment in the teaching environment seems to be at odds with how many scientists view science education. Most scientists seem to highly value physical presence and physical interaction with the materials and equipment in the teaching laboratory (Cooper, 2005). A recent search of Google Scholar for the term *remote laboratory education* in articles published between January 1, 2013, and September 9, 2014, revealed that 60 of the top 100 results were explicitly about current practice in engineering education. Most of the remainder concerned the analysis of remote laboratories from a purely educational perspective, and most of those articles necessarily dealt with engineering-related remote laboratories. There were no articles about remote laboratories in college-level science, although there were a few concerning the use of remote labs in secondary education. This seems odd to us, because a great deal of real-world science is done remotely. For example, all deep-space and most deep-sea exploration is accomplished using remotely controlled equipment, as is all Earth observation and a significant fraction of astronomy. Most research-grade laboratory equipment cannot be operated without the use of computers, and experimenters are often located in rooms or buildings separate from the equipment itself.

The real question is as follows: Does this approach enhance learning, engage students, or have any other positive learning effect? In an excellent study published by Lindsay and Good (2005), the performance of 120 students was measured across three different modes of laboratory curriculum delivery: traditional, simulated, and remote. Students were roughly equally distributed across the different modes. The same experiment was done in all three cases, and the same outcomes were used as a basis for measuring students' performance by analyzing their written reports:

Specific Outcomes:

1. Appreciation of the hardware involved
2. Reasons for calibration
3. The complexity of signals

Generic Skills:

4. Identification of assumptions
5. Exception handling
6. Processing of data
7. Limitations of accuracy
8. Comparison of data

Lindsay and Good (2005) found that the remotely accessed laboratory was statistically as good as, or better than, traditional delivery (which they termed *proximal*) and that simulations were as good as, or worse than, the traditional delivery. The ability to deal with experimental results that differ from expectation (termed *exception handling*) in simulations and in remote scenarios dramatically outperformed that of traditional delivery, with an effect size greater than 0.8. As a point of reference, an effect size of 0.4 is generally classified as large, so 0.8 would be a very large effect (Cohen, 1988). Remote delivery of the lab activity also significantly outperformed traditional delivery for outcomes 3, 6, and 8. There are many other publications illustrating the potential effectiveness of remote laboratory access as a teaching and learning tool (Baran, Currie, & Kennepohl, 2004; Corter et al., 2007; Lowe, Murray, Li, & Lindsay, 2008; Ogot, Elliott, & Glumac, 2003). Even though remote lab access can be effective, it isn't shown to be better than traditional lab delivery for all possible learning objectives. This is the case for ISEs as well. For those who maintain that a new approach needs to be as good as or better than the traditional approach across the board, this may seem to be an indictment of remote laboratories in education. However, remote laboratories can be effective teaching tools for the learning outcomes for which they are appropriate. Of course, if one of the learning outcomes of a laboratory activity involves physical interaction with the system by, say, touch or smell, then a remote laboratory approach may not be the best way to deliver that activity to a student. We discuss this more in a later section. Actually setting up and operating a remote access science lab is a significant challenge, so are there any successful examples that we can learn from?

Two Examples of Remote Access Science Laboratories

Because the authors of this chapter operate two large-scale remote access science laboratories, we would like to highlight our facilities and use them as an illustration of how this can be done successfully.

The OpenScience Laboratory

The Open University (OU) in the United Kingdom has put together a collection of online laboratory resources to serve distance learning undergraduates in science. The OpenScience Laboratory (OSL; www.opensciencelab.ac.uk) is an intellectual descendant of the PEARL project and was officially unveiled in the summer of 2013, with generous funding from The Wolfson Foundation. OSL contains many diverse resources. It provides access to remote laboratory equipment, as well as virtual laboratories and instruments, online field investigations, and citizen science projects. Currently (May 2016), OSL offers five pieces of remotely controlled equipment. There is a 5-meter radio telescope (ARROW) located on the OU and a 430-millimeter (17-inch) optical telescope (PIRATE) located in Mallorca, Spain, and currently being relocated to the IAS observatory on Tenerife; both use browser-based interfaces. Three sets of benchtop Compton scattering experiments are accessed through a LabVIEW client or bespoke HTML5 interface. Access to these pieces of equipment must be coordinated through the faculty at OU, so they are only available through a registered booking system. OSL also offers access to data from an autonomously running biochemical oxygen demand apparatus so it can determine the biological activity of wastewater as a function of dissolved oxygen levels. To get around the difficulty of adapting real laboratory equipment to online access, while still giving a realistic set of results, OSL has created a number of ISEs. To give the effect of controlling real equipment, OSL provides a real experimental setup from archives of hundreds or thousands of results generated by varying experimental variables on the apparatus. Then, using this matrix of real data, OSL created an interface that allows students to change various parameters, which then produces the real-world result that was previously recorded. Two examples of this are an ISE that allows students to gather data from an electron beam to calculate the charge-to-mass ratio of an electron, and a flame-test activity that shows the visible light spectrum of flame colors produced by various chemical elements. OSL also provides access to citizen science (big data) projects developed in-house such as Treezilla (www.treezilla.org), iSpot (www.ispotnature.org/communities/global), and the Field Network System (weblab .open.ac.uk/blog/projects/field-network-system). The Field Network System has been deployed in environmental fieldwork, enabling remote e-connectivity between observers. Many of the OSL assets, including citizen science projects and various virtual microscope slide sets, are openly available for third-party use, and all of the OSL materials are openly licensed. In the same period, about 200 OU students (in pairs and again not in the same location) used the remote Compton scattering experiment. In the each of the last two years, around 250 OU students have completed a short project on either PIRATE or ARROW, the radio telescope. This cohort then moved on to work in pairs on the Compton scattering experiment. Marcus Brodeur, a doctoral student, has actively followed these student groups and has been conducting surveys of their developing skills and changing perceptions.

North American Network of Science Labs Online

The other remote access science laboratory we wish to highlight is the North American Network of Science Labs Online (NANSLO; wiche.edu/nanslo), which has three physical laboratories, or nodes, containing lab equipment that can be accessed through the web. NANSLO began as a single site at North Island College under the direction of Albert Balbon and Ron Evans. NANSLO was expanded to include the Denver Node in 2012, with funding from EDUCAUSE. The Montana Node was established in 2014, with funding from the U.S. Department of Labor. NANSLO offers only remote laboratory access and does not currently provide any simulations or ISEs. Like OSL, NANSLO is operated by academic institutions. NANSLO is currently serving over 600 students per semester in undergraduate biology, chemistry, and physics courses to the following sets of equipment through the Internet, using LabVIEW:

- Nikon Eclipse microscopes with robotic slideloaders
- Ocean Optics UV/Visible spectrometers with temperature controllable six-position sample carousels from Quantum Northwest
- Air track assemblies for physics experimentation
- Helmholtz coil apparatus for measuring the charge and mass of an electron
- Tabletop gas chromatographs from Vernier
- Photosynthesis apparatus
- Titration apparatus
- Speed of light apparatus
- Reflection and refraction of light apparatus

With these various pieces of equipment, there are in excess of 25 different lab activities that can be performed, and more are being developed. For each lab activity, NANSLO personnel create a laboratory procedure that can be used by students to perform the activity. The procedure includes prelab assignments, background information and theory, and postlab analysis assignments, in addition to the basic instructions for performing the experiment. These documents are created through a collaborative, peer-review effort, involving faculty from many institutions. Once created, these procedures are licensed under a Creative Commons "CC-BY" license (creativecommons.org/licenses/by/3.0/us/), which means they can be used or modified by anyone, as long as the original source is attributed. In the past two years, over 1,500 students have used the NANSLO lab equipment, with the longest distance access being from Sri Lanka to Denver, Colorado, although the vast majority of students accessing the system were located in the United States. Data are currently being gathered on student performance to see if any positive learning outcomes can be attributed to the use of the NANSLO remote laboratories.

Seven Guiding Principles of Successful Remote Access Science Laboratories

From the literature (Cooper, 2005; Trevelyan, 2004), as well as from our own experience at OSL and NANSLO over the past several years, we present seven guiding principles that need to be considered in providing remote science laboratory access for teaching purposes.

1. Allow Learning Objectives to Drive Everything Else

The question should not be, "Can we do this remotely?" That answer is almost always "yes," if enough time and money are available. The question should be, "What do you want your students to learn and be able to do?" This question is much harder for most faculty members to answer than one would initially imagine. Most laboratory curricula are basically canon, based on "what has always been done," and this often makes it difficult to determine what actual learning outcomes are being addressed. In our collaborative process of generating laboratory activities and procedures for remote implementation in the NANSLO project, we have found that identifying learning objectives has been one of the more challenging aspects of the process. Often, it requires a very low-level analysis of the standard laboratory activity to identify what is important about it, whether it should be done at all, and other, sometimes uncomfortable, questions. But this is something that must be established even before a judgment can be made about the appropriateness of a suggested activity for remote implementation. Once the learning objectives have been identified, the work to determine how best to present the activity in a remote environment, and the appropriate tasks and analysis to ask of students, can proceed. This type of rigorous learning design is also well established in OSL.

2. Recognize That Controlled Access to the Laboratory Is a Necessary Limitation, and It Requires a Robust Scheduling and Resource Allocation System

Allowing fully open, 24-hours-a-day, 365-days-a-year access on demand is an attractive idea for the convenience of students and optimal scalability of the resource, but it is challenging in the case of remote science laboratories. Until laboratory instrumentation can be designed from the ground up as autonomous, remotely accessible, and self-supporting, it will be necessary to have mediated access. This both ensures the safety of the equipment and creates an optimal experience for students. To access the NANSLO or OSL equipment, users must reserve time on the system so that resources can be made available and monitored appropriately. Even when monitored, students sometimes manage to push equipment beyond its limits. In fact, the reservation system is at least as important as the laboratory.

Because all of the NANSLO equipment is real (i.e., not virtual), it is not as scalable as a virtual lab or ISE such as the ones included in OSL. With real equipment, there needs to be downtime for recalibration, maintenance, and so on. Even with 24-hours-per-day availability, the number of people who can use a single instrument at any given time is limited by both bandwidth and pedagogy. In some cases, four to six people can work together synchronously on a collaborative project using one piece of equipment, but in others, the single-user experience is important.

Most laboratory instrumentation appropriate for undergraduate science education is not designed to be accessed or controlled or reset remotely. Therefore, that capability must be provided through software (e.g., LabVIEW) or hardware adaptations. Besides the inherent difficulty in providing the remote capability to deal with troubleshooting situations, it is also not reasonable to expect an undergraduate science student to be able to deal with such situations, which brings us to our next principle.

3. Be Student Focused, Not Technology Focused

It is extraordinarily easy to become so focused on the technology involved that you lose sight of the needs of the students. This is a factor both in designing the interface for students to use and in assisting students with difficulties. The temptation to become facilities or equipment focused exists also in a traditional teaching laboratory. Principle 1 (objectivity) and Principle 3 (student focus) call for careful design of the equipment control and data collection. A corollary is the fact that lab assistants or technicians must be on call and require the ability to monitor the students' activity. Though this is another constraint on access to the equipment, staff members provide a human component to the technology-heavy remote environment. NANSLO initially planned on having lab technicians present only to handle equipment malfunctions. What was discovered is that the students highly value the presence of a human being who can watch over them during the laboratory activity and provide assistance if necessary. More than 60% of the positive comments from NANSLO surveys reference the lab technicians directly and express appreciation for them, even if no direct assistance was provided. The lab technicians do not provide any teaching assistance, beyond general encouragement to adhere to good laboratory practice. However, they can watch exactly what the students are doing, effectively looking over their shoulder, and they are physically present in the laboratory facility in case something goes wrong with the equipment. The OSL model currently provides asynchronous forum support from lab teachers with the aim of providing real-time online support only in emergencies. In both approaches, the ability to see what the students are seeing gives optimal opportunity for assistance.

4. Give Access to Appropriate Equipment and Data Functions

In the absence of equipment and systems designed specifically for teaching undergraduates in a remote environment, we must adapt existing equipment and software to make it accessible. As we do this, we must ask ourselves questions such as the following: What do we want the students to be able to control or access? What do we not want them to be able to control or access? What do we want them to be able to control or access that isn't directly related to the equipment itself? We learned two very important lessons when we started to address these questions.

Lesson 1: Allow learning from mistakes. In the case of the NANSLO remote access Nikon Eclipse microscopes, we realized that students could break slides with the objectives if they didn't pay attention to what they were doing. We considered putting limits in place so that the microscope would not physically be able to break the slide. However, after we talked with faculty members, it became clear that the risk of breaking slides was a reality they wanted their students to experience. This was an important revelation. Accordingly, we did not limit the system, and students have, indeed, broken microscope slides. Although we strive to give students control over anything that they would be able to control if they were physically present in the laboratory, there are some items that we choose to leave out. For example, we could also give them the capability of powering the equipment down and restarting it. This would really serve no purpose and does not meet any identified learning objectives.

Lesson 2: Keep the science in the foreground. When we set up the NANSLO air track apparatus, we had a lot of questions about how to mediate the students' capabilities. There are no air tracks available that are built for online access. One of the very important factors in using an air track in many experiments is making sure it is completely level. In the traditional physical laboratory, students spend most of their time leveling the air track. Did we want to replicate that in the remote environment, or did we want to have the air track leveled automatically so the students could instead focus on gathering data and analyzing it? After discussing it with faculty, we decided that leveling an air track was not actually an important learning objective for this activity.

5. Have a Well-Structured Pedagogy and Encourage Instructor Involvement

One of the strong points of remote access is its flexibility in scheduling, but this is also a weak point. The chance that a given student's instructor will be available to answer a question when the student is performing the lab activity is very slim. Therefore, the procedure must be robust and give enough information and guidance that students will be able to work through the procedure without the need for intervention by their instructor. We have found that guided or scaffolded inquiry works very well in these situations. We provide detailed background information and gradually increase the difficulty of the questions and analysis that the students are asked to address during and after the procedure. Unsurprisingly, we have also found that when instructors are very familiar with the lab procedure and with how the remote laboratory works, they are much better able to prepare their students for the experience, and the students seem to be much more at ease with the activity.

6. Create Remote Activities That Are Easy to Integrate Into Courses

This is hugely important, because integration must occur for the user base to increase and achieve sustainability. Forcing activities into a course may be all right for short-term proof of concept, but it doesn't work for the long term. Instructors must be able to (a) identify what learning objectives are addressed by the activity and (b) modify the activity to suit their own needs. This reinforces the importance of open source licensing for lab procedures and software. Instructors may want to add different prelab activities and questions or change the focus of the postlab analysis. Investigation of some other aspect of the phenomenon under consideration is fine provided it does not alter the fundamental nature of the activity (instrument, samples, etc.). For example, if instructors want to use a different chemical solution in a Beer–Lambert Law activity, they would need to contact the laboratory administration to find out if such modification is possible.

This also makes it necessary that the original procedure be independent of any particular text or course curriculum and be as self-contained as possible. It would not be practical to produce an unreasonably long lab procedure, so we make good use of web-accessible sources of information, online simulations, animations, and other resources to help explain the necessary principles to support the lab activity. If instructors wish to tie the activity to their textbook or other source material, they can easily do this by adding references to the appropriate sources. On more than one occasion, instructors felt the need to reduce the complexity of the procedures we prepared, because they were using the activity in a nonmajor's course. We believe that it is much easier to remove information than to add it; therefore, we always write the core procedure with science-major students in mind.

Facilitating easy integration also means making the procedures and other necessary information freely and easily available. The documents can be posted to a wiki or a blog or some other type of webpage for easy and free access.

7. Make It Easy to Get Feedback and Make Adjustments

It is vital to get feedback from students and instructors, whether formally or informally, and make necessary adjustments. We have made adjustments to the core laboratory procedures for our activities nearly every semester. We have done this in a variety of ways. We strive to maintain good contact with the instructors and administrators using our system so we can obtain their input through e-mails or phone calls. We send out a link for our 10-question survey after every lab activity. Students also have access to this survey directly in the NANSLO remote interface if they have time during their lab period to fill it out. Feedback from faculty and students doesn't always lead to modification of the procedure, but it might help us refine the user interface, for example.

It is also necessary to gather faculty and student feedback during the development phase of a remote activity. This can be done through the use of discipline panels or test groups at various intervals of development. At NANSLO, we also make use of our laboratory technicians as a "student test group" before finalizing any procedure and interface. The OSL approach is for initial usability testing in special observation labs together with built-in learning analytics tools during regular student use monitoring time spent on various stages, sequences of activity, and so on. The input of faculty is important not only from a usability standpoint but also for subject matter guidance. It is very easy for the interface developers to get off task (see Principle 3) when they are writing the program. Having faculty help us stay focused on the learning objectives is extremely valuable to avoid "feature creep" where more and more features are added that are "cool" but unnecessary.

The Future of Remote Access Science Laboratories

The areas where remote access science laboratories will see the biggest improvement in the near future are connectivity and collaboration, specifically the impact of improving and emerging network technologies.

Truly Networking Remote Laboratory Facilities Together: The "Internet of Things" for Lab Work

Many others have envisioned "smart" equipment that can communicate using standardized network protocols, almost since the beginning of the remote laboratory idea, and this is one of the goals of the NANSLO project. It is very difficult to do in practice, but we believe it will be possible to have remote laboratory equipment that is source agnostic from the student perspective. Imagine that one group of students from Institution X could use a remote spectrometer in Denver, Colorado, while another group from the same institution is using a remote spectrometer in Queensland, Australia. Creating a network of instruments that is this flexible and transparent from a user perspective is a daunting task when there may be differing types and models of equipment available on the network. The improvements in single-board computers like the Intel Edison, Raspberry Pi, and Arduino, coupled with the even smaller Systems on a Chip, will allow the addition of full computer integration with little or no increase in size.

Easy Addition of Equipment From Other Labs: Connectivity

At the moment, making a piece of laboratory equipment available on the Internet seems dismayingly difficult. It requires programming and may involve modification of the equipment in some way or augmentation with various kinds of robotics and automation hardware that may or may not have been designed for the task. In addition, it requires an infrastructure of information technology hardware and software to allow controlled and secure access to the facility and enough bandwidth to accommodate a large number of simultaneous connections. However, with properly designed modular and object-oriented software, many of these hindrances can be minimized or eliminated. To allow access to and control of the laboratory equipment, the equipment must be able to communicate directly with the controlling computer. Unfortunately, many necessary pieces of equipment are currently limited to USB or even RS-232 communication protocols, which dramatically limits the distance that can be placed between the equipment and the controlling computer and also makes it nearly impossible for one computer to control more than one suite of equipment simultaneously, all of which limits options for scalability and drives up cost. However, there are devices available that allow such devices to be accessed through the Internet.

Cloud-Based Services for Access and Control

If the laboratory equipment physically located at multiple institutions can be accessed through the Internet, then the distance between the equipment and the computer is virtually unlimited. This could enable the software that provides access and control of the equipment to be a virtual system located in the cloud. This would additionally decrease the cost of operation borne by individual institutions and give economies of scale that could not be reached otherwise. This kind of infrastructure would give the ability to expand the networked system of laboratory equipment to a truly global scale.

Big Data, Citizen Science Collaborative Projects

With a very large-scale network of laboratories and globally accessible software services, we could enable institutional and student-built hardware to contribute to big data projects easily and flexibly. Student-built devices could be added to and taken from the network as needed, but the underlying backbone of the network would still be there, generating data and contributing to the science. For example, student-built environmental sensors could be joined to the network and their data made accessible in a large database. After a year or two, when the student has moved on to other things, that sensor may degrade or stop working entirely, but in that period, more devices will have been added, contributing to a network enabling global environmental data gathering. And then it will be truly self-sustaining.

With all of these exciting possibilities, it is our belief that properly constructed, remote access laboratories can have a significant positive impact on science education at all levels.

References

Aktan, B., Bohus, C. A., Crowl, L. A., & Shor, M. H. (1996). Distance learning applied to control engineering laboratories. *IEEE Transactions on Education, 39*(3), 320–326.

Baran, J., Currie, R., & Kennepohl, D. (2004). Remote instrumentation for the teaching laboratory. *Journal of Chemical Education, 81*(12), 1814–1816.

Chen, X., Song, G., & Zhang, Y. (2010). Virtual and remote laboratory development: A review. In G. Song, & R. B. Malla (Eds.), Proceedings of Earth and Space. Paper presented at the 12th Biennial International Conference on Engineering, Construction, and Operations in Challenging Environments, Honolulu, Hawaii, United States, 14–17 March (pp. 3843–3852). United States: American Society of Civil Engineers.

Cohen, J. (1988). The effect size index: f. In *Statistical power analysis for the behavioral sciences* (2nd ed., pp. 285–288). Hillsdale, NJ: Lawrence Erlbaum.

Cooper, M. (2005). Remote laboratories in teaching and learning: Issues impinging on widespread adoption in science and engineering education. *International Journal of Online Engineering (iJOE), 1*(1), 1–7.

Cooper, M., & Ferreira, J. (2009). Remote laboratories extending access to science and engineering curricular. *IEEE Transactions on Learning Technologies, 2*(4), 342–353.

Corter, J. E., Nickerson, J. V., Esche, S. K., Chassapis, C., Im, S., & Ma, J. (2007). Constructing reality: A study of remote, hands-on, and simulated laboratories. *ACM Transactions on Computer-Human Interaction, 14*(2), Article 7.

Eikaas, T. I., Schmid, C., Foss, B. A., & Gillet, D. (2003). A global remote laboratory experimentation network and the experiment service provider business model and plans. *Modeling, Identification and Control, 24*(3), 159–168.

Kara, A., Ozbek, M. E., Cagiltay, N. E., & Aydin, E. (2011). Maintenance, sustainability and extendibility in virtual and remote laboratories. *Procedia: Social and Behavioral Sciences, 28,* 722–728.

Kirstein, J. (1999). *Interaktive Bildschirmexperimente—Technik und Didaktik eines neuartigen Verfahrens zur multimedialen Abbildung physikalischer Experimente* (Unpublished doctoral dissertation). Technische Universität Berlin, Berlin.

Kirstein, J., & Nordmeier, V. (2007). Multimedia representation of experiments in physics. *European Journal of Physics, 28*(3), S115–S126.

Lindsay, E. D., & Good, M. C. (2005). Effects of laboratory access modes upon learning outcomes. *IEEE Transactions on Education, 48*(4), 619–631.

Lowe, D., Murray, S., Li, D., & Lindsay, E. (2008). *Remotely accessible laboratories: Enhancing learning outcomes.* Strawberry Hills, Australia: Australian Learning and Teaching Council.

Lustigova, Z., & Zelenda, S. (1997). Remote laboratory for science education. In S. Oblak et al. (Eds.), *Proceedings of the GIREP-ICPE International Conference on New Ways of Teaching Physics* (Ljubljana, Slovenia, August 21–27, 1996) (pp. 260–262). Slovenia: GIREP-ICPE.

Ma, J., & Nickerson, J. (2006). Hands-on, simulated, and remote laboratories: A comparative literature review. *ACM Computer Surveys, 38*(3), Article 7.

Ogot, M., Elliott, G., & Glumac, N. (2003). An assessment of in-person and remotely operated laboratories. *Journal of Engineering Education, 92*(1), 57–64.

Potter, C., Brady, R., Moran, P., Gregory, C., Carragher, B., Kisseberth, N., . . . Lindquist, J. (1996). EVAC: A virtual environment for control of remote imaging instrumentation. *Computer Graphics and Applications, IEEE, 16*(4), 62–66.

Pradyumna, P. R., Tarun, C. K. S., & Bhanot, S. (2012). Remote experimentation of "no-load tests on a transformer" in electrical engineering. In *IEEE International Conference on Engineering Education: Innovative Practices and Future Trends (AICERA)* (Kottayam, Kerala, July 19–21, 2012) (pp. 1–6). India: IEEE.

Prieto, G. A., & Mendoza, J. P. (2013). Low cost didactic robotic platform based on player/stage software architecture and la fonera hardware. *IEEE Revista Iberoamericana de Tecnologias del Aprendizaje, 8*(3), 126–132.

Salzmann, C., & Gillet, D. (2007). Challenges in remote laboratory sustainability. In *Proceedings of the International Conference on Engineering Education* (Coimbra, Portugal, September 3–7, 2007). Retrieved from www.ineer.org/Events/ICEE2007/papers/331.pdf

Santana, I., Ferre, M., Izaguirre, E., Aracil, R., & Hernandez, L. (2013). Remote laboratories for education and research purposes in automatic control systems. *IEEE Transactions on Industrial Informatics, 9*(1), 547–556.

Sauter, M., Uttal, D., Rapp, D. N., Downing, M., & Jona, K. (2013). Getting real: The authenticity of remote labs and simulations for science learning. *Distance Education, 34*(1), 37–47.

Theyßen, H., Schumacher, D., & von Aufschnaiter, S. (2002). Development and evaluation of a laboratory course in physics for medical students. In D. Psillos & H. Niedderer (Eds.), *Teaching and learning in the science laboratory* (pp. 91–104). Dordrecht, the Netherlands: Kluwer Academic Publishers.

Trevelyan, J. (2004). Lessons learned from 10 years experience with remote laboratories. In R. Farana et al. (Eds.), *International Conference on Engineering Education and Research "Progress Through Partnership"* (Ostrava, Czech Republic, June 27–30, 2004) (pp. 687–698). Czech Republic: Technical University of Ostrava. Retrieved from www.ineer.org/Events/ICEER2004/Proceedings/body.pdf

10

SITUATED SCIENCE LEARNING FOR HIGHER LEVEL LEARNING WITH MOBILE DEVICES

Brett McCollum
Mount Royal University

Abstract

Mobile learning (mLearning) and the mobile devices that support it are still in their infancy, and yet the field is rapidly emerging. Educators across the planet are refining or reinventing their teaching practices to integrate mobile devices and mLearning. Examples of the use of mobile devices in science education are presented across seven categories. The reader is challenged to consider each example based on Koole's FRAME model. With an aim of science-informed public policy, science education can benefit from increased focus on the socially collaborative component of mLearning.

Mobile technology is becoming ubiquitous around the world. The International Telecommunication Union (ITU) estimates that 95% of the global population is covered by a 2G mobile-cellular network or better, with more than 3.2 billion global Internet users and more than three quarters of them using a mobile device (ITU, 2015). Although the number of Internet users is far behind the predicted 2015 global adult literacy rate of 86%, it is increasing at a faster rate (UNESCO, 2013). As this chapter will endeavor to demonstrate, each of us can take advantage of this mobile revolution to enrich the learning of our students.

Considering the pace of technological advancement and the evolving ways such devices are used in the context of the learning experience, it is doubtful that a widely accepted definition for *mLearning* will be established. However, an excellent model for discussing the technical, personal, and social aspects of mLearning is FRAME (Koole, 2006, 2009). In this model, Koole argued that mLearning occurs at the center of a three-aspect Venn diagram, in the overlap of device, learner, and social aspects.

With the FRAME model in mind, at the present time we will define an *ideal mLearning experience* as learning that involves collaboration among learners, includes a deep contextualization of learning, and is mediated through ubiquitous portable handheld digital devices that can wirelessly connect to the Internet and that an individual regularly keeps on his or her person. mLearning devices must be more than tools for retrieving information; they should help the learner filter through the mass of digital information to make meaning. Smartphones and tablets are common examples of mLearning devices, but they do not exhaust the options. Laptops and tablet PCs, on the other hand, do not fulfill the criteria for mLearning devices; users generally carry these items only for a specific purpose and for a limited amount of time.

Learning Resources

mLearning resources may be an option when considering user properties such as the functionality of the user's device, the user's physical location, or the user's preferred learning approach and history. The Joint Information Systems Committee (2011) established a list of "tangible benefits" of mLearning in 2011, which can guide any discussion on what constitutes an mLearning resource:

- Is personal, private, and familiar
- Is pervasive and ubiquitous
- Fits into the lives of learners
- Is portable to allow anywhere, anytime learning
- Provides immediacy of communication
- Allows access to learning by those in dispersed communities and isolated situations
- Provides contextualization through location-aware features such as GPS
- Allows data to be recorded and learning processes captured wherever they happen
- Provides access to mentors, tutors, and other learners on the move
- Is perceived as an acceptable way for learners to receive reminders and chasers and to manage their time
- Provides bite-sized eLearning resources that can be delivered to learners
- Provides abstract (representational) and concrete (environmentally situated) knowledge that can be integrated
- Offers peer-to-peer networks that make learning more student centered
- Promotes active learning
- Enables new learning environments
- Increases accessibility for learners with special educational needs
- Encourages reflection in close proximity to the learning event
- Reduces technical barriers to eLearning

As an example, consider modern molecular modeling software packages. Chemistry students cannot take a desktop computer with its impressive molecular modeling software from the computer laboratory into a lecture. They may have that same software installed on their laptop, but as we have already discussed, laptops do not fit the definition for *mLearning devices*. In contrast, a rudimentary version of molecular modeling software available for the iPad could be considered an mLearning resource depending on the features of the software: mobile, contextual, and social.

An mLearning resource must be designed with mobile devices in mind; for example, wireless access, limited memory, processing power and battery life, and an interface different from that of a standard desktop computer. The resource should permit peer-to-peer synchronous or asynchronous collaboration and be contextualized by offering information germane to the user's current needs. mLearning resources support context-specific situated learning (Lave & Wenger, 1991). The current shift from Java to HTML5 illustrates the desire of eLearning content providers to deploy their materials to all digital platforms, be that computers, laptops, tablets, or smartphones. However, it does not signify a transition into well-designed mLearning resources that use the special features of mobile devices.

Situated Science Learning With Mobile Devices

The remainder of this chapter is structured to highlight seven grouped examples of the ways that mobile devices are currently being used for eLearning and mLearning in science education. Many of these innovations can be applied to distance education and campus-centric instruction. As you read through each example, you are encouraged to consider if it illustrates eLearning or matches the *mLearning* definition.

1. Collecting, sharing, and accessing data
2. Wirelessly connecting to instrumentation with mobile devices
3. Collaborative learning through digital video
4. Collaborative learning through screen sharing
5. Connecting learners with peers and experts
6. Citizen science and participatory sensing
7. Representational training and concept mapping

Collecting, Sharing, and Accessing Data

As a group-based learning project in a graduate environmental biology course, students at the University of Florida developed UF Campus Tree Guide, a mobile app for identifying trees on the University of Florida campus (Palumbo et al., 2012). The app, available free on the Android marketplace, contains information on animal–tree interactions, a glossary, quizzes, and GPS-enabled maps.

An app with a similar purpose, GreenHat, was developed at the University of California, Berkeley, and uses the GPS feature of modern smartphones to "encourage exploration of the natural environment through experts' perspectives" (Ryokai, Agogino, & Oehlberg, 2012). Examining how users engaged with the app while outdoors, they found that learners will not read long articles or watch long videos on the small screens of a mobile device, but they will access these more detailed resources after returning to a stationary learning environment. By shadowing the learners during a 90-minute nature exploration, they observed that mobile learners shifted their attention back and forth between the app on their phone and the physical environment. Students reported that the contextualization of being in the outdoor environment while learning about it on their mobile device made the experience more personal than it would have been accessing the same information at a desktop computer indoors. The researchers explained that their goal was not for the learners to have a desktop experience while being mobile but rather for the mobile resources to "motivate and inspire educational curiosity" and concluded that learning resources must be optimized for short user-driven experiences (Ryokai et al., 2012, p. 1121).

Both of these apps are clearly designed to be used on a mobile device and are contextualized. However, with static data and no social component, they would be categorized as an eLearning resource accessed on a mobile platform, which was earlier referred to as "mobile eLearning." An example of a field-based activity that included a social component to the mobile experience occurred in a second-year environmental science course at the University of Northampton, when students traveled to Wicken Fen Nature Reserve and Stonehenge (Gordon, Jackson, & Usher, 2014). Using their mobile devices, learners recorded their observations of the locations, including photos with GPS tags and notes. These were uploaded to Flickr and Blackboard to share with peers. Unfortunately, limited connectivity hindered the experience with long upload and download times for data sharing in the field. The faculty supervisors noted that the portability of the mobile devices still provided value in the data-gathering process and recommended sharing data in a timelier manner when a solid Internet connection is available.

Wirelessly Connecting to Instrumentation With Mobile Devices

Memorable learning experiences expose us to new contexts. This is exactly what Andrew Dodson envisioned for his Year 7 and 8 middle school geography students when he planned a lesson where leaners would use an iPad to fly a drone with a mounted camera up to 50 meters above a feature to collect, share, and analyze local geographic data (Dodson, 2013). Dodson argued learner collection of data in real time provides context for subsequent analysis. Although the drone could be controlled from a PC, the intimate proximity afforded by the iPad control made the experience feel more personal for learners. Having learners generate their own maps of their community enables them to make meaning through the study of places that are familiar and important to them. In addition, this approach allows learners to strengthen their representational competence skills (Kozma, 2000) and establish connections between the concrete images from the drone and the abstract representation of maps.

With the rapid expansion and popularity of mobile devices such as the iPad, commercially available probeware for science education has adapted to permit probe data collection to be wirelessly controlled and analyzed on the iPad (Pasco, 2014; Vernier, 2014a). Although probeware is more commonly found in the K–12 system, it is also having an impact in STEM higher education. At Fort Hays State University, preengineering students undertake an integrated science project that requires them to "focus on bacteria collection, exposure of bacteria to cosmic rays, temperature and pressure profiles of the atmosphere" (Vernier, 2014b). Students design their own balloon system that includes Vernier probeware, safely launch and recover the system, and then analyze the data. Teaching and learning activities using Pasco probeware have also been conducted in chemistry, with instructor-to-instructor workshops recently held by the Federation of African Societies of Chemistry in Ethiopia (Shelton & Mason, 2014).

Collaborative Learning Through Digital Video

Since the time of Stanford and Muybridge's (1878) film *Sallie Gardner at a Gallop*, video recordings of a body's movements have long been an important part of the study of motion for sport, physical education, and kinesiology. At Mount Royal University, smartphones and Google Drive have made the study of human movement an mLearning experience (J. Parnell, personal communication, May 30, 2014). Using a smartphone, students were filmed performing various types of strokes in the swimming pool. These videos were then uploaded to Google Drive using the iPhone app. The video files were shared with preassigned groups and analyzed according to theory taught in the lectures. Students shared written analysis with their group through Google Docs, permitting asynchronous collaboration. If needed, individual frames could also be extracted from the videos and annotated with additional feedback. The course instructor chose to use her own iPhone for all video collection to avoid the possibility of student phones getting wet. Sealable plastic bags have been used in chemistry laboratories to avoid contamination of electronic tablets and protect against spills, and such an approach might be considered for video capture at a pool as long as the phone is not intentionally submerged. Such precautions are likely not necessary for nonaquatic activities.

Using the context of Canada's national pastime, students in Winnipeg used the iPad and Vernier's Video Physics application (Vernier, 2014c) to record and analyze the motion of a hockey puck during a pass (Hechter, 2013). The objective of the activity was to build on learners' existing understanding of the motion of a saucer pass for an authentic physics problem-solving exercise. Previously, the learning activity had required a video camera, a computer, transfer software and equipment, and analysis software. The iPad with its integrated camera and inherent mobility simplified the setup so that the lesson could be conducted anywhere.

These physics students used their finger on the touch screen to mark data points for each frame of the video. The data were then used to generate distance-time and velocity-time graphs. Learners could then compare their real-world data with theoretical fits predicted by the corresponding mathematical formulas found in their textbook. Hechter (2013) argued, "The real strength of this scaffolding activity is creating the forum to discuss and learn from student comparisons of the digitally constructed graphs from the iPad application with hand-drawn ones" (p. 347). The exercise also provides the context for conversations about the relationship between the distance-time and velocity-time graphs, the determination of slope, the physical interpretation of numerical and graphical data, and the options available for symbolic representation of data.

Collaborative Learning Through Screen Sharing

The film *Bill and Ted's Bogus Journey* (Kroopf & Hewitt, 1991) opens with a scene of a utopian future with students wearing the obligatory metallic gray clothing and learning from touch screen tablets. Although the futuristic fashions have not yet captured the imaginations of the masses, mobile touch screen tablets are shaping the evolving higher education landscape. Two features of particular interest are the front- and back-facing cameras and the advancing ability to share content as it is being created.

Penn State University (Penn State) established a Video Learning Network (VLN) in 2011 with the goal to help learners acquire the knowledge and skills they need at a Penn State campus close to home while reducing the need to replicate programs at multiple campuses (Penn State, 2011). Rooms outfitted with the VLN system include a large-screen television, multiple cameras and microphones, and computer software that permit the instructor to switch between projecting the desktop computer screen or a document camera. The instructor wears a microphone and stands in front of a camera so that his or her voice and image can be transmitted to all connected campuses. When students on any campus want to ask a question, they press a button on their desk, and a camera in the room zooms in on their location while a microphone turns on to capture audio. The traditional chalkboard is missing from this learning situation; all written information is projected to the television from the desktop computer or document camera. More recently, iPad and Doceri software have been added to the VLN (Silverberg, 2013; S.P. Controls, Inc., 2014) and used in chemistry instruction at multiple campuses simultaneously. Doceri allows users to project their iPad screen to the desktop computer, freeing the instructor to move about the room. In addition, the instructor can hand the iPad to students in the same room to permit them to contribute to the lecture and broadcast their solution to all connected campuses. The software costs $30 for the computer license and another $5 to remove the Doceri watermark in the associated iPad app.

Similar work has been carried out at Mount Royal University. The software in use at Mount Royal University is Reflector, which has the advantage that up to six iPad screens can be simultaneously projected (Air Squirrels, 2014). For Reflector to function, the Wi-Fi network must have the Bonjour gateway enabled. Although all devices must be connected to the same network, functionality extends across the entire campus, permitting sharing of data between different rooms, such as the laboratory and lecture hall. The software costs $13 (Canadian dollars) for the desktop license. No additional app is required for the iPad, as the software uses the iPad's native AirPlay feature, and the associated computer acts as an AirPlay receiver for wireless mirroring and streaming. Anecdotal evidence has suggested that students are more willing to share their work with a large class by projecting their iPad screen to the classroom front screen and describing their solution from their seat as compared to presenting at the front chalkboard. Groups of students can be invited to share their iPad screens with the class while they are working on a problem, permitting small-group discussion throughout the room to be informed by the solutions being derived live. In return, students can be encouraged to shout out suggestions for the groups broadcasting their tablet screens. Reflector can also be used to demonstrate how to use a new app or, in combination with QuickTime, to create an iPad screen recording.

Connecting Learners With Peers and Experts

In professional programs, such as engineering and medicine, students are expected to build personal bridges between theory and practical application. In addition, learners are often confronted with contrasting or complementary approaches to the field, with professors emphasizing an academically informed vantage in contrast to practitioners' focus on pragmatic problem-solving. Researchers in Australia are investigating the possibility of using cameras on mobile devices to connect university classrooms to locations of professional practice (Dalgarno, Kennedy, & Merritt, 2014). They proposed that mobile videos can be used primarily in two ways. First, videos prepared ahead of time using mobile devices at a site of practice can act as a hook for discussing both theoretical and practical issues within the field. Second, web conferencing between the classroom and a site of practice using software such as Skype can permit live discussions with a mobile practitioner without the need for hardware beyond the classroom computer and the practitioner's smartphone. Perhaps the most important benefit is allowing simultaneous learning between classroom and practice environment sites.

Dalgarno and colleagues (2014) identified current concerns with this approach to learning. In many areas of the world, wireless bandwidths cannot handle high-definition video, which can influence a learner's perception of the interaction as being sufficiently authentic. The use of specialized devices for video and audio capture, such as head-mounted cameras or Google Glass, requires investigation on how to best help the learner feel connected to the site of both the practice and the practitioner. Ethical and legal considerations also must be resolved. How should practitioners manage the privacy and anonymity of participants at the site of practice, such as patients at a hospital? If a participant or practitioner agrees to a live discussion with a class, can that video be captured and reused in future years? What responsibility does the institution have to secure archived video? Dalgarno and colleagues argued that university educators and professionals already have the tools in place to initiate collaborative projects of this type. Careful documentation of the design and execution of novel learning projects between classrooms and sites of practice using mobile video is needed at this time.

The Mobile Malawi Project at Virginia Tech also aims to connect learners with practitioners. Tapping into the wealth of experience passed down through generations of farmers in Africa, the project facilitates learning about organic agricultural practices and connects learners with farmers in Malawi (Glasson, 2014). As place-based education, it draws on local community knowledge and culture (Glasson, Frykholm, Mhango, & Phiri, 2006). It "provides the context for learning, student work focuses on community needs and interests, and community members serve as resources and partners in every aspect of teaching and learning" (Rural School and Community Trust, 2003, p. 1). Content is delivered through a highly contextualized mobile application designed for smartphones. Learners can access videos from organic farmers and upload images and notes related to their own garden, which are then shared with other users through a related blog. Course grades are determined based on learners' documentation submitted to the blog and their success at applying the concepts to growing an organic garden at the school site. As more people worldwide are able to access the Internet (ITU, 2015), open education resources (OERs) in electronic repositories are increasing access to learning materials for almost all learners through mobile technology. OERs, such as the Mobile Malawi Project, can "have a significant impact on education through social inclusion and justice so that everyone can achieve a basic level of education" (Ally & Samaka, 2013, p. 22).

As exemplified in both of these cases, connecting learners and practitioners has numerous benefits. Using video on mobile devices brings classroom learning and practical settings together for simultaneous learning experiences. These approaches can help resolve the issue of limited practicum opportunities that occurs in most educational settings. In addition, with the ubiquity of mobile devices, OERs may reduce the educational opportunity divide that exists between affluent and less affluent communities.

Citizen Science and Participatory Sensing

Can smartphones help rediscover a species that hasn't been observed since 2000? The New Forest cicada (*Cicadetta montana s. str.*) is the only cicada native to the United Kingdom (Zilli, Parson, Merrett, & Rogers, 2013). A number of factors have made it difficult to determine if the insect has gone extinct. First, its habitat is New Forest (approximately 600 square kilometers), an area too large for a small number of experts to search during the few summer days that the males sing. Second, the insect grows in its larva stage for a period of seven to eight years, emerging as an adult for only four to six weeks during the months of May to July. The New Forest cicadas do not emerge in a synchronized fashion like some other cicada species, and thus the number present at any time is smaller. Finally, the cicada sings at a frequency of 13 to 14 kilohertz, at the bottom of audible frequency range of humans. These challenges of large habitat coverage, limited detection time period, and audible limited frequency have stimulated a citizen science participatory sensing project.

New Forest has approximately 13 million day visits each year. Park visitors can download the Cicada Hunt mobile app, which has an imbedded acoustic classification algorithm designed to detect and distinguish the New Forest cicada (Zilli et al., 2013). During the summer months of 2013, over 4,000 audio surveys were conducted, but no cicadas were detected. Although some experts had concerns about the reliability of crowdsourced scientific data, even with an automated program, the project successfully lowered the barrier of citizen participation in a scientific endeavor.

Another citizen science participatory sensing project is taking place in Australia. In 2014, World Turtle Day was celebrated with the launch of TurtleSAT (Turtle Survey and Analysis Tools), a free mapping app designed for users to identify the species of an observed turtle and submit photos with GPS location (Ecological Society of Australia, 2014; TurtleSAT, 2014). A companion website (TurtleSAT.org.au) permits those without mobile technology to also report sightings. The objective of the resource is to help users learn more about the specific turtle they have encountered (contextualization) and help scientists better protect turtles by gathering GPS data on turtle populations (peer-to-peer data sharing). Ricky Spencer, a zoologist at the University of Western Sydney and one of the app's developers, explained the importance of crowdsourcing the data collection by saying, "If people report lots of sightings near busy roads or frequent road kills, there are some simple and inexpensive measures we can introduce at those locations, which help direct turtles and other wildlife to safer areas" (Ecological Society of Australia, 2014).

Representational Training and Concept Mapping

Development of representational competence skills is important in all scientific fields (Uttal & Cohen, 2012). Whereas symbolic chemical representations are the primary mode of communication for chemists (Habraken, 2004), representational competence skills are particularly important for learners in chemistry (Kozma, 2000; Kozma & Russell, 1997; Wu, Krajcik, & Soloway, 2001). Faculty at Mount Royal University are using the Molecules iOS app to introduce university general chemistry students to common molecular geometries (McCollum, 2014; McCollum, Regier, Leong, Simpson, & Sterner, 2014). They found that learners were measurably better at matching molecular representations, known as *representational translation*, when using the ball-and-stick representations on the iPad as compared to similar images found in print textbooks. In addition, even after the iPad was put away, the learners who had used the iPad earlier demonstrated increased representational construction skills when building a plastic molecular model to match a provided structural formula. Surprisingly, it took students only 15 minutes working through a series of training exercises using ball-and-stick representations, structural formulae, and plastic models for these gains to be observed.

One of the challenges of using mobile devices for deployment of learning materials is that resources must be sized for small screens. Many OERs are simply text and multimedia tied together using hyperlinks (Waycott & Kukulska-Hulme, 2003). Although mLearning is contextual, the limitations of electronic delivery of learning materials can lead to information fragmentation (Nelson & Palumbo, 1992). To assess if image-based concept mapping as compared to text-based concept mapping has an impact on student achievement or engaged cognitive processes, 86 computer science students in Taiwan were randomly assigned in a study to one of the two concept-mapping strategies (Yen, Lee, & Chen, 2012). The students used their mobile phones to prepare their concept maps and document their experience. To support image-based concept mapping, the researchers developed an Android phone app that permitted users to collect a gallery of images and then create concept maps that included both images and text. After six weeks of concept mapping, no statistical difference was found in student achievement on the course test. Students in the two groups demonstrated the same cognitive levels for remembering, applying, analyzing, and evaluating information. However, the image-based group performed better than the other group when asked to construct meaning from a concept map. They demonstrated enhanced levels of interpretation, exemplification, classification, summarization, inference, comparison, and explanation. Yen and colleagues went on to say, "The group using image-based concept mapping was adept at reorganizing concepts into a new pattern or structure through generating, planning or producing new outlines" (p. 318).

Going Forward

Not all educators have a strong affinity for technology, and there is disagreement on how and to what degree technology should be integrated into classroom learning (Parker, Bonney, Schamberg, Stylinski, & McAuliffe, 2013). How much time should be devoted to learning to use the technology as opposed to using the technology to learn? Is the technology used to facilitate learning of course content, or is the objective to develop career-oriented technical skills? Shifts toward inclusion of technology have been categorized using binary views of educator approaches and technology types. The first categorization considers if the changes in educator pedagogy to include technology are incrementalist or transformational (Schofield & Davidson, 2002). The second categorization considers technology "Type I" if it supports traditional teaching methods by making them "faster, more efficient, or otherwise more convenient," and "Type II" makes it "possible to teach or learn in new and better ways" (Maddux & Johnson, 2005, p. 3). Mobile technology is helping advance education on both sides of these categorizations. With technology's permeating presence in our lives, the barrier to including it in the learning experience has been lowered. Educators can incorporate mobile devices to their comfort level, doing it incrementally or completely changing their pedagogical approach as budgets, expertise, and passions dictate.

As we incorporate mobile devices in science education, we must keep in mind that science is a social endeavor. Scientific knowledge impacts societies. It is scientific advances in chemistry, physics, and computer science that have enabled distance education, eLearning, and mLearning to become part of the educational landscape. Despite this, "communication [of scientific knowledge] often remains an afterthought, a by-product of scientific endeavor somehow removed from the scientific process itself and often funded by a different mechanism than the scientists who perform the research" (Borchelt, 2001, p. 200). Perhaps this is the untapped strength of ideal mLearning. Although the mobility and contextualization of mobile devices provides access to knowledge to more learners in more places, it is the social aspect of mLearning that has the power to elevate science as a connected and participatory human activity in our knowledge-based society. The use of mLearning for the communication of science through formal and informal education settings has the potential to motivate more science-based policy and less policy-based science.

References

Air Squirrels. (2014). Reflector [Software]. Retrieved from www.airsquirrels.com/reflector

Ally, M., & Samaka, M. (2013). Open educational resources and mobile technology to narrow the learning divide. *The International Review of Research in Open and Distance Learning, 14*(2), 14–27.

Borchelt, R. E. (2001). Communicating the future: Report of the Research Roadmap Panel for Public Communication of Science and Technology in the Twenty-First Century. *Science Communication, 23*, 194–211.

Dalgarno, B., Kennedy, G., & Merritt, A. (2014). Connecting student learning at university with professional practice using rich media in practice-based curricula. In M. Gosper & D. Ifenthaler (Eds.), *Curriculum models for the 21st century: Using learning technologies in higher education* (pp. 213–232). New York, NY: Springer.

Dodson, A. (2013). Applications of the iPad and Drone in the middle-school geography classroom. *Interaction, 41*(2), 47–49.

Ecological Society of Australia. (2014). New app helps track turtles. *ESA eNews.* Retrieved from www.ecolsoc.org.au/news/2014/05/new-app-helps-track-turtles

Glasson, G. E. (2014). Is there an app for that? Connecting local knowledge with scientific literacy. In M. P. Mueller, D. J. Tippins, & A. J. Stewart (Eds.), *Assessing schools for Generation R (responsibility): A guide for legislation and school policy in science education* (Vol. 41, pp. 215–225). Dordrecht, the Netherlands: Springer.

Glasson, G. E., Frykholm, J. A., Mhango, N. A., & Phiri, A. D. (2006). Understanding the earth systems of Malawi: Ecological sustainability, culture, and place-based education. *Science Education, 90*(4), 660–680.

Gordon, A., Jackson, J., & Usher, J. (2014). Learning across contexts: Mobile for fieldwork in environmental sciences. In J. Ahmed et al. (Eds.), *Mobile learning: How mobile technologies can enhance the learning experience* (pp. 2–5). Oxford, UK: University and Colleges Information Systems Association.

Habraken, C. L. (2004). Integrating into chemistry teaching today's student's visuospatial talents and skills, and the teaching of today's chemistry's graphical language. *Journal of Science Education and Technology, 13*(1), 89–94.

Hechter, R. P. (2013). Hockey, iPads, and projectile motion in a physics classroom. *The Physics Teacher, 51*(6), 346–347.

International Telecommunication Union. (2015). *The world in 2015: ICT facts and figures.* Retrieved from www.itu.int/en/ITU-D/Statistics/Documents/facts/ICTFactsFigures2015.pdf

Joint Information Systems Committee. (2011). *Mobile learning infoKit.* Retrieved from www .jiscinfonet.ac.uk/infokits/mobile-learning/

Koole, M. (2006). *Framework for the rational analysis of mobile education (FRAME): A model for evaluating mobile learning devices* (Master's thesis). Athabasca University, Athabasca. Retrieved from dtpr.lib.athabascau.ca/action/download.php?filename=MDE/aaa_FINAL_VERSION_ mkoole_thesis_edited_May9_2006.pdf

Koole, M. L. (2009). A model for framing mobile learning. In M. Ally (Ed.), *Mobile learning: Transforming the delivery of education and training* (pp. 25–47). Edmonton, Canada: AU Press.

Kozma, R. B. (2000). The use of multiple representations and the social construction of understanding in chemistry. In M. J. Jacobson & R. B. Kozma (Eds.), *Innovations in science and mathematics education: Advanced designs for technologies of learning* (pp. 11–46). Mahwah, NJ: Lawrence Erlbaum.

Kozma, R. B., & Russell, J. (1997). Multimedia and understanding: Expert and novice responses to different representations of chemical phenomena. *Journal of Research in Science Teaching, 34*(9), 949–968.

Kroopf, S. (Producer), & Hewitt, P. (Director). (1991, July). *Bill and Ted's bogus journey* [Motion picture]. United States: Orion Pictures.

Lave, J., & Wenger, E. (1991). *Situated learning: Legitimate peripheral participation.* Cambridge, UK: Cambridge University Press.

Maddux, C. D., & Johnson, D. L. (2005). Information technology, Type II classroom integration, and the limited infrastructure in schools. *Computers in the Schools, 22*(3–4), 1–5.

McCollum, B. (2014). *Visualizing molecular geometries: Research-based study using molecules app.* Retrieved from itunes.apple.com/ca/book/visualizing-molecular-geometries/id863239256 ?mt=11

McCollum, B. M., Regier, L., Leong, J., Simpson, S., & Sterner, S. (2014). The effects of using touch-screen devices on students' molecular visualization and representational competence skills. *Journal of Chemical Education, 91*(11), 1810–1817.

Nelson, W. A., & Palumbo, D. B. (1992). Learning, instruction, and hypermedia. *Journal of Education Multimedia and Hypermedia, 1*(3), 287–299.

Palumbo, M. J., Johnson, S. A., Mundim, F. M., Lau, A., Wolf, A. C., Arunachalam, S., . . . Bruna, E. M. (2012). Harnessing smartphones for ecological education, research, and outreach. *Bulletin of the Ecological Society of America, 93*(4), 390–393.

Parker, C., Bonney, C., Schamberg, M., Stylinski, C., & McAuliffe, C. (2013). *Exploring the elements of a classroom technology applications implementation framework.* Paper presented at the American Educational Research Association Conference, San Francisco, CA. Retrieved from www.ltd.edc.org/sites/ltd.edc.org/files/Parker_etal_2013_AERA.pdf

Pasco. (2014). SPARKvue (Version 2.1) for iOS [Software]. Available from itunes.apple.com/ca/ app/sparkvue-hd/id552527324?mt=8

Penn State. (2011). New Penn State Video Learning Network expands to 16 campuses. *Penn State News*. Retrieved from live.psu.edu/story/53894

Rural School and Community Trust. (2003). *Engaged institutions: Impacting the lives of vulnerable youth through place-based learning*. Washington, DC: Author.

Ryokai, K., Agogino, A. M., & Oehlberg, L. (2012). Mobile learning with the engineering pathway digital library. *International Journal of Engineering Education, 28*(5), 1119–1126.

Schofield, J. W., & Davidson, A. L. (2002). *Bringing the Internet to school: Lessons from an urban district*. San Francisco, CA: Jossey-Bass.

Shelton, G. R., & Mason, D. (2014). ICT in teaching and learning chemistry activities on the iPad [Special Issue (Part II)]. *African Journal of Chemical Education, 4*(3), 182–188.

Silverberg, L. J. (2013). Use of Doceri software for iPad in polycom and resident instruction chemistry classes. *Journal of Chemical Education, 90*(8), 1087–1089.

S.P. Controls, Inc. (2014). Doceri [Software]. Available from doceri.com/

Stanford, L. (Producer), & Muybridge, E. (Director). (1878). *Sallie Gardner at a gallop* [Motion picture]. United States.

TurtleSAT. (2014). TurtleSAT [Software]. Available from turtlesat.org.au/turtlesat/default.aspx

UNESCO. (2013). *Adult and youth literacy: National, regional, and global trends, 1985–2015* (UIS Information Paper prepared by F. Huebler & W. Lu). Retrieved from www.uis.unesco.org/Education/Documents/literacy-statistics-trends-1985-2015.pdf

Uttal, D. H., & Cohen, C. A. (2012). Spatial thinking and STEM education: When, why, and how? In B. H. Ross (Ed.), *The psychology of learning and motivation* (Vol. 57, pp. 147–181). Cambridge, MA: Academic Press.

Vernier. (2014a). *iPad for data collection and analysis*. Retrieved from www.vernier.com/platforms/mobile/ipad/

Vernier. (2014b). *Vernier/NSTA technology award winners*. Retrieved from www.vernier.com/grants/nsta/2014-winners/

Vernier. (2014c). *Video physics for iPad, iPhone, and iPod touch*. Retrieved from www.vernier.com/products/software/video-physics/

Waycott, J., & Kukulska-Hulme, A. (2003). Students' experiences with PDAs for reading course materials. *Personal and Ubiquitous Computing, 7*(1), 30–43.

Wu, H. K., Krajcik, J. S., & Soloway, E. (2001). Promoting understanding of chemical representations: Students' use of a visualization tool in the classroom. *Journal of Research in Science and Teaching, 38*(7), 821–842.

Yen, J.-C., Lee, C.-Y., & Chen, I.-J. (2012). The effects of image-based concept mapping on the learning outcomes and cognitive processes of mobile learners. *British Journal of Educational Technology, 43*(2), 307–320.

Zilli, D., Parson, O., Merrett, G. V., & Rogers, A. (2013). A hidden Markov model-based acoustic cicada detector for crowdsourced smartphone biodiversity monitoring. In F. Rossi (Ed.), *Proceedings of the Twenty-Third International Joint Conference on Artificial Intelligence* (pp. 2945–2951). Palo Alto, CA: AAAI Press.

11

ONLINE DELIVERY OF FIELD- AND LABORATORY-BASED ENVIRONMENTAL AND EARTH SCIENCES CURRICULUM

Ron Reuter
Oregon State University

Abstract

Baccalaureate online degree programs and course offerings are continuing to grow. Notably slow to add both programs and courses are the earth sciences, especially those with traditional laboratory- and field-based experiential components. Challenges to developing earth science experiential learning courses revolve around online student access to laboratory facilities and specialized equipment, student location impeding field observations, and lack of one-on-one instruction for nuanced skills that are required to demonstrate proficiency in earth science topics. With thoughtful course development, utilization of technology, and incorporation of various methods to address learning styles, instructors can offer successful experiential courses, especially at the introductory level.

Studies in environmental and earth sciences are couched in many different degree program names. Degree names are natural resources, or environmental science, as well as more specific disciplines like geology, ecology, agricultural science, and forestry. Statistical reviews of reported U.S. Department of Education degree data demonstrate the difficulty in aligning and categorizing these degree topic areas. A review of degrees awarded between 1981 and 2010 lists degree categories of agriculture and natural resources, biological and biomedical sciences, and physical sciences and science technologies ("Growth in Number of Bachelor's Degrees Awarded," 2012). A subsequent review uses categories of natural resources and conservation, biological and biomedical sciences, agriculture and related sciences, and physical sciences ("Change in Number of Bachelor's Degrees Awarded," 2013).

Although majors such as geology, geography, and agricultural production have likely remained in their traditional category, the advent of interdisciplinary degree programs with names like natural resources and environmental science make it difficult to tease out growth and apply one generic degree title. In the former review, agriculture and natural resources degrees gained by 20%. In the latter review, where natural resources is given a distinct separation from agricultural science, degree growth is 300%—fourth highest in a list of 44 degrees. Growth in physical sciences in these two studies saw a decrease of 2% in the first review and a 59% increase in the second review. Growth in natural resources and environmental science is reflected in the rebranding and degree creation that occurred in higher education between the 1980s and 2000s, when schools were developing degrees specific to natural resources and environmental sciences. Indeed, many academic schools within universities rebranded themselves to include natural resources or environmental science in their names. For example, the University of Minnesota in 2006 combined its agricultural college and forestry college to create a College of Food, Agricultural, and Natural Resource Sciences (www.cfans.umn.edu/about).

This chapter deals with teaching experiential online lab- and field-based courses in the natural resources and environmental sciences, such as fisheries and wildlife or ecology, as well as traditional earth sciences like geology. The term *environmental and earth sciences* (EES) will be used to cover the broad grouping of programs.

Although the number of awarded EES degrees has grown in the past decade, online offerings of EES degrees have been slow to develop. EES courses that have a lab or field component may be more difficult to offer online because of their interdisciplinary nature or their specificity. An online student in an introductory cellular biology course can replicate a lab assignment using a mail-order lab kit and detailed instructions. A regional field course in bird identification is a little more difficult to replicate because students are expected to observe the behavior and habitat of the organism in its native environment. A lab demonstrating the block and pulley system in physics is easier to do at home than a plant identification course or a stream entomology course. Therefore, teaching these experiential courses online requires deliberate planning and creative thinking to help the students learn.

This chapter introduces the development of online education in the EES arena, covers the challenges and benefits of teaching these courses online, and provides examples of teaching methods that have proved effective in online EES education. Last, an EES online degree program at Oregon State University is examined.

Challenges and Benefits of Online Field- and Lab-Based Earth Science Courses

Kolb (1984) expressed that experiential learning allows the learner to use reflection on observations and collected data to synthesize concrete ideas. By accumulating and comparing assembled concrete ideas, the learner can refine understanding of complex systems. In the realm of EES, the role of experiential education falls to the laboratory and the field trip. Darwin (1859) may never have written *The Origin of Species* if he had not had the experience of exploring the world's ecosystems on the HMS *Beagle*.

Experiential learning in EES is difficult in any setting, on campus or online. One way to describe the complexity is exploring the ecoregion concept. Ecoregions are geographic areas designated by ecologists to group natural systems that share similar biotic and abiotic characteristics. In general, the delineations are based on commonalities in climate, vegetation, geology, topography, and soils. The systems we observe have developed over tens to hundreds of thousands of years, and each variable controls and is controlled by feedback loops, making the task of separating the controlling variable difficult. For example, mountain ranges on the western coast of North America intercept atmospheric moisture, which supports the establishment of vigorous coniferous forests, including the redwood (*Sequoia sempervirens*) and giant sequoia (*Sequiadendron giganteum*) forests. The soils in the region reflect both the influence of the conifers and increased moisture. Increased moisture over time results in erosion, which alters the topography and fertility of the soil and so on. The variables are intertwined, to say the least.

Already, before experiencing an ecosystem, the concept is complex. Plant science, geomorphology, hydrology, meteorology, and soil science, as well as the sciences of biology, chemistry, and physics, are all required to make these connections. A well-rounded student in EES would have a basic understanding of the processes and controlling variables that exist in those environments. North America, at a very broad scale (Level III), can be mapped as having 182 ecological regions—from tundra to tropical (Commission for Environmental Cooperation, 1997). Reducing the mapping resolution (Level II) reduces the number of ecoregions to 50. Driving cross continent at a latitude of 40° north, a traveler experiences only 10 Level II ecoregions driving at 60 miles per hour, and that journey takes three nonstop days. Very little learning of these complex environments can occur in that manner of experience. Experiential education in EES is therefore a challenge to do in person, let alone in an online environment.

Degree programs in EES have a long history of field- and laboratory-based experiential learning for many degree-required courses. Geomorphology, methods of field biology, wildlife survey, forest mensuration, surveying, GPS, and compass are all examples of courses that have hands-on and field trip components. Because of the hands-on nature of the course work and the diverse field experiences required for proficiency in EES, these academic offerings have been slow to develop for online education; replication and testing of those key experiences is difficult in the online environment.

An example of a difficult lab- and field-based course is introductory soil science (Reuter, 2007). This course covers topics involving chemistry, biology, and physics, and the laboratory component includes accurate measurements; chemical and physical manipulations of soil samples; in-lab examination of different soil properties, including samples from diverse geographical areas; and field surveys of soil pits and landscapes. Getting an online student to experience that range of materials poses a problem when approaching education from a traditional classroom perspective. However, with intentional and thoughtful consideration by the course designer and instructor, an online student can have the same learning success as an on-campus student (Murdock & Williams, 2011; Reuter, 2009; Werhner, 2010).

With specific regard to online earth science lab- and field-based courses, there are general challenges to these courses in the online method. At the same time, there are often innovative or commonsense benefits that counter the challenge. Challenge categories discussed here are (a) location, space, and time; (b) tools; (c) audience; and (d) instructor contact.

Location, Space, and Time

Online students are not in a single, central location. Often, students are in very disparate locations, from a rural ranch with intermittent Internet connection via phone modem to urban centers with high-speed Wi-Fi Internet. Reliable digital access is one concern. Early digital classes often heavily relied on video lectures or synchronous broadcasts. However, much of online education has moved away from that delivery type to asynchronous delivery, and video formatting has improved so that Internet connection speed and reliability has become less of an issue.

The disparate locations also affect student observation of natural world phenomena. Whereas the ranch student can walk outside and see plant species and insects and dig a hole in the ground, the urban center dweller may not have access to an environmental setting, certainly not one without drastic alteration by human activity. Neither ranch nor urban dwellers have an instructor to gather them in a van for a field trip. The location of students may impact their ability to observe and interact with the natural environment in the traditional way that an educator may desire.

When dealing with ecosystems in general, location impacts both online and on-campus courses; an instructor in the Mediterranean-like climate of Sacramento, California, is no more able to lead students to a tropical rain forest than an instructor in San José, Costa Rica, can lead students to the arctic tundra. One advantage of on-campus instruction is the immediate, in-the-field compare-and-contrast conversations that can be had regarding the present and the distance ecosystems—assuming the instructor has enough knowledge about both systems to make viable comparisons (e.g., a graduate teaching assistant may not have a broad perspective because of lack of experiences).

Interestingly, this challenge can be used to enhance student experiences in a thoughtfully designed course. With the exception of outer space, biology is everywhere, even in the densest metropolitan area. For example, there are an estimated 2,000 coyotes in the Chicago metropolitan area, home to 9 million people (Maher, 2012). Surely ecological earth science lessons can be experienced in urban settings; in fact, a scientific journal, *Urban Ecosystems*, is dedicated to that concept. A thoughtful instructor can take advantage of the disparate situations via collaborative learning to teach students through first-hand accounts of earth science lessons from the ranch and urban settings.

An example laboratory lesson these two students could perform is an evaluation of impervious surfaces in a one-mile radius of their location. Impervious surfaces are restrictive to precipitation and result in increased surface runoff, which can lead to flooding and erosion issues. An urban setting will have a considerably more impervious surface than a ranch. The evaluation can be done with simple, web-based mapping tools. Having students in the class review the evaluations for each unique location and reflect on how the local surfaces influence surface hydrology forces students to consider a system that they are not necessarily familiar with. Furthermore, it is a type of collaborative learning network, a useful tool in student success (Lou, 2004; Mason & Watts, 2012).

Tools

The sciences have tools of the trade: microscope and Petri dish for biology, atomic absorption spectrometer for chemistry, block and tackle for physics, X-ray diffractometer for geology, radio collar and antenna for wildlife, tree-ring corer for forestry, and total station for mapping. Current teaching faculty learned on these instruments and equipment and place value in the lessons that hands-on use of the tools provides. Collection of data from and handling of the instruments results in a better comprehension of the science and technology that serve as a basis for these subject areas (De Jong, Linn, & Zacharia, 2013).

Employers in the EES fields often desire graduates who have experience using equipment similar to that mentioned. Distance education students, without direct access to the same resources of on-campus students, may be at a disadvantage in the job market. Online programs need to develop courses that can compensate for these limitations.

Typically, these specialized instruments are expensive—prohibitively expensive for students. Centers of learning have the financial resources to purchase the equipment and use the tools of the trade. To teach these experiential skills online requires innovation to replicate or supplant the field tools. An example of an approach is the student lab kit such as Quality Science Labs's QSL Biology Lab Kit (www.qualitysciencelabs.com/biology-labs/qsl-biology-lab-kit). However, even these kits can cost in the hundreds of dollars, whereas an on-campus lab fee at a school will be substantially less (Phipps, 2013) (e.g., $29 for introductory biology at Oregon State University, fall 2014). In terms of sustainability, these lab kits are often onetime-use kits, so consumer generation of waste is also an environmental concern. Some tools are so specialized and maintenance heavy or sensitive that they could never be provided to an online student. A basic total station used in surveying retails for more than $2,500. A tree-ring corer is hundreds of dollars and assumes the student has access to a tree to core. In short, the tools used in on-campus experiential education for the EES are neither easily accessible nor affordable for online students.

This challenge area may be one of the most difficult to overcome for EES online education. At the introductory level, educators have found success combining simple, affordable lab kits with commonly accessible household products (Reuter, 2007). Online students' use of preassembled mail-order lab kits can standardize the experience for them (Jeschofnig, 2009); however, costs to students increase (Phipps, 2013).

Use of virtual technology will likely be where online students will be learning to use and manipulate expensive yet critical laboratory and field equipment. Ramasundaram, Grunwald, Mangeot, Comerford, and Bliss (2005) developed a virtual field laboratory based on a 42-acre Florida landscape where students were able to simulate ecological processes and observe predicted ecological outcomes. The simulation results were based on 25 years of empirical data collected on-site. This method actually has an advantage over a onetime visit, in that students observe the influence of the fourth dimension, time, in landscape processes (Ramasundaram et al., 2005). Other virtual tools are being used to engage students in the EES, such as 3D imaging of natural systems (Gilford, Falconer, Wade, & Scott-Brown, 2014). Researchers are attempting to collect 3D representations of landscapes and combine these representations in mapping programs, like Google Earth, to enhance student learning (D. Hirmas, personal communication, December 15, 2013).

De Jong and colleagues (2013) reviewed examples of studies where student learning between in-person and virtual laboratory was compared. One common theme about the use of virtual technology is that students completing both hands-on and virtual components demonstrate better comprehension than students using either only hands-on or only virtual components (Clary & Wandersee, 2010; De Jong et al., 2013; Gonzalez, 2014; Mawn, Carrico, Charuk, Stote, & Lawrence, 2011). For online courses in EES, a successful course will require students to do some sort of hands-on manipulation or in-person investigation, in addition to well-structured virtual activities.

Audience

Educators have demonstrated success in online student learning when a course has been thoughtfully developed. Indeed, in some circumstances, online students demonstrate higher degrees of learning success (Reuter, 2009), whereas in other comparisons, students perform with no significant difference between online and traditional delivery modes (Al-Qahtani & Higgins, 2013; Porter, Pitterle, & Hayney, 2014; Werhner, 2010). Maturity and educational experience can certainly affect student success, with freshmen enrolled in an online course being outperformed by upperclassmen (Levy, 2007; Urtel, 2008). Client audience is an important factor in determining how successful students will be in an online class.

Two basic online course user categories are students intentionally pursuing an online degree program (intentional) and students using online course work for ease of scheduling or overcrowding in on-campus courses (convenience). Online intentional students typically have a different demographic than convenience students (Wang, Shannon, & Ross, 2013). Intentional students are often older, have worked in another career path, or are forced to complete an online degree because they are place bound (Edge & Sanchez, 2011). Convenience students are often younger, are taking mostly in-person classes, and are traditional (e.g., have entered college directly from high school). Because of their self-selection for online degree programs, intentional students often perform at a higher level than convenience students. As universities develop more online-based degree programs, for both budgetary and convenience reasons, the distinction between intentional and convenience students will blur.

Attrition from online courses at universities is an issue of concern (Lee & Choi, 2011; Marshall, Greenberg, & Machun, 2012). Attrition rates studies for online courses report normal attrition rates between 25% and 40%, compared to 10% to 20% for on-campus courses (Levy, 2007; Marshall et al., 2012). Lee and Choi (2011) examined 35 empirical studies on online course retention and dropout and identified three factors in student retention rates: (a) student factors, (b) course and program factors, and (c) environmental factors. In their analysis, they found student factors contributed to 55% of the cause for student dropout (Lee & Choi, 2011). So the audience factor of online courses is especially important. Course development of online earth science lab and field courses needs to strongly consider the audience.

To demonstrate audience complexity, consider an earth science course taught at two different institutions. The author has taught the same online lab-based course at a California community college and an Oregon university and also taught the course on campus for an Oregon community college with a mix of university and junior college students. An earlier study compared the student learning success of the Oregon students and found that online university students demonstrated higher learning success than the community college students learning face-to-face (Reuter, 2009). The online students were all natural resource or science students and intentional students. The author then taught the course online for four terms for the California college. Enrollment attrition was over 70% by midterm, and student learning success and course completion was low. The Oregon on-campus students would likely outperform the California students, although a comparative study was not done. Students enrolling in the California course were generally nursing students or other students not majoring in earth sciences and were taking the course to meet a general education laboratory science requirement because other, more topic-relevant lab courses were overenrolled. The course population was mostly convenience students not engaged in the topic for their degree, and therefore they had lower commitment and interest.

Instructor Contact

An argument against online lab classes, or even lecture classes, for that matter, has been the loss of instructor contact time. A preconceived notion has the on-campus lab instructor as a font of knowledge and experience that the student has access to for three to four hours per week during the assigned lab period. This one-on-one interaction is considered highly valuable for exchanging ideas and concepts and solidifying the learning outcomes for the lab and enhancing experiential learning. Online students do not have this beneficial face-to-face contact.

This argument is a myth, especially at larger institutions. The lab instructor has a class of 20 to 30 students for the three-hour period and, when not giving instructions to the group, will likely spend most of his or her time providing instruction to the least prepared students, whereas more competent students will complete the assignment as quickly as possible and vacate the laboratory. On a field trip, some students will be attentive, whereas others will not participate. In addition, the lab instructor may be a graduate teaching assistant who has little to no real-world experiences from which the students will benefit.

In the online environment, student participation can be structured and required. If students are completing a lab or field component, they become responsible for independent completion of the assignment. Requiring digital photographic evidence of completion of hands-on and field components means that students must perform the tasks assigned and cannot "sit in the back of the classroom." In a thoughtfully designed lab and field course, the instructor will be able to provide some feedback to each student on an individual basis, meaning perceived instructor contact in the online environment may actually be higher. In the on-campus environment, inevitably there will be students who do not actively participate in the assigned task and choose to only observe or not participate. In the online class, because each student is completing the lab assignment individually, student success should be improved. Dishonesty is always a potential issue in both online and on-campus courses and needs to be taken into account in course development.

In summary, there are some perceived issues with offering lab- and field-based courses in an online setting. Specialized equipment, access to environmental settings, and in-person guidance are definite issues to overcome for successful learning. And advanced courses in EES face these challenges to a higher degree than introductory courses, due to the depth to which a topic should be covered. But there are also benefits to offering online EES courses. Instructors have time to construct coherent answers to student inquiry. Development of a section of frequently asked questions in the course materials ensures that all students have access to answers, whereas face-to-face instruction may not be as inclusive. In online labs, some skill sets may develop that will be useful in career fields, such as remote-controlled lab equipment (deep-sea and space research, laparoscopic surgery, etc.).

Example Online Lab Class: Introduction to Soil Science

Introductory soil science is a staple course in agriculture and environmental science programs. At many institutions, this course will often meet the degree requirements for the specific major but will also count toward a general education lab-based physical or biological science course (much like introductory physics or biology). Therefore, the audience in this course can include students with the aforementioned majors, as well as students from other less science-based majors.

In the *Glossary of Soil Science Terms, soil science* is defined as "that science dealing with soils as a natural resource on the surface of the earth including soil formation, classification, and mapping; physical, chemical, biological, and fertility properties of soils per se; and these properties in relation to the use and management of soils" (www.soils .org/publications/soils-glossary). As the definition implies, the science covers chemistry, biology, and physics; therefore, it behooves students (and instructors) to have a background in those subjects prior to taking introductory soils. This example is for a soils course without prerequisites in those subjects, so the student audience will have students with and without formal background in those sciences, making the education task for the instructor difficult because of the multiple levels of science comprehension in the class. An earlier iteration of this course was described previously (Reuter, 2007, 2009).

The soils course has 11 laboratory modules (see Table 11.1), which include a combination of web-directed labs, kitchen labs, and field labs. The labs include quantitative calculations for common formulas used in soil science (e.g., slope, velocity, volume, density) and quantitative measurements of soil properties (e.g., pH, texture, color). Kitchen labs are completed with a combination of lab kit materials and student-supplied materials. With students supplementing the lab kit, the cost of the mail-order kit is minimized. Importantly, students are required to perform some of the labs in the field, including soil collection and preparation, density measurements, and a full soil profile description. These are all activities a successful student would be required to demonstrate competence in following an on-campus course. A breakdown of lab content, including supplementary resources and student supplies, is found in Table 11.1.

Critical in the course management is feedback from the instructor. The feedback needs to be timely to assist students in figuring out if they are performing the lab correctly. To this end, each lab includes example outcomes for calculations or uses a lab kit sample that has a premeasured property. For example, when students are calculating density, a sample problem is worked through. When students are trying to hand texture soil texture on their collected samples, they are provided demonstration videos and a set of known soil samples so that they can calibrate their method. Including these calibration examples allows students to complete the laboratory without immediate feedback from the instructor, an important consideration for an asynchronous online lab and field course.

TABLE 11.1

Lab Topics, Activities, and Resources for Introductory Soil Science, a Laboratory- and Field-Based Experiential Learning Course

Lab Topic	Activities	Lab Kit Components	Web Resources	Student Supplies
Landscapes and mapping tools	Perform introduction to satellite imagery and programs (e.g., Google Earth), landscape measurements, calculations of slope and velocity, tracking landscape changes over time	—	Google Earth	—
Chemistry of rocks and soils	Perform introduction to chemical formulas of rock-forming minerals, identification of mineral features, of minerals, plant nutrients in minerals, mineral weathering	Minimal rock and mineral samples	Online lessons (Mamo et al., 2011; McCallister et al., 2009), multiple chemistry and mineral sites	—
Rocks and minerals	Perform introduction to mineral and rock formation, weathering, rock identification, plant nutrients from rock type	Rock and mineral samples	Online lessons (Mamo et al., 2011; McCallister et al., 2009), rock and mineral informational sites	—
Concepts of soil formation	Perform introduction to soil profile development, the five soil-forming factors, soil geographic relationships	—	Online lessons (Kertler et al., 2009; Reuter et al., 2009), The Twelve Soil Orders (University of Idaho College of Agricultural and Life Sciences, Soil and Land Division, n.d.)	—
Soil collection	Identify sample site from aerial imagery, collect soil systematically, describe sites, map coordinated, record data	—	Google Earth	Shovel Collection bags Camera
Bulk density	Perform introduction to density and soil bulk density, particle size, calculate density, field measurement of bulk density, work with buoyancy and displacement methods for density calculations	Graduated cylinder Rock samples Digital pocket scale	—	Soil samples Tin can Wooden block Mallet or hammer Thread Camera
Soil moisture	Systematically measure and dry soil samples calculate soil moisture contents of samples	Sponge Digital pocket scale	—	Soil samples Camera

Soil color and pH	Determine soil color for collected and provided samples, interpret soil color measure soil pH	Soil samples Graduated cylinder pH strips Standardized color sheets	—	Soil samples Glass jar Vinegar Baking soda Bottle caps Camera
Soil texture and structure	Observe settling rates based on particle size in collected and kit samples, develop hand-texturing skills using samples, postulate on impacts of soil texture and structure on soil behavior (e.g., drainage, compaction), construct hydrometer	Soil samples (two) Graduated cylinder Scale	—	Soil samples Straw Camera
Soil survey	Investigate information in a digital soil survey, including land-use interpretations	—	Web Soil Survey (U.S. Department of Agriculture, Natural Resources Conservation Service, n.d.), Google Earth, SoilWeb Earth (University of California–Davis Soil Resources Lab, n.d.)	
Soil description	Excavate; describe soil profile, including horizons, color, texture, pH; describe landform; develop land-use interpretations for site	pH strips Standardized color sheets Field description sheet	—	Shovel Tape measurer Camera

Each laboratory that has a hands-on component requires photographic evidence of the task being performed, and these photos are included in the submitted lab report. The photos serve a dual purpose. First, the instructor has evidence that the student has carried out the lab assignment, and second, the photos can assist the instructor when the student reports a problem with the outcome of a lab assignment. For example, a student having difficulty interpreting a soil profile during the concluding lab can submit photos to the instructor, who can ask pointed questions and help direct the student in his or her interpretation. In this way, the online lab mimics the interactions that would occur between instructor and students in an on-campus course.

Case Study: Oregon State University EES-Related Degrees Online

Distance learning for Oregon State University (OSU) is managed by OSU's Extended Campus, or Ecampus. Various colleges at OSU began offering Ecampus degrees in 2002, and as of spring 2016, there were 20 undergraduate bachelor degree programs offered online. These programs typically also have an on-campus version. Of these majors, five require students to complete hands-on lab- and field-based courses: agricultural sciences, environmental sciences, fisheries and wildlife sciences, and natural resources.

Enrollment in Ecampus courses has grown rapidly since inception (see Table 11.2; oregonstate.edu/admin/aa/ir/enrollmentdemographic-reports), with total student credit hours taken via Ecampus courses quadrupling since 2002.

All the major programs shown in Table 11.2 traditionally have a suite of lab- or field-based courses that students are required to take. With the adaptation of these programs to the online environment, the inclusion of the experiential courses has not always followed suit. Although teaching experiential courses online may not require more time or effort than the on-campus version, getting the online course developed can be resource consuming and time-consuming. Faculty and administration need to find a balance of return on investment. Faculty fully committed to regular course and research load would need incentive to develop the course, such as release time or salary adjustment (Herman, 2013). To justify this investment, administration needs evidence that student enrollment will pay back the investment costs.

OSU's Ecampus accepts course proposals from programs and will offer development funds if the course has merit for long-term delivery. As of spring 2016, programs proposing an acceptable course are eligible for up to $4,000 in development funds per course. These are discretionary funds that can be used for faculty salary, course release, or supplies. The program must ultimately decide if development of an experiential online course is viable.

Experiential learning courses at OSU are somewhat limited, given the number of majors offered online. Some departments have been reluctant to develop online experiential courses because of the complexities in course development and lab requirements (Edge & Sanchez, 2011). Oregon has a strong online community college presence, and these institutions have often developed some of the introductory experiential courses before the university system. Where this has occurred, students can take a community college course that articulates to the OSU course at a much lower cost. At OSU, a prime example of this is in the introductory biology courses, a requirement in many EES

TABLE 11.2
Student Credit Hours for Oregon State University, OSU Ecampus, and Specific Experiential Education Programs

Unit	Student Credit Hours	
	Fall 2002	Fall 2008
Oregon State University, university-wide	243,564	260,806
All Ecampus courses	7,688	16,115
Agriculture Ecampus courses	160	1,951
Forestry Ecampus courses	53	247
Science Ecampus courses	656	3,280
Earth and oceanic sciences Ecampus courses	20	208

TABLE 11.3
Online Courses Offered Through Oregon State University's Ecampus That Include Laboratory- or Field-Based Experiential Learning

Course Designator	Course Title	Quarter Credit Hours
BOT 220	Introduction to plant biology	4
BOT 350	Introductory plant pathology	4
BOT 440	Field methods in plant ecology	4
CH 121	General chemistry I	5
CH 122	General chemistry II	5
CH 123	General chemistry III	5
CH 130	General chemistry of living systems	5
FE 208	Forest surveying	4
FE 430	Watershed processes	4
FES 240	Forest biology	4
FES 241	Dendrology	5
FES 445	Ecological restoration	4
FW 255	Field sampling of fish and wildlife	3
FW 312	Systematics of birds	2
FW 318	Systematics of mammals	2
GEO 221	Environmental geology	4
PH 205	Solar system astronomy	4
RNG 353	Wildland plant identification	4
SOIL 205	Soil science	4

degree programs; OSU has developed online chemistry lab courses but no online biology courses. At least one Oregon community college offers biology lab courses at lower levels. A review of OSU's Ecampus catalog identifies 19 courses that are lab or experiential courses (see Table 11.3).

OSU's Ecampus offers over 900 online courses. Experiential courses represent less than 2% of the total courses. An examination of OSU's 10 peer institutions (oregonstate .edu/admin/aa/ir/peer-institutions) reveals that only two have developed online baccalaureate degree programs that might include EES experiential courses. The online course catalogs for these institutions show that only one has significant online field and lab courses. One has one evident course, and another only offers limited course work at the master's level. One interpretation from these findings is that development of successful online courses of this type is difficult and requires an investment of time and money and that, administratively, course development in this learning arena does not offer a viable return on investment.

Conclusion

Development of successful, quality online courses and degree programs requires significant investment of time, energy, and money. Online education has advanced greatly in the past decade in programs that do not have extensive field- and lab-based courses. However, online experiential courses can be developed and successfully deployed, with students gaining appropriate skill sets, especially with more introductory-level courses.

For online experiential EES courses to be meaningful, the course developer must be thoughtful and intentional. Experiments and field exercises need to be clearly explained for setup and learning outcomes. Such attentiveness will assist online learners in correctly executing the exercises and gleaning the intended skills and knowledge. Such courses do not lend themselves well to large class sizes without extended instructional support—the learners need to receive timely feedback on their progression through the exercises. Creative thinking on the part of developers can help them overcome some equipment and facility limitations they encounter when offering experiential learning courses online.

Caution is needed for development of these types of courses, especially in regard to learner safety. And, indeed, there are likely many field- and lab-based courses, especially at upper levels where delicate, complex, or instrumented activities are considered vital to learner success (J. Gautschi, personal communication, September 23, 2014), which do not lend themselves to teaching in the online environment. And institutions need to remember that the variety of learning types means that some students learn better face-to-face, and some learn better online. The balancing act is determining the degree of investment in on-campus and online learning to serve the targeted learners.

References

Al-Qahtani, A. A. Y., & Higgins, S. E. (2013). Effects of traditional, blended and e-learning on students' achievement in higher education. *Journal of Computer Assisted Learning, 29*(3), 220–234.

Change in number of bachelor's degrees awarded, by field of study, 1991–2011. (2013). [Table in Almanac of Higher Education 2013]. *The Chronicle of Higher Education.* Retrieved from chronicle.com/article/Change-in-Number-of-Bachelors/140745/

Clary, R. M., & Wandersee, J. H. (2010). Virtual field exercises in the online classroom: Practicing science teachers' perceptions of effectiveness, best practices, and implementation. *Journal of College Science Teaching, 39*(4), 50–58.

Commission for Environmental Cooperation. (1997). *Ecological regions of North America: Toward a common perspective.* Montréal, Québec. Retrieved from www.cec.org/storage/42/3484_eco-eng_en.pdf

Darwin, C. (1859). *The Origin of Species.* London: John Murray.

De Jong, T., Linn, M. C., & Zacharia, Z. C. (2013). Physical and virtual laboratories in science and engineering education. *Science, 340*(6130), 305–308.

Edge, W. D., & Sanchez, D. (2011). An online fisheries and wildlife degree: Can you really do that? *Wildlife Society Bulletin, 35*(1), 2–8.

Gilford, J., Falconer, R. E., Wade, R., & Scott-Brown, K. C. (2014). 3D visualisation and artistic imagery to enhance interest in "hidden environments": New approaches to soil science. *European Journal of Engineering Education, 39*(5), 467–482.

Gonzalez, B. Y. (2014). A six-year review of student success in a biology course using lecture, blended, and hybrid methods. *Journal of College Science Teaching, 43*(6), 14–19.

Growth in number of bachelor's degrees awarded, by field of study, 1981–2010. (2012). [Table in Almanac of Higher Education 2012]. *The Chronicle of Higher Education.* Retrieved from chronicle.com/article/Growth-in-Bachelors-Degrees-Awarded/133413/

Herman, J. H. (2013). Faculty incentives for online course design, delivery, and professional development. *Innovative Higher Education, 38*(5), 397–410.

Jeschofnig, L. (2009, Fall). Lab science courses can now be fully online. *Community College Week,* 16.

Kettler, T., Zanner, W., Mamo, M., Ippolito, J., Reuter, R., McCallister, D., . . . Soester, J. (2009). Soil genesis and development, Lesson 5: Soil classification and geography. *Journal of Natural Resources and Life Sciences Education, 38,* 240.

Kolb, D. A. (1984). *Experiential learning: Experiences as the source of learning and development.* Englewood Cliffs, NJ: Prentice Hall.

Lee, Y., & Choi, J. (2011). A review of online course dropout research: Implications for practice and future research. *Educational Technology Research and Development, 59*(5), 593–618.

Levy, Y. (2007). Comparing dropouts and persistence in e-learning courses. *Computers and Education, 48*(2), 185–204.

Lou, Y. (2004). Learning to solve complex problems through between-group collaboration in project-based online courses. *Distance Education, 25*(1), 49–66.

Maher, J. L. (2012, December 13). Watch out urbanites, here come the carnivores. *Discovery News.* Retrieved from news.discovery.com/animals/zoo-animals/urban-carnivores-121005.htm

Mamo, M., Ippolito, J. A., Kettler, T. A., Reuter, R., McCallister, D., Morner, P., . . . Blankenship, E. (2011). Learning gains and response to digital lessons on soil genesis and development. *Journal of Geoscience Education, 59*(4), 194–204.

Marshall, J., Greenberg, H., & Machun, P. A. (2012). How would they choose? Online student preferences for advance course information. *Open Learning: The Journal of Open, Distance and e-Learning, 27*(3), 249–263.

Mason, W., & Watts, D. J. (2012). Collaborative learning in networks. *Proceedings of the National Academy of Sciences of the United States of America, 109*(3), 764–769.

Mawn, M. V., Carrico, P., Charuk, K., Stote, K. S., & Lawrence, B. (2011). Hands-on and online: Scientific explorations through distance learning. *Open Learning: The Journal of Open, Distance and e-Learning, 26*(2), 135–146.

McCallister, D., Geiss, C., Mamo, M., Kettler, T., Ippolito, J., Reuter, R., . . . Soester, J. (2009). Soil genesis and development, Lesson 1: Rocks, minerals, and soils. *Journal of Natural Resources and Life Sciences Education, 38*, 238.

Murdock, J. L., & Williams, A. M. (2011). Creating an online learning community: Is it possible? *Innovative Higher Education, 36*(5), 305–315.

Phipps, L. R. (2013). Creating and teaching a web-based, university-level introductory chemistry course that incorporates laboratory exercises and active learning pedagogies. *Journal of Chemical Education, 90*(5), 568–573. doi:10.1021/ed200614r

Porter, A. L., Pitterle, M. E., & Hayney, M. S. (2014). Comparison of online versus classroom delivery of an immunization elective course. *American Journal of Pharmaceutical Education, 78*(5), 1–9.

Ramasundaram, V., Grunwald, S., Mangeot, A., Comerford, N. B., & Bliss, C. M. (2005). Development of an environmental virtual field laboratory. *Computers and Education, 45*(1), 21–34.

Reuter, R. (2007). Introductory soils online: An effective way to get online students in the field. *Journal of Natural Resources and Life Sciences Education, 36*(1), 139–146.

Reuter, R. (2009). Online versus in the classroom: Student success in a hands-on lab class. *American Journal of Distance Education, 23*(3), 151–162.

Reuter, R., Mamo, M., Kettler, T., Ippolito, J., McCallister, D., Zanner, W., . . . Soester, J. (2009). Soil genesis and development, Lesson 4: Soil profile development. *Journal of Natural Resources and Life Sciences Education, 38*, 239.

University of California–Davis Soil Resources Lab. (n.d.). *Soil web: An online soil survey browser.* Retrieved from casoilresource.lawr.ucdavis.edu/gmap/

University of Idaho College of Agricultural and Life Sciences, Soil and Land Division. (n.d.). *The twelve soil orders.* Retrieved from www.cals.uidaho.edu/soilorders/index.htm

Urtel, M. G. (2008). Assessing academic performance between traditional and distance education course formats. *Journal of Educational Technology and Society, 11*(1), 322–330.

U.S. Department of Agriculture, Natural Resources Conservation Service. (n.d.). *Web soil survey.* Retrieved from websoilsurvey.sc.egov.usda.gov/App/HomePage.htm

Wang, C.-H., Shannon, D. M., & Ross, M. E. (2013). Students' characteristics, self-regulated learning, technology self-efficacy, and course outcomes in online learning. *Distance Education, 34*(3), 302–323.

Werhner, M. J. (2010). A comparison of the performance of online versus traditional on-campus earth science students on identical exams. *Journal of Geoscience Education, 58*(5), 310–312.

12

ENABLING REMOTE ACTIVITY

Widening Participation in Field Study Courses

Trevor Collins, Sarah Davies, and Mark Gaved
The Open University

Abstract

Field courses provide opportunities for students to engage with the world as part of the learning process. This chapter explores the use of a portable Wi-Fi network and mobile technologies to support the inclusion of students with physical disabilities in field study courses. The Enabling Remote Activity approach, which has been developed through multiple field courses at The Open University in the United Kingdom, is introduced, and a case study involving two field courses from a second-level undergraduate environmental science module is presented. The findings are discussed in regard to inclusive education, and recommendations for facilitating social inclusion are proposed.

Field study courses are a valued aspect of authentic practical science that offers opportunities for learning and problem-solving in contexts comparable to those that students will face during their subsequent professional practice (Butler, 2008; Whitmeyer, Mogk, & Pyle, 2009). Within geology, for example, fieldwork education is considered to provide opportunities for students to synthesize and apply their knowledge, acquire professional field skills and techniques, develop the values and ethics of practicing geoscience, and gain exposure to a variety of geological phenomena (Pyle, 2009). Similarly, Mogk and Goodwin (2012) argued that field education improves students' knowledge and problem-solving skills, enhances their ability to reflect on their own understanding, generates positive feelings toward the subject that help motivate learning, offers direct and immersive experiences, and introduces students to professional practice. Residential fieldwork has been found to help develop generic and subject-specific skills (e.g., teamwork, decision making, and autonomy) and interpersonal skills (Stokes & Boyle, 2009). Petcovic, Stokes, and Caulkins (2014) reported on a survey of 172 geoscientists attending the Geological Society of America Annual Meeting (in

2010 or 2011), which found that 89.5% agreed that fieldwork should be a fundamental requirement in undergraduate degree programs.

Fieldwork is also viewed as a central component within the biosciences, supporting the development of key biological skills and transferable skills that are linked with graduate employability (Mauchline, Peacock, & Park, 2013). On the basis of the findings of a comparative case study, G. W. Scott and colleagues (2012) argued that fieldwork enhances undergraduate learning within the biosciences. They asked one group of students to collect organisms from the field and create labeled drawings of them and asked another group to create labeled drawings of specimens they had not collected. Through questionnaires and written exercises, they found that students who collected the organisms themselves were better at constructing a taxonomic list of the organisms, recalling the structural details of those organisms and the ecological sampling method that they had used to collect them, than were the students who created labeled drawings of specimens they had not collected and had the sampling method described to them in a classroom setting.

Although field courses are recognized as beneficial within science education, the costs involved in running these courses has brought increased pressure to consider alternate learning experiences (Çaliskan, 2011). A further pressure is the accessibility of such courses. Within the United Kingdom, the Special Educational Needs and Disability Act requires educational institutions to ensure that students with disabilities are not placed at a disadvantage in comparison with students without disabilities. M. Fuller and colleagues (2009) presented an extensive study of UK university practices to support students with disabilities and argued the case for developing inclusive curricula and a supportive environment for all students.

Hall, Healey, and Harrison (2002) critically reviewed the representation of fieldwork by geography, earth, and environmental science departments in UK universities and presented the findings of a postal survey of departmental experiences of supporting students with disabilities (*N* = 88). They found that departments typically adopted a mixture of two approaches, defined as a *responsive approach* and an *enabling approach*. Responsive approaches instigate measures in reaction to situations or problems as they arise to overcome the barriers excluding students with disabilities. Enabling approaches seek to reconstruct fieldwork in an inclusive way so that the barriers excluding students with disabilities are not inherent in the first place. In fact, an action undertaken when planning fieldwork could be classified as an enabling approach (preventing barriers) or as a responsive approach when undertaken to overcome a barrier. Hall and colleagues (2002) noted that responsive approaches are not necessarily less effective at including students with disabilities than enabling approaches and that "it is unlikely that all eventualities can ever be foreseen and planned for" (p. 227).

One aspect that was rarely addressed in the survey responses was the social problems that students with disabilities may encounter. Typically, there was a focus on physical access to the extent that more complex and challenging barriers to social inclusion were overlooked (Ash, Bellew, Davies, Newman, & Richardson, 1997; Borland & James, 1999). The following section introduces a range of approaches that have been developed to support access to field courses for students with disabilities.

Accessible Fieldwork and Alternate Experiences

A spectrum of approaches can be used to provide accessible fieldwork learning, ranging from offering immersive virtual reality fieldwork through multimedia-based virtual field trips and technology-assisted field experiences to simply providing more accessible fieldwork. Gardiner and Anwar (2001) outlined the following five strategies to use when a student with mobility impairments cannot directly access a field site or carry out a fieldwork activity:

1. Facilitate the activity so the student can participate in it. This may involve offering alternate routes, assistance such as off-road wheelchairs for rough terrain, or helpers who can take notes or make measurements under a student's direction.
2. Facilitate the activity so the student can participate in it but at a different location (i.e., find a new, accessible location for the whole cohort of students to use).
3. Substitute an alternative activity with the same learning outcomes. For example, Cooke, Anderson, and Forrest (1997) provided geological specimens in a laboratory as a small-scale substitute for the field.
4. Provide additional time for the activity and/or for gaining access.
5. Do virtual fieldwork in place of on-site fieldwork.

Gardiner and Anwar (2001) also emphasized the importance of students with mobility impairments being able to share all the experiences available to the other students, including the social life and domestic arrangements of a residential trip. It is recognized that social interactions during fieldwork are an important part of the whole learning activity (Stokes & Boyle, 2009).

Multimedia-based virtual field trips can be created as websites and on CDs and DVDs using a combination of photographs, videos, text-based information, and data. These may involve linear, narrative-led approaches, such as the CD-ROM-based tide pools virtual field trip discussed by Spicer and Stratford (2001), or more free-form exploratory approaches, such as the web-based geography virtual field trip reported by Dykes, Moore, and Wood (1999).

Stitching together photographs using software such as Gigapan and Photosynth can create panoramic views of field sites. The use of high-resolution photography with these tools allows students to explore a site and zoom in on details. An advantage of this approach is that students are presented with the whole scene. They are able to investigate and decide on their own what to examine in detail (Stimpson, Gertisser, Montenari, & O'Driscoll, 2010).

A similar form of open inquiry is supported through virtual reality systems. Atchison and Feig (2011) discussed the development of an immersive virtual reality model of a series of field locations within the Mammoth Cave National Park in Kentucky. Their system, designed as an alternative learning environment for students with mobility impairments, uses a stereographic surround display system (CAVE) and supports real-time synchronous interaction between users.

More recently, as part of The OpenScience Laboratory, the Open University (OU) has produced a multiuser three-dimensional (3D) virtual geology field trip of Skiddaw, a mountain in the UK Lake District (see www.open.ac.uk/researchprojects/open-science/3d-virtual-geology-field-trip). This system, built in Unity 3D, is intended to provide users wider access to fieldwork and preparative support for actual field trips. It is based around a 10 kilometer × 10 kilometer model of the terrain produced from LiDAR data with overlaid aerial photography. The project also explores what can be done on virtual field trips that can't be done on actual field trips, such as flying over the terrain, looking at rock sections in the field using a virtual microscope, and raising 3D geological sections out of the ground.

Virtual field trips are most often used to complement existing field activities, either to prepare students for going into the field or to reinforce learning after fieldwork (e.g., McMorrow, 2005; Rumsby & Middleton, 2003; Stainfield, Fisher, Ford, & Solem, 2000). It is worth stating that the aims, objectives, and learning outcomes of virtual field trips can differ significantly from those of traditional field activities (Qiu & Hubble, 2002). Studies of student and tutor perceptions of actual field experiences versus virtual field trips show that virtual field trips are seen as valuable activities but not as direct replacements for actual fieldwork because of the variety of physical, social, and real-world experiences involved (I. Fuller, Gaskin, & Scott, 2003; I. Scott, Fuller, & Gaskin, 2006; Spicer & Stratford, 2001).

The Enabling Remote Activity Approach to Accessible Fieldwork

Healey, Jenkins, Leach, and Roberts (2001) provided a guide for teaching and support staff at higher education institutions on the provision of learning support for students with disabilities undertaking fieldwork and related activities. Emphasizing the application of the social model of disability, their approach prioritizes the development of an inclusive curriculum that is appropriate for all students. For example, when selecting fieldwork locations, staff should consider accessibility in terms not just of the numbers of students accessing the site but also of their modes of access. The approach introduced here draws extensively on the guidelines presented by Gardiner and Anwar (2001).

The Enabling Remote Activity (ERA) approach was devised in response to an inquiry from OU's Earth Sciences Department in 2006:

> We are trying to make the fieldwork components of the residential school programme more accessible to students with severe mobility impairment. Currently the fieldwork involves walking distances of several kilometres across moorland and on coastal sections, all inaccessible to students in wheelchairs. We would like to set up an alternative learning experience for students in wheelchairs that matches as closely as possible that experienced by the other students. We envisage the possibility of using two-way audio and video communication between the student (positioned on the nearest roadside) and a tutor (on the hill/beach). (OU curriculum manager, personal communication, January 2006)

This was initiated in response to a request from a student using a wheelchair, and therefore the initial work was part of a responsive approach to address a given situation. However, the accessibility of fieldwork courses was identified as a broader issue, and therefore an enabling approach was subsequently adopted to produce a flexible tool kit that could be deployed in a variety of ways on any field course.

Within the context of use, fieldwork takes place over multiple days as part of a residential course. Students work in groups (typically between four and six students per group). The fieldwork activities typically follow a problem-based learning approach in which the students are required to undertake an investigation involving field observations, group communication, and interpretation. During the day, the students are transported to specific locations to undertake fieldwork, returning to a residential center in the evening for lab work, data analysis, and lectures. Group work is a core aspect of the learning experience, and therefore it is critically important to facilitate the social inclusion of students in all aspects of the course. Although accessible fieldwork locations are used when available, this is not always feasible. For locations that students who are mobility impaired are unable to access directly, our approach is to get them as close as possible and then use technology to provide remote access to the inaccessible field site.

The technology aspects of the ERA approach include a portable communications network and a flexible set of communication tools (Collins, Gaved, & Lea, 2010). The portable communications network comprises at least one battery-powered outdoor Wi-Fi router mounted on photography lighting stands. This creates a temporary wireless local area network at each location, enabling communication without depending on mobile phone coverage or Internet connectivity (neither of which is available in more rural field locations). Mobile devices are then used to provide a set of communication tools. A netbook computer runs a web server application and a voice over Internet protocol (VoIP) telephony application, creating a local web and phone service. Internet protocol (IP) video cameras and video encoders provide live video streams, and Wi-Fi cameras (or mobile phone cameras) are used to upload photographs to the web server as they are taken. The students and tutors can then use VoIP phone applications to make free phone calls over the network on mobile devices, and they can also view the live video streams and photographs using a standard web browser (see Figure 12.1).

The rapid deployment of the equipment is crucial, as the students' time in the field is precious, and students often visit multiple locations in a day. Typically, the approach requires two additional roles: One staff member is responsible for setting up the equipment, and a second member provides additional tutoring support. Voice communication is the most important service, as it maintains a direct link between the individuals involved. The video streams bring a strong sense of live interaction. Placed at a wide-angle shot position, video cameras can provide a sense of presence, and handheld (high-resolution) cameras can be used to zoom in on detailed parts of a site. Photographs are also used to capture wide views of a site or macro-level detail views of specific items. The choice of tools and use made of them varies according to the demands of the learning activity, the tutor's teaching approach, and the preferences of the students involved.

The ERA system has been used in a range of undergraduate field study courses, including Ancient Mountains (OU course code SXR399) at Kindrogan in 2006 and 2008, Environmental Change: The Record in the Rocks (SXR369) at Durham in 2009, and the Practical Environmental Science course (SXE288) at Preston Montford and Malham Tarn in 2014. The following section presents a case study of the most recent example, where the tool kit was used to support a student with mobility impairments on two separate field courses undertaken as part of a practical environmental science course.

An Environmental Science Case Study

In 2014, the ERA system was used to support a student on two field courses on the OU's Practical Environmental Science module (SXE288). This distance learning module, which is compulsory for the BSc degree in environmental science, is taken at the end of the second level, and, as such, students already have some experience of practical scientific observations and measurements. The aim of the module is for students to undertake scientific inquiry into environmental relationships through observation and experimentation. The module involves on-screen and home-based practical work, as well as two compulsory field courses: Hydrology and Meteorology in the Field and Vegetation and Soils in the Field. These take place in the United Kingdom at the Field Studies Council residential field centers at Malham Tarn in Yorkshire and Preston Montford in Shropshire, respectively.

The Hydrology and Meteorology in the Field course concentrates on how to collect and interpret hydrological and meteorological data. Students measure the flow of water in rivers and through soils and analyze water quality. They collect meteorological data, examine cloud formations, and explore relationships between weather and hydrology. Students work in small groups of five or six on an assessed project in which they investigate the water balance of a river catchment.

The Vegetation and Soils in the Field course focuses on how to describe and interpret vegetation and soils. Students learn to identify plant species, map plant communities, investigate soil properties, and study the interactions between soils and vegetation in upland environments. For the assessed project work, students work in small groups to investigate the differences between two contrasting vegetation stands.

Each field course is composed of a group of 30 students, supported by 3 tutors, and runs over 3 and a half days. One additional field tutor and one educational technologist were needed to run the ERA system. The student using the ERA system (referred to here as the ERA student) had mobility, coordination, and speech impairments and also had the support of a personal caregiver and a note taker. The ERA student used a wheelchair but was able to walk short distances over flat ground. The ERA student had some speech capability and sometimes used a text-to-speech device.

Accessible field sites were used wherever possible, and in those situations, and in the classrooms and laboratories, the ERA student took part in activities alongside his peers. However, when the field sites were inaccessible for the student (e.g., because the terrain was too uneven or the slope too steep), the ERA system was used to connect the student to the field sites through audio and video links (see Figure 12.1).

The system was used flexibly, depending on the fieldwork activity involved, in one or more of the following configurations:

- For field site descriptions and more didactic teaching situations, a tutor talking to the whole class was fitted with an audio headset and video recorded by a field tutor. The ERA student (or helper) could talk to either tutor.
- For group working, a field tutor acted as the remote eyes and ears of the ERA student, relaying the activity of the student group to the ERA student using audio, video, and still images and acting as an audio conduit between the student group and the ERA student.

- For group working, the field tutor stayed with the ERA student, while another helper operated the field audio and video. The tutor could then help the ERA student understand what was happening in the field and relay queries to the helper.
- For group working, the students in the field used the audio headset and talked directly to the ERA student or a colocated helper.
- For group working, some students stayed at one site with the ERA student and used the system to communicate with other students or a helper at the remote field site.

After each course, a follow-up e-mail questionnaire was sent to the ERA student, the other members of the ERA-associated project group, the tutors, and the note taker to elicit information about their experiences with the technology and their reflections. Feedback showed the ERA approach helped the student not only to attend but also to participate actively in the field courses: "The ERA technology was superb; without it, I would have been a spectator, instead, I was a contributor" (ERA student).

The student appreciated the audio and visual features of ERA that enabled him to view remote environments that he could not access and to communicate with the tutors and other students: "To be able to see environments which I wasn't able to access myself. . . . There was no way I would have been able to get inside the bracken, but with the ERA equipment, I could see most things, which was useful" (ERA student). He also noted, "The ability for me to see what the other students were being shown was great. To be able to hear the tutors and questions from students was also of great benefit."

As the field courses were about learning through scientific inquiry, it was important that the student could engage in that aspect. The ERA student commented that the technology helped him "to see scientific processes in the field." As the note taker commented, this helped to provide a more meaningful learning experience than simply providing the student with the field data:

Figure 12.1 ERA technology in use.

Note. An accessible base location (left) is connected to an inaccessible field site (right) using a portable wireless local area network (middle). A camcorder is used (right) to produce a live video stream, and VoIP calls are used to provide a two-way audio link. Photographs taken on a Wi-Fi camera can also be uploaded over the network to a web server at the base location.

> The technology allowed [the ERA student] to see how different measurements and readings were taken in the field. I took many of the readings whilst [he] used ERA to watch from a distance. Having watched the readings being taken, the results were, I believe, more meaningful to [him] than just pure data recordings. (note taker)

It was important that ERA acted as an enabling system and, as such, was available to the student when he needed it. Therefore, the requirement for the ERA system may well depend on the capability of the student at a particular time and place. For example, on one occasion, the ERA system was set up to provide remote access to a river site, but it was not needed, as the student wanted and was able to get to the river. On another occasion, the student was able to access one vegetation stand in the morning but later that day felt unable to access another vegetation stand. At that point, the ERA system was brought into use. The ability to rapidly deploy the system meant that it could be used to visit a number of sites within a fieldwork period: "It was very helpful to have such a lightweight system that's easy to set up and take down, and therefore can be available when the student needs to use it, and on standby when the student may or may not want to use it," one field tutor reported. "Travelling to more than one site meant that knowledge acquired could be used in more than one area, leading to better understanding of field techniques," the ERA student noted.

Other students most closely involved with the ERA technology were those in the ERA student's project group, so it was important to explore how the technology affected them and their learning experience. None of those students found the ERA system distracting or felt that it interfered with their work at all: "After the initial few seconds of "Oh there is a camera," I forgot it was there, it was just another person" (project group student). "I was pleased with the way it wasn't too intrusive with the rest of the students and that some students used it to talk to me when I had a question from . . . [the ERA student] that I could relay to them, they seemed happy to talk to me using the headset" (field tutor). None of the tutors who were teaching the whole group of students felt that ERA distracted or interfered with their work during the field courses.

Group working and peer discussion are important parts of these field courses but are also more generally important for social inclusion. One of the aims of the ERA project is to enable students to take part in fieldwork experiences alongside their peers, and the questionnaire responses showed an appreciation of this aspect:

> The opportunity to work with other students, in an environment like Malham, is invaluable. Taking readings and interpreting data can be done on an individual basis but working in a group environment and having the opportunity to discuss ideas helps a great deal. (note taker)

> Attending the residential gives students the chance to feel like part of a community and I believe that it is important for everyone to be able to experience that. (project group student)

> The technology was superb. It was very unobtrusive and certainly made it easy to include [the ERA student] in all the group activities. I felt that he was an integral part of the group, I hope he did too. It was very important to all members of the group that he felt included and able to make some very insightful and useful contributions to our discussions. I feel sure that without the technology this would not have been the case. (project group student)

We also explored how the project group students interacted with the ERA technology. The students reported that they helped the ERA student by ensuring that what they were doing was relayed clearly through the video back to the ERA student and, where necessary, repeated some of what was said to ensure the ERA student heard and understood what was happening at the field site. "[We showed] the camera what we had in our hands so [the ERA student] could see what we had found whilst having a discussion with the group as to what it was" (project group student).

Interestingly, the process of selecting information to share with the ERA student and relaying it to him was recognized by students as being useful in terms of reinforcing their own learning:

> In terms of interaction with the ERA, I hope that I helped the OU staff in ensuring that what we were doing was relayed clearly and, in doing so, repeated some of what was said. As we were learning the scientific names of the vegetation around us, I think this helped me, and perhaps others in my group, to commit them to memory. (project group student)

Using such technology in fieldwork isn't without problems. There were minor technical issues with using ERA in the field due to glare from laptop screens, wind noise on microphones interfering with the audio, and occasional loss of video. However, these issues did not cause major problems with the fieldwork learning. The main teaching concern was the social aspect of how best to involve the student when he was remote from the group, and this was noted both by the field tutor and by other students:

> The main issue was facilitating [the ERA student] to participate in the group work; although I could show him what was going on in the field, the fast pace of group work made it difficult for me to involve him fully. This may just need more consideration of how this could be achieved better. (field tutor)

> It would have been nice if [the ERA student] could have contributed more to the plant discussions by perhaps someone asking any questions he had as he contributed when he was able to get to the quadrats we were studying. (project group student)

However, despite these issues, the overall use of ERA in these field courses was a success. The student completed the two field courses and afterward stated, "Without ERA technology, my participation, inclusiveness and general enjoyment would have been lower" (ERA student).

Discussion: Sociotechnical Solutions for Inclusive Field Courses

The ERA approach involves a combination of social and technological interventions to improve the accessibility of field courses. This section discusses the issues raised by the comments and feedback presented in the previous section to identify the factors that contribute to a sense of inclusion and the remaining areas of difficulty within these courses.

The students in each course came from all over the United Kingdom and in most cases did not know one another beforehand. The course designs emphasize group work and require students to work effectively in teams to undertake their fieldwork. Afterward, each student writes up the work individually in a report, which is assessed and contributes to that student's overall course result. There is therefore an incentive for the students to work well together. The group dynamics are a primary concern for tutors, and the importance of effective teamwork is underlined in the course text and in the guidance provided by the tutors.

In this case study, the ERA student's group worked well together, and the overall result was a sense by all of the students that the course was inclusive. Notably, the students took ownership and responsibility to make it work. The ERA student commented on being a contributor rather than a spectator; the other members of his group commented that he was an integral member of the group and that he had made insightful and useful contributions. The level of active participation by all members of the group made the course inclusive in this case.

The presence of additional access technologies inevitably affects the learning context, but in this case, the field tutor commented that it "wasn't too obtrusive." One of the students noted that after an initial surprise, the use of the camera was ignored. Another said that she tried to ensure that what she was doing was relayed clearly and felt that this had benefited her and the other members of the group. The field tutor also commented that the students seemed to be happy to use the technology to discuss what they were doing with her and the ERA student.

Another important theme was flexibility, specifically in regard to the optional use of the equipment and the adaptability of the field tutor. Although the field locations had been surveyed and plans were made for how to use the system for each activity, the students decided at each location what they were going to do and how they would do it. The role of the field tutor and educational technologist was to guide and facilitate activities but not determine them. The field tutor commented that it was helpful having the system "on standby when the student may or may not want to use it."

One area of difficulty that was not fully resolved was the pace of group work and the facilitation of discussion between all students. At the field locations the ERA student accessed directly, the impact of his speech impairment was minimized, but nonetheless repeating or clarifying his questions at times did affect the pace of the group's discussion. The field tutor commented that it was difficult to fully involve the ERA student in some of the remote group activities. Some of the visual communication cues that the students used when face-to-face were not well supported by the system. As noted previously, not every eventuality could be planned for, but two-way video calls had been used in previous courses, and this may have been helpful in this context.

Conclusion: Reflections and Recommendations

This chapter has explored inclusive fieldwork through the discussion of related approaches and a case study on the optional use of portable network and web technologies to support remote access to inaccessible field locations. An action-oriented approach has been used to develop and deploy the ERA system that involves students and tutors in a process of technology appropriation to support their active participation in distributed group work at field locations. In drawing together the comments and observations of the participants involved, we extend the following conclusions for others seeking to develop inclusive teaching practices facilitated through technology.

Unobtrusive Simple Technology

Minimizing the negative impact of additional access technology can be difficult, but using tools in a way that foregrounds and facilitates the learning objectives of the course is critical to helping tutors and students engage with the technology and adapt their teaching and learning practices accordingly. When introducing the technology, staff will find it useful to draw comparisons with recognizable examples to alleviate anxieties around technology failure. For example, the portable network was directly comparable to domestic Wi-Fi routers that people use at home, the telephony service could be likened to Skype, and the video cameras were comparable to camcorders.

Flexibility of Use and Adaptability of Teaching Approaches

Maintaining an active and flexible approach to "making things work" that focused on what people could do, rather than what they could not do, helped develop a sense of group responsibility and engagement. The positioning of the tutor and educational technologist as facilitators with relevant expertise, rather than instructors, helped create and maintain the student group's sense of autonomy. A major advantage of residential courses is that there are multiple opportunities to make things work, so the tutor can explore different ways of working with students to help them make the most of their learning opportunities.

Active Participation in Groups and Social Inclusion

Working with the whole group, rather than individuals, helped engage everyone in the learning process. Within the courses' inquiry-based learning activities, the students' agency and responsibility for the decisions made by the group contributed in this case to the success of the group work. Although technical interventions can be used to improve physical access to field locations, it is only through active participation that social inclusion can be achieved. Interestingly, this is not totally within the control of tutors or institutions. They can create an environment that encourages participation, but it is the individuals who ultimately choose to engage (or not). Arguably, social inclusion is a shared responsibility, and setting students' expectations around active participation is important in all group-learning contexts.

Preparation, Expectation, and Hindsight

Finally, coordinating tutor and student preparation and setting realistic expectations is difficult. Hindsight is generally clearer than foresight. Every student who has used the ERA system had an individual set of requirements, and when a course is taking students to new and unfamiliar environments, their specific needs are difficult to predict. When a course has been undertaken previously at a specific site, drawing on example cases and illustrative photographs or recordings can help tutors and students prepare for the course. Ultimately, the ERA approach combines elements of enabling and responsive approaches (Hall et al., 2002); the portable network and use of the communication tools are planned and prepared to meet a wide range of needs, but individual differences and day-to-day variations require the tutor to adapt to meet all the students' needs as they emerge.

References

Ash, A., Bellew, J., Davies, M., Newman, T., & Richardson, L. (1997). Everybody in? The experience of disabled students in further education. *Disability and Society, 12*(4), 605–621.

Atchison, C. L., & Feig, A. D. (2011). Theoretical perspectives on constructing experience through alternative field-based learning environments for students with mobility impairments. *Geological Society of America Special Papers, 474*, 11–22.

Borland, J., & James, S. (1999). The learning experience of students with disabilities in higher education: A case study of a UK university. *Disability and Society, 14*(1), 85–101.

Butler, R. (2008). *Teaching geoscience through fieldwork.* Plymouth, UK: The Higher Education Academy. Retrieved from www.gees.ac.uk/pubs/guides/fw/fwgeosci.pdf

Çaliskan, O. (2011). Virtual field trips in education of earth and environmental sciences. *Procedia—Social and Behavioral Sciences, 15*, 3239–3243.

Collins, T., Gaved, M., & Lea, J. (2010, October). *Remote fieldwork: Using portable wireless networks and backhaul links to participate remotely in fieldwork.* Paper presented at the Ninth World Conference on Mobile and Contextual Learning (mlearn 2010), Valletta, Malta. Retrieved from oro.open.ac.uk/24711

Cooke, M. L., Anderson, K. S., & Forrest, S. E. (1997). Creating accessible introductory geology field trips. *Journal of Geoscience Education, 45*, 4–9.

Dykes, J., Moore, K., & Wood, J. (1999). Virtual environments for student fieldwork using networked components. *International Journal of Geographical Information Science, 13*(4), 397–416.

Fuller, I., Gaskin, S., & Scott, I. (2003). Student perceptions of geography and environmental science fieldwork in the light of restricted access to the field, caused by foot and mouth disease in the UK in 2001. *Journal of Geography in Higher Education, 27*(1), 79–102.

Fuller, M., Georgeson, J., Healey, M., Hurst, A., Kelly, K., Riddell, S., . . . Weedon, E. (2009). *Improving disabled students' learning: Experiences and outcomes.* London, UK: Routledge.

Gardiner, V., & Anwar, N. (2001). *Providing learning support for disabled students undertaking fieldwork and related activities.* Gloucestershire, UK: University of Gloucestershire, Geography Discipline Network. Retrieved from www2.glos.ac.uk/gdn/disabil/mobility/mobility.pdf

Hall, T., Healey, M., & Harrison, M. (2002). Fieldwork and disabled students: Discourses of exclusion and inclusion. *Transactions of the Institute of British Geographers, 27*(2), 213–231.

Healey, M., Jenkins, A., Leach, J., & Roberts, C. (2001). *Issues in providing learning support for disabled students undertaking fieldwork and related activities.* Gloucestershire, UK: University of Gloucestershire, Geography Discipline Network. Retrieved from www2.glos.ac.uk/gdn/disabil/overview/overview.pdf

Mauchline, A. L., Peacock, J., & Park, J. R. (2013). The future of bioscience fieldwork in UK higher education. *Bioscience Education, 21*(1), 7–19.

McMorrow, J. (2005). Using a web-based resource to prepare students for fieldwork: Evaluating the Dark Peak virtual tour. *Journal of Geography in Higher Education, 29*(2), 223–240.

Mogk, D. W., & Goodwin, C. (2012). Learning in the field: Synthesis of research on thinking and learning in the geosciences. *Geological Society of America Special Papers, 486*, 131–163.

Petcovic, H. L., Stokes, A., & Caulkins, J. L. (2014). Geoscientists' perceptions of the value of undergraduate field education. *GSA Today, 24*(7), 4–10.

Pyle, E. J. (2009). The evaluation of field course experiences: A framework for development, improvement, and reporting. *Geological Society of America Special Papers, 461*, 341–356.

Qiu, W., & Hubble, T. (2002). The advantages and disadvantages of virtual field trips in geoscience education. *The China Papers, 13*, 75–79.

Rumsby, B., & Middleton, R. (2003). Using C & IT to support fieldwork on Tenerife. *Planet, 9*(1), 4–6.

Scott, G. W., Goulder, R., Wheeler, P., Scott, L. J., Tobin, M. L., & Marsham, S. (2012). The value of fieldwork in life and environmental sciences in the context of higher education: A case study in learning about biodiversity. *Journal of Science Education and Technology, 21*(1), 11–21.

Scott, I., Fuller, I., & Gaskin, S. (2006). Life without fieldwork: Some lecturers' perceptions of geography and environmental science fieldwork. *Journal of Geography in Higher Education, 30*(1), 161–171.

Spicer, J. I., & Stratford, J. (2001). Student perceptions of a virtual field trip to replace a real field trip. *Journal of Computer Assisted Learning, 17*(4), 345–354.

Stainfield, J., Fisher, P., Ford, B., & Solem, M. (2000). International virtual field trips: A new direction? *Journal of Geography in Higher Education, 24*(2), 255–262.

Stimpson, I., Gertisser, R., Montenari, M., & O'Driscoll, B. (2010). Multi-scale geological outcrop visualisation: Using Gigapan and Photosynth in fieldwork-related geology teaching [Abstract]. *European Geosciences Union (EGU) General Assembly Conference Abstracts, 12,* 4702. Retrieved from adsabs.harvard.edu/abs/2010EGUGA..12.4702S

Stokes, A., & Boyle, A. P. (2009). The undergraduate geoscience fieldwork experience: Influencing factors and implications for learning. *Geological Society of America Special Papers, 461,* 291–311.

Whitmeyer, S. J., Mogk, D. W., & Pyle, E. J. (2009). An introduction to historical perspectives on and modern approaches to field geology education. *Geological Society of America Special Papers, 461,* vii–ix.

13

COLLABORATIVE e-LEARNING IN PHARMACY

Design, Evaluation, and Outcomes of a European Cross-Border Project

Marion Bruhn-Suhr, Dorothee Dartsch, and Jasmin Hamadeh
University of Hamburg

Abstract

The development, evaluation, and presentation outcomes of a cross-border e-learning course in clinical pharmacy are outlined. The course originated as a European Union–funded project among the universities in Cracow, Poland; Montpellier, France; Barcelona, Spain; and Hamburg, Germany. The aim was to develop a course for graduate pharmacists working in hospitals or community pharmacies. Details of the initiative include course content, didactical concept, learning outcomes, and intercultural aspects, as well as an evaluation and conclusion. The case provides an example of how to balance the different aspects, cultures, and learning targets, leading to new learning experiences for all stakeholders involved.

This chapter outlines the development, presentation, and evaluation outcomes of a cross-border e-learning course in clinical pharmacy. Clinical pharmacy has only in recent years become part of undergraduate pharmacy programs at universities in most European Union (EU) countries. In addition, the steady increase in medical and pharmaceutical knowledge requires constant updating of pharmacists' professional competence. As a consequence, there is an EU-wide demand for this subject in universities' continuing education programs. Given this situation, the University of Cracow successfully applied for project funding from the Leonardo da Vinci program of the European Commission, which supports practical projects in the field of vocational education and training (ec.europa.eu/education/tools/llp_en.htm).

The project started in 2006, and the universities in Cracow, Poland; Montpellier, France; Barcelona, Spain; and Hamburg, Germany, developed a course for the target group of graduate pharmacists working either in hospitals or in community pharmacies. In this chapter, we address the

- content covered in the course,
- didactical concept for teaching the subject,
- special advantages and challenges for the target group,
- learning outcomes,
- intercultural aspects,
- evaluation of the course presentations, and
- short- and long-term conclusions and perspectives.

Because of the special relevance of intercultural issues, we will analyze them from different perspectives with respect to the participants and students with a German-speaking background (i.e., participants from Germany, Austria, and Switzerland or expatriates living in other European countries). We examine the following:

- *German-speaking participants and students:* The cultural differences between pharmacists in hospitals and community pharmacies, on one hand, and the professional guild of medical doctors, on the other hand, that were widely discussed.
- *Profession cultures:* The geographical variety in the student group provided insights into different perspectives regarding the status of pharmacy in different European countries.
- *Differences in learning habits and continuing education infrastructure:* These were revealed and discussed in regard to the feasibility of different e-learning concepts.

When we use the term *students* in this chapter, we are referring to pharmacy graduates with at least one year of working experience in a hospital or community pharmacy.

Background

Pharmacists' work both in hospitals and in community pharmacies has been undergoing a radical change toward patient-oriented activities since the 1990s (e.g., individualized drug and unit dose supply in hospitals and medication therapy management in community pharmacies). Thus, pharmacists require new skills in addition to their traditional focus on drug chemistry and technology. For example, they require more in-depth pharmacology and knowledge about patient characteristics (e.g., laboratory data, kidney and liver function, pharmacogenetics) that influence the outcome of drug therapy (see Table 13.1). As a follow-up, the profile or role of the pharmacist is developing toward becoming a member of the health care team. The EU project partners involved aimed to create a harmonized program to support the potential of high-profile counseling activities by providing the means for pharmacists to acquire the new competencies they need.

Knowledge and skills in clinical pharmacy are required for safe and optimal patient care in community and hospital pharmacies, as clinical pharmacy is the discipline that

TABLE 13.1
Clinical Pharmacy Course Curriculum

Chapter	Topic	Contents
1	Clinical pharmacokinetics	Factors affecting the pharmacokinetic behavior of drugs, therapeutic drug monitoring, methods of optimizing drug dosage, new trends in dose optimization
	Special patient populations	Physiological, functional, and formal differences in neonates and children, pregnant and breast-feeding women, seniors, patients with renal or hepatic insufficiency, multimorbid patients in intensive care, and pharmacogenetically different patients compared with the "standard" adult patient; consequences for optimal pharmacotherapy
2	Laboratory data	Clinical chemistry, hematology, coagulation, drugs affecting lab data
	Drug interactions	Mechanisms of drug interactions, compatibility, interactions with medical devices, relevance of interactions
	Adverse drug reactions (ADRs)	Terminology of adverse drug events, causes, causality and prevention of ADRs and medication errors, pharmacovigilance
3	Pharmacoepidemiology and economy	History, aims, and methodology of epidemiology and economy, risk assessment, and evidence-based practice
	Medical literature	Sources and quality of medical information, literature research, and critical appraisal of medical literature
4	Immune system	Physiology and pathophysiology of the relevant organ systems, diseases with their etiology, signs and symptoms, current drug use, and relevant international guidelines
	Bacterial infections	
	Blood and cancer	
	Pain	
5	Cardiovascular system	
	Respiratory tract	
	Gastrointestinal tract	
	Endocrine system	
6	Communication and counseling	Complementation of medical and pharmaceutical knowledge, basic elements and effective tools of communication, the clinical interview, the impact of counseling on patient concordance
	Pharmaceutical care	Concepts and the process of pharmaceutical care
7	Drug formulation	Aseptic drug formulation and sterilization techniques, handling of cytostatics, quality assurance, production-related medicines safety
	Clinical nutrition	Relationship between clinical nutrition, prognosis and therapy outcome, nutritional assessment, indications, admixtures and administration of enteral and parenteral nutrition, drug administration with clinical nutrition

(Continues)

TABLE 13.1 *(Continued)*

Chapter	Topic	Contents
8	Clinical investigations and research	Laws and ethics of clinical trials, good clinical practice, trial design and study protocol, practical tasks of the clinical pharmacist in clinical trials, and handling of study medication
9	Drug management in hospitals	Comparison of different drug distribution systems, advantages and disadvantages in terms of economy and safety
	Tasks of the clinical pharmacist	Participation in ward rounds and multiprofessional teams, education, and training
	Cooperation between hospital and community pharmacy	Interface between hospital and ambulatory care, ensuing problems and safety issues, pharmacist cooperation across the interface

addresses the adaptation of pharmacotherapy to the individual characteristics and needs of patients. Additional aspects adding to the need for continuing education in clinical pharmacy include (a) the fact that this subject is the youngest among the pharmaceutical subjects and covers but a small percentage of the total pharmacy curriculum at most universities and (b) the fact that the inertia of university curricula, especially when regulated by law as in Germany, slows down any adaptation to newly developing professional demands. Consequently, undergraduate pharmacy studies lay the foundations for a successful professional life in clinical pharmacy, but building on these foundations needs to be achieved by postgraduate education.

Suboptimal pharmacotherapy has been recognized worldwide as a relevant source of human suffering and an economic burden on health care systems. Projects like "high fives," "medication reconciliation," "medication therapy management," and "medication therapy safety" have thus been launched in many countries and require health care providers, including pharmacists, to ensure that patients take their medications correctly. For pharmacists, this means the detection and solution of drug-related problems, like the recognition of drug interactions, wrong dosages in a medication regimen, occurrence of adverse drug reactions, neglected contraindications, and monitoring requirements or adherence problems. To fulfill this task, pharmacists need not only the knowledge but also the skills to find current and valid information, judge the relevance of drug-related problems they identify, develop an adequate solution to the problem, and finally communicate this solution to the patient and doctor if necessary. Therefore, concepts for lifelong learning programs in clinical pharmacy need to transfer knowledge, these skills, and the ability both to critically judge one's own competence in the field and to apply it in real professional life. The project partners successfully applied for funding within the European Commission Leonardo da Vinci program to compile a postgraduate training program for pharmacists in Europe to acquire the necessary knowledge and skills. This project is therefore named the "Leonardo Project."

The center for continuing university education and distance learning of the University of Hamburg, *Arbeitsstelle für wissenschaftliche Weiterbildung* (AWW), is the institution in charge of programs in the areas of

- traditional general university education (lecture series open to the public and a program for senior citizens),
- subject-specific postgraduate programs continuously assessed and certified (art history, general management, management of conflicts, train the e-trainer, etc.), and
- a cooperation contract (the AWW is a local contact point for students and inquirers for The Open University United Kingdom, in Hamburg, northern Germany).

The AWW has long-standing expertise in the area of designing and running e-learning modules for postgraduates. The Leonardo partner at the University of Hamburg, Dr. Dorothee Dartsch, professor and licensed pharmacist, contacted the AWW at the beginning of the project to make sure that the AWW's e-learning expertise was widely used.

The Leonardo Project (2006–2009)

Within this project, titled Standards of Continuing and Professional Development Education in Specific Fields of Pharmacy on the European Level, pharmacists from the universities in Cracow, Poland; Barcelona, Spain; Montpellier, France; and Hamburg, Germany, developed a joint curriculum for an e-learning training program in clinical pharmacy (Dartsch, 2008). The target groups were graduates in pharmacy working in hospitals or in community pharmacies. The involved partners aimed primarily at a harmonized curriculum including specific learning objectives for all fields within the program. In addition, they developed the actual material for the first module (solving drug-related problems). This consisted of a concise textbook component to specifically accompany the topics covered in the module, exercises, tasks, tests to solve in different social settings (e.g., single learner, small group, all participants), and the tutor's script containing the expected problem solution.

English was the module and project language. The four universities agreed that the English material would be available in a repository for each partner. Because of the differences in the country conditions regarding the costs and fees of continuing university education, the partners stipulated that each university would offer a course in its native language to avoid possible international competition and to safeguard its own market. However, to the best of our knowledge, the project has been realized only in Germany.

Curriculum

The harmonized curriculum consists of the following four clinical pharmacy modules (150-hour workload each) that could be developed into the foundation of a master program in clinical pharmacy:

- *Module 1:* Solving drug-related problems (Chapters 1 and 2 in Table 13.1)
- *Module 2:* Information and counseling (Chapter 3 in Table 13.1)
- *Module 3:* Pharmacotherapy (Chapters 4 and 5 in Table 13.1)
- *Module 4:* Special aspects of hospital pharmacy; special aspects of community pharmacy (Chapters 6–9 in Table 13.1)

The development of the content of each module was managed by an academic from each of the countries involved. Dr. Dartsch of the University of Hamburg was the project manager for Module 1.

Pharmacy is a work in progress as an area of active research: New drugs, new insights into old drugs, new molecular pathways, increasing understanding of diseases, and constantly changing therapy guidelines all lead to the necessity of continuously updating the course material.

Module 1: From Project to Pilot Course Presentation

First, Module 1 documents and materials were translated into German. The course design combined cooperation and communication activities for the learner. There was the text material, as well as articles, to read in combination with tasks to fulfill and case studies to be analyzed and solved by the students. A task could also be the preparation of a summary of an article. The course language was German, with significant numbers of English articles and references involved. Discussions and other activities were actively moderated by two specially qualified moderators (in this case, the two authors Dorothee Dartsch and Jasmin Hamadeh): one in the role of a pharmacy expert, and one in the role of a group process observer and moderator.

Part of the AWW's e-learning concept was an interdisciplinary course to prepare the students for the special needs of successfully participating in a collaborative course setting (Bruhn-Suhr, 2005). The preparation of students for these special needs focuses on three areas: (a) use of an e-learning platform (the University of Hamburg uses the Online Learning and Training [OLAT] learning management system), (b) time management, and (c) working in virtual teams. Because of the mix of students (across academic and professional backgrounds, age, working experience, media competence, cultural background, etc.), it cannot be assumed that all are equally well prepared for our concept of web-based academic postgraduate education (Reglin & Severing, 2003). To meet these needs, all students had to complete a compulsory course titled Virtual Teamwork. The topics covered were: familiarization with the learning platform and its tools; time management issues; web-based group work; web-related communication skills; reading and note taking; and basic knowledge of learning styles and their influence on efficient learning, individually and in groups. The didactic concept is based on employing and experimenting with the different tools, experiencing virtual teamwork, and reflecting on all these experiences. Although the AWW's target groups are postgraduates, these individuals tend to behave like students at school until they learn how to learn differently. More bluntly, they are passively waiting for the teacher to tell them what to do. The preparation module is used to motivate and train them on how to become active self-determined learners. In the case considered here, the results become very clear when the students start with one of the subject-specific modules like pharmacy. Students familiarize themselves with the learning platform, as well as the "dos and don'ts" of online communication and collaboration by experiencing and training in it. For the preparation module, there is a mix of students across different subjects. The advantage of running this compulsory course for mixed groups across subjects and cultural and professional backgrounds lies in the assumed mix of learning styles and types in combination with diverse cultures. All students profit from this diversity. The OLAT platform used requires only Internet access and a browser without any additional software. It is important to use a stable running platform that is easy to use to avoid students becoming distracted from the course contents. For the target group of pharmacists, we designed a 30-hour preparation course followed by the 150-hour pharmacy course (Module 1) over a period of six months.

e-Learning Concept

The e-learning concept is based on mostly asynchronous communication, collaboration, and teamwork in a moderated process.

Interlocking Methods and Social Forms in a Problem-Solving Approach

The interplay of different didactical methods and social forms of learning reflects an activity-oriented, problem-solving approach: Students are confronted with realistic cases and asked to find answers to these problems that can be realized in their workaday lives. Case-based tasks are the kickoff points for studying the technical literature and for an exchange of experience. (For an analysis of the benefits of training with case studies, see Beyer, Bruhn-Suhr, and Hamadeh [2004].)

With Each Other: Tasks for Teams and the Plenary

Because the module aims at competencies to analyze, make decisions, and act accordingly, team tasks are an integral element. Typical team tasks are analyzing a case study or writing the abstract of an article. Teams of five students are formed by the course moderators according to all or some of the following guidelines:

- They should not be colleagues.
- There should be a mix of female and male students.
- They should come from different geographical areas.
- There should be a mix of pharmacists from hospitals and from community pharmacies.

Feedback received covers not only the students' and teams' results but also their approaches to solve the problems. To focus on their approaches strengthens the students' problem-solving ability as they are supported to find their own ways based on their perspective to look at the problems. In addition, there are group tasks that comprise sharing experience and discussing different approaches. For insights into designing and conducting discussions in moderated, asynchronous online trainings, see Bremer (2003). To facilitate intensive exchange among the participants, groups are limited to 20 participants.

Individual Learning

The concept also integrates elements of individual learning, especially when it comes to acquiring basic theoretical knowledge. There are opportunities to work through the teaching material, to work through an extensive multiple-choice test, and to solve cases individually. The focus on individual tasks is a less complex context compared to the team tasks.

Profiting From Structure and From Flexibility

Flexibility in learning periods is generally perceived as a huge benefit in asynchronous training formats. But experience shows that, at the same time, it is one of the major pitfalls when training competes with everyday work and life. Therefore, a structure is provided that sets binding periods for each task but that has flexible times of activities within those periods. The structure of the course is laid out in a course calendar, which specifies the different tasks for the individual and team or plenary. It also provides information about the estimated workload and fixed deadlines for every task to enable intensive cooperation. The clear and rather restricted timetable provides a working basis for both students and moderators, which reduces the flexibility on the one side but guarantees interaction on the other side (see Figure 13.1).

Participants Take Responsibility

Students have clear responsibilities, including

- regularly checking e-mail and discussion forums,
- informing the group and tutors about times of absence,
- appointing a person to be responsible for handing in the results of the group work on time and in a version agreed on by all group members,
- contacting the tutor in case of difficulties, and
- contacting the tutor when there are difficulties in time management or group organization.

Figure 13.1 A typical course timetable.

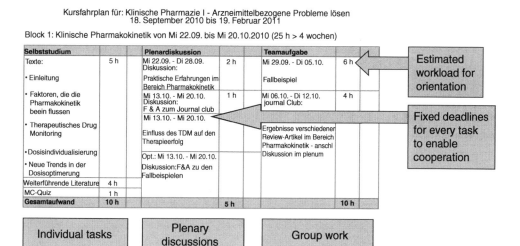

These transparently communicated responsibilities have proven to strengthen the participants' commitment to the module.

Moderators Act as Experts and Facilitators

Moderators regularly and reliably support the students in the areas of

- team building at the face-to-face meeting,
- facilitating participants' online activities and group work,
- giving feedback to group solutions (content, process, team), and
- providing input and feedback by external experts.

Most moderators are experts in their field of content, but for moderators to qualify to fulfill these tasks appropriately, they need a "train the e-trainer" qualification. A three-month online training course that covers theory and moderating e-learning formats is offered by the University of Hamburg (AWW) to meet this requirement (Beyer & Hamadeh, 2003). Besides conceptual abilities, an important field of this qualification is for moderators to benefit from the potential of e-moderating in asynchronous online scenarios (Salmon, 2000).

Assessing Learning Success

Besides the individual targets of each student, there are defined learning targets for each module. The participants, as well as the trainers, need to be able to assess if these targets are being met. Relating to the different levels of targets are the different means to assess learning success. There are methods referring to the results of tasks given (e.g., individual case, multiple-choice test, team task), whereas others refer to the process of finding results. Additionally, in the plenary discussion forums, as in the process of the team task, it becomes evident how the participants use the tools and information at hand. This process-based approach provides the additional benefit of the moderator supporting participants effectively and efficiently according to the needs observed (for more about focusing on the learners' needs, see Ehlers, 2002). The following example illustrates the relationship among learning objectives, tasks, and assessment of student skills. One of the learning objectives in the module "drug-drug interactions" is that students will be competent to give an adequate recommendation of how to avoid a problematic drug interaction in a given medication regimen. The first plenary discussion reveals feasible approaches to the analysis of medications for drug interactions; the second compiles different instruments that are helpful in this analysis. In a single-learner exercise, the students evaluate the nature and severity of a binary drug combination and receive individual feedback. If necessary, they have the chance to correct and complete their answer until it matches the expected model solution. In a multiple-choice test, students are required in several exercises to explain important drug interactions, to apply the information from an interaction analysis tool to realistic case reports, and to give adequate recommendations. In a small-group scenario, students finally solve a drug-interaction-related problem within a complex case report by discussing and agreeing on adequate recommendations. Process-related support is given by the tutor, thus ensuring a correct and complete solution to the given problem.

Pilot Presentations

The University of Hamburg decided to run the pilot in the winter semester of 2008–2009. Overall, there were four presentations of the first module, with 47 students from five different countries: Austria, Germany, Luxembourg, Norway, and Switzerland. Most students were female (approximately 80%). Of the whole population 34% were hospital pharmacists, and 44.7% were community pharmacists. Slightly over 21% had working experiences both in hospitals and in community pharmacies (see Figure 13.2). The majority (62%) was younger than or equal to 40 years old, but there were also students older than 56 years old (see Figure 13.3).

Compared to other students with different professional backgrounds in the joint interdisciplinary preparation course Virtual Teamwork, the group of pharmacists had more difficulties with teamwork. This is not particularly surprising considering their work situation; they regularly have to make decisions at very short notice without the luxury of time or colleagues to consult or to discuss issues. Their focus was to learn facts

Figure 13.2 Previous pharmacy experience of pilot participants.

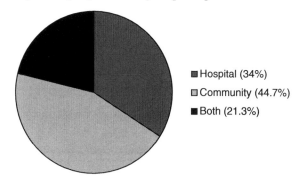

Figure 13.3 Age distribution of pilot participants.

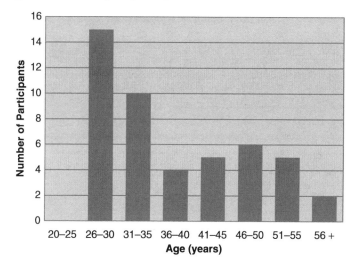

and figures about clinical pharmacy, and in the beginning, they did not see any advantage of working in groups.

Evaluation

Whether the students gained abilities and competencies that are listed in the curriculum can be definitively assessed. According to the level of learning targets, there are

- results of individual tasks like multiple-choice tests and (mostly case-based) assignments for assessing targets on the level of "knowing how" and "knowing how to in simple contexts" and
- processes and results of team tasks (case based, following a problem-solving approach) for assessing targets on the level of "knowing how to in complex contexts."

Although there will never be indisputable proof that a particular training was directly responsible for students' gaining new competencies, the reactions and evaluations show that most students appraise the quality and effectiveness regarding the aims focused on in the modules. The experiences in the preparation module Virtual Teamwork showed pharmacists new ways of working together. The students reported that they

- accepted the provided team settings,
- appreciated the team-building activities,
- realized the potential benefit of group work,
- disapproved of the tight online schedule, and
- approved of the organizational support by tutors.

How well students integrated the new competencies was clear by the intensive interaction in the pharmacy module; for example, there were 84 relevant postings in only one forum within the first online week. Students intensively discussed topics such as

- routine interaction checks (databases used: ABDA database, Pharmavista, Up to Date, Micromedex).
- dosage adjustment.
- databases, literature, checklists, fax templates.
- typical problems and possible measures to be taken: problems arise mainly with the clinical relevance of interactions (polypharmacy, flood of interaction warnings, incongruent classifications in a different database, etc.) and lack of data (customer cards may be helpful, but electronic patient records are optimal); measures include informing the prescribing doctor (e.g., by phone, fax) about major interactions, counseling the patient about intermediate interactions, and recommending the observation of specific symptoms if possible.

The first group activity (writing a summary of an English review article on pharmacokinetics) demonstrated the advantage of working in a team. Some of the students were fluent in English, whereas others felt less comfortable with the language. Students divided the task among group members and thus experienced that the team is more than the sum of the individuals. To summarize, we observed that

- group work was very profitable,
- knowledge sharing became very important,
- shared labor was appreciated,
- there was deeper reflection on all topics discussed,
- mutual motivation through groups must not be disregarded, and
- organizational support was necessary for some groups.

Lessons Learned

Although pharmacists tend to be solitary workers, they quickly noticed how enriching working in teams can be. Group work also reduces pressure. Moreover, the mix of hospital-and community-based pharmacists inspired all participants to review their working style and opened new paths for them. One student in the end said, "You managed to guide our international team in an optimal way and you successfully provoked everyone to perform in the best possible way. Thank you very much!" All students said that they were much more confident and felt themselves on par with medical doctors because they realized that they have special knowledge that medical doctors do not have. Some of the students even managed to start a process of change: Pilot projects were set up in hospitals to include pharmacists in the ward rounds. Some countries were more open to such projects than others, but the students learned from the exchange how to initiate and support a change and even develop strategies on how to move forward. About 80% of the students remain in touch with each other. They set up a learning group within the platform and continue to discuss cases or share different upcoming projects in hospitals and to keep each other informed about new scientific findings and ongoing changes in the different countries.

Extending the view from pharmaceutical topics and target groups to other faculties, we summarize our main experiences (as described in Dartsch, 2011):

- Collaborative e-learning supports achieving abilities and competencies in complex contexts.
- Key elements are
  o avoidance of information technology problems with highly sophisticated applications;
  o real-life questions and answers;
  o ways to convince participants of the benefit of exchange of experiences and perspectives;
  o manageable complexity of tasks in closely regulated, discrete periods of time;
  o clear instructions and support to follow them;
  o a well-designed interplay of tasks and social forms of learning;
  o continuous facilitation on course form and content, as well as social and organizational components;
  o feedback to approaches of problem-solving and achieving final results;

- o facilitators who are concerned with every participant;
- o opportunities to ask questions and address problems arising in the participants' work context; and
- o opportunities to cross-check contents and learning objectives in the participants' real work life.
- Creating a friendly, open, and encouraging atmosphere in the online communication space is a precondition of success.

Current Situation and Perspectives

In 2012, the program evolved into the CaP Campus Pharmazie GmbH. The curriculum and basic concept of the seminars remained largely unaffected by the change of the institutional provider. Virtual Teamwork for explicit student preparation was retired, and the program was split into individually bookable four-week seminars with a total workload of 32 hours each. Seven different seminars were offered in the first years of the CaP Campus Pharmazie GmbH, and about 50 students successfully completed single modules in 2013.

The CaP Campus Pharmazie GmbH decided to resign Virtual Teamwork, as it was considered to be an entry barrier, especially for those students who were interested in booking single modules as a first trial of the format. Instead, in each module, the teams are provided with organizational guidelines and asked to organize their work in the week before they are actually confronted with their task. Moderators support their organization and give expert feedback to their collaboration and to preliminary results. Focus of the guidelines and support is the benefit of the multiple perspectives and experience the collaboration allows for. In this context, the group work is well accepted and generally successful. The participants anonymously evaluate all seminars offered by CaP Campus Pharmazie GmbH. Here we discuss the most current evaluation (i.e., of all seminars in the year 2013).

The objectives pursued individually by the participants were described as fully achieved or mostly achieved by 93% of the participants. All participants confirmed the completeness of the curriculum and the suitability as vocational training. More than 95% judged the exercises as adequately practice oriented. The team exercises were emphasized as being most valuable for the learning process. Throughout all seminars, 99% of the participants self-reported achieving the learning objectives predefined in the curriculum. None of these items showed a significant difference between hospital and community pharmacists. Finally, the participants rated the seminar on a scale between 1 (*outstanding*) and 5 (*inadequate*). The seminars scored a mean of 1.38 ± 0.6.

Meeting the Needs

The growing number of networking partners of the CaP Campus Pharmazie GmbH (i.e., federal Chambers of Pharmacists and professional pharmaceutical associations in Germany and Austria) shows that an urgent need is met regarding training that

- is related to practice and meets academic standards in terms of achieving problem-solving competence and skills,
- is flexible regarding time and place, and
- offers active learning by employing exchange and discussion as didactical means in a quality-assured institutional context.

CaP Campus Pharmazie GmbH aims at expanding this network to methodically complement the traditional postgraduate education offered (e.g., by the Chambers of Pharmacists) and to develop common standards of continuing education that facilitate orientation for potential participants, including the disclosure of conflicts of interest that are ubiquitously present in continuing pharmacy education.

References

Beyer, K., Bruhn-Suhr, M., & Hamadeh, J. (2004, February). *Praxisbezug in Online-Kursen: Lernen mit Fallstudien und Fallbeispielen.* Paper presented at the Tagungsdokumentation Learntec, Karlsruhe, Germany.

Beyer, K., & Hamadeh, J. (2003, December). *It's not only the "e" that is new but also the "teaching": How to enable traditional professors and lecturer to become didactical correct e-teachers; Insights into a guided process.* Paper presented at the Online-Educa Berlin: 9th International Conference on Technology Supported Learning and Training, Berlin, Germany.

Bremer, C. (2003). Lessons learned: Moderation und Gestaltung netzbasierter Diskussionsprozesse in Foren. In M. Kerres & B. Voß (Eds.), *Digitaler Campus: Vom Medienprojekt zum nachhaltigen Medieneinsatz in der Hochschule. Medien in der Wissenschaft* (Vol. 24, pp. 191–202). Münster, Germany: Waxmann Verlag.

Bruhn-Suhr, M. (2005). *Projekt–OLIM, Online-Perspektiven für das weiterbildende Studium "Management für Führungskräfte": Schlussbericht.* Retrieved from www.aww.uni-hamburg.de/de/dokumente/olim_abschluss.pdf

Dartsch, D. (2008). *Curriculum Klinische Pharmazie: Konzept für einen europäischen postgradualen Online-Kurs.* München, Germany: AVM-Verlag.

Dartsch, D. C. (2011). A first online postgraduate course in clinical pharmacy: Impressions and experience. *European Journal of Hospital Pharmacy: Practice, 17*(2), 54–57.

Ehlers, U. (2002). Qualität—Im Mittelpunkt steht der Lernende. *LIMPACT: Leitprojekte Informationen Compact, 5*(1) 17–20. Retrieved from www.bibb.de/dokumente/pdf/a12ptiaw_limpact05_2002.pdf

Reglin, T., & Severing, E. (2003). Konzepte und Bedingungen des Einsatzes von E-Learning in der betrieblichen Bildung. In E. Nuissl, C. Schiersmann, & H. Siebert (Eds.), *Erfahrungen mit neuen Medien: Literatur- und Forschungsreport Weiterbildung* (Vol. 26, Report 2, pp. 9–20). Bonn, Germany: Deutsches Institut für Erwachsenenbildung.

Salmon, G. (2000). *E-moderating: The key to teaching and learning online.* London, UK: Kogan Page.

14

ONLINE PROFESSIONAL DEVELOPMENT FOR AUSTRALIAN SCIENCE TEACHERS

Developing and Deploying a Curriculum Evaluation Model

Karen Spence, Jennifer Donovan, and P. A. Danaher
University of Southern Queensland

Abstract

A crucial element of enhancing science education and maximizing science literacy is the capacity to implement successful programs of online professional development for science teachers. Despite the recently acknowledged dearth of research about this topic, there is a growing number of in-service programs of varying duration that aim (and claim) to use contemporary information and communication technologies to augment the knowledge and skills of practicing science educators at all educational levels and across educational sectors. The diversity of these programs notwithstanding, their common focus is on assisting science teachers to develop and refine strategies to boost their students' learning outcomes.

This chapter presents the findings of an examination of carefully selected online professional development programs for science teachers, with special but not exclusive focus on those programs offered in Australia. We develop and deploy a curriculum evaluation model applied to two representative online programs, one from Australia and one from the United States. The chapter concludes with some suggested implications for designing and delivering effective online professional development for contemporary science teachers in Australia and internationally.

Traditionally, meetings, seminars, and workshops at the district level and conferences such as the Conference of Science Teachers' Association of Western Australia (CONSTAWA) and the Science Teachers' Association of Queensland (STAQ) at the state level and the Conference of the Australian Science Teachers Association (CONASTA) at the national level have provided professional development for Australian science teachers. Such meetings involve well-intentioned presenters freely sharing science knowledge and innovative teaching ideas, usually to a receptive audience, but evidence is lacking concerning harnessing the transformative power of such techniques in massified school-ing systems, in teaching as a whole (Desimone, 2009) and in science teaching specifically (Wilson, 2013). This is not to say that such meetings should be abandoned; conferences provide important networking opportunities, a chance to be away from the cloister of the classroom and engage with other like-minded teachers. However, in terms of improv-ing science teaching and hence the science learning outcomes of students, success is less certain (Lumpe, Czerniak, Haney, & Beltyukova, 2012). Clearly, different methods of delivering professional development are needed.

Literature Review

Garet, Porter, Desimone, Birman, and Yoon (2001) published the results of a survey of 1,027 mathematics and science teachers, the first to provide empirical evidence of the influence of different characteristics of professional development on teachers' learning. Three core features were found: first, a focus on content knowledge; second, opportuni-ties for active learning; and third, coherence. Within these, three structures were also found to affect teacher learning: the format (e.g., workshop or study group), the col-lective participation of like-minded teachers, and the duration of the activity (sustained professional development being more effective).

Harwell (2003) also concluded that professional development that unfolds over time is more successful than one-off events. She contended that time is needed for teachers to change their beliefs and that they are more likely to do so in a supported social setting. Drawing on many scholarly sources, Harwell described several characteristics of appro-priate professional development, including that it

- is based on sound, current research;
- involves teachers who realize and share the need for change;
- provides strong content focused on addressing identified gaps in student achievement and increasing the breadth and depth of teachers' knowledge;
- focuses on strategies likely to influence student learning that will also enhance teachers' classroom skills;
- keeps up with innovations in education and in specific fields;
- generates and contributes new knowledge to the teaching profession;
- increases the monitoring of student work to provide improved regular feedback to students about their learning;
- is delivered using the same strategies that are considered optimal for the classroom;
- uses familiar contexts in which the information is useful; and
- is communal and provides opportunities for teachers to practice new behaviors in a safe setting with peer feedback.

Harwell (2003) suggested that an optimal strategy is to combine face-to-face meetings with online programs. The face-to-face meetings provide opportunities to expose teach-ers to new information and strategies, while online components provide further informa-tion and asynchronous communication opportunities to discuss how well their adoption of new teaching strategies is proceeding. Harwell made a strong case that teacher professional development needs to change. However, she provided no new empirical evidence that her recommended changes work. Her argument was also not specific to science teachers.

In 2007, Duncan-Howell's dissertation considered the role of online communities of practice in the professional development of teachers (not science teachers specifically). Her collective case study of three online communities of practice of varying size and membership indicated that online communities of practice were valuable, particularly because they are self-sustaining and generate relevant ideas. Their flexibility and freedom from the constraints of time allowed teachers to access them according to need. Participants in Duncan-Howell's (2007) study suggested that ongoing professional development was important, and the finding that the average membership of a community of practice was three years indicated its fulfillment of this perceived need. Participants saw the communities as authentic and worth the average one and a half hours per week that they spent there. Relationships were forged as members participated actively in topics of interest. Most members had over 20 years of teaching experience; they were willing to offer the fruits of that experience to the community, but they also sought to update their own skills through engaging in the community. Participants ranked changing their practices first and improving student learning second as the aims of professional development. The findings of Duncan-Howell's (2007) study supported Harwell's (2003) contention that teachers are unwilling to implement changes suggested by outsiders in one-off sessions, but they are more likely to experiment with changes advocated by peers in a participatory manner. However, the communities of practice do not always provide opportunities for the face-to-face meetings proposed by Harwell (2003).

An attempt to combine face-to-face synchronous communication with an online community of practice without participants having to travel was reported by Marrero, Woodruff, Schuster, and Riccio (2010). Their case study investigated live, online short courses developed with support from the U.S. National Aeronautics and Space Administration (NASA) for science teachers in NASA Explorer Schools within a social constructivist paradigm. The courses were specifically designed to be relevant, provide opportunities for collaboration, contribute to professional growth, and be widely accessible. Research drove the design in terms of the courses' compact length and the critical inclusion of live (synchronous) interaction between instructors and participants. The seven short courses involved four to six hour-long episodes of synchronous communication via teleconference while participants were logged into an online classroom. Follow-up assignments were given for participants to complete between sessions. Courses were designed to develop participants' science content knowledge and their pedagogical content knowledge (PCK); that is, what to teach and how best to teach it.

Marrero and colleagues' (2010) mixed methods study found that teachers viewed the short courses as valuable but were particularly interested in participating in a collaborative community of practice with other teachers, instructors, and scientists. Flexibility and the capacity to receive immediate feedback and responses to questions were seen as strengths. In terms of transformative practice, nearly 80% of the participants reported using what they had learned in their school in the current year, and 96.6% anticipated doing so within the current year. All were interested in taking future short courses. Most preferred live online courses to those that were asynchronous and self-paced. Evidence of relationship formation included the exchange of e-mail addresses between participants and the development of preclass conversation to the point where, at the end of the study, the instructor had to break into the animated chatter to begin the class. The main limitations involved technology issues.

In June 2014, EdSurge (an independent information resource and community for everyone involved in education technology) published its own report on the influence of technology on teachers' learning. Supported by the Gates Foundation, associate editor Christina Quattrocchi, chief executive officer Betsy Corcoran, and others surveyed more than 400 educators and interviewed more than 50 educators to establish their perceptions of what support they liked and needed versus what did not work for them. They then mapped the tools available on the market for professional development, comparing the tools with what the teachers had told them. From this, they developed a simple cyclical framework for professional development. Finally, they profiled 28 tools, describing them in detail and mapping them to their framework. Unfortunately, relatively few of these tools were specific to science teachers. The mapping was intended to assist teachers and administrators to put together a program that covered all stages of professional development, as it was noted that few, if any, programs covered all aspects. A wide range of pricing was found, from free information to packages that could cost a district hundreds of thousands of U.S. dollars.

Developing a Model and Evaluating Packages

We considered the insights obtained in all of these studies. Although some were not specifically about science teachers and teaching, the generalized findings seemed applicable to that discipline. We sought to combine the findings into one model (see Figure 14.1) against which online professional development packages for science teachers could be mapped and evaluated.

We call this framework the 4Cs model of curriculum evaluation, given its focus on the four iterative and interdependent overall categories of high-quality curriculum packages. To be successful, packages must be content-rich, cooperative, coherent, and contextual. Each of these categories is associated directly with a set of accompanying criteria that can be used to evaluate a package's quality in relation to each selected criterion. These categories and criteria are distilled from, and align with, the contemporary scholarship in science education and online professional development, some of which was highlighted earlier in this chapter.

We reasoned that most science teachers would simply use a common search engine to locate online science professional development, so this was how we selected packages for evaluation. We intended to survey several online packages in detail to evaluate them against the model. However, it rapidly became apparent that most of the packages were extremely limited and addressed only small sections of the model. This in itself was useful information, in that it supported the claim from EdSurge (2014) that no one package addressed all aspects. Therefore, we assessed only two packages in detail: one from Australia from the Australian Science Teachers Association (ASTA) called "ASTA Online Professional Learning" (moodle.asta.edu.au/course/index.php?categoryid=3), and one from the United States called "Annenberg Learner" (www.learner.org). We chose

Figure 14.1 The 4Cs model for evaluating online professional development packages for science teachers.

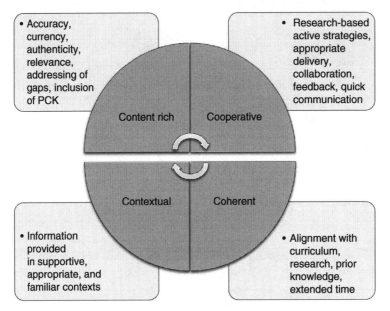

to use the Australian term *primary* when referring to the Australian materials and the American equivalent *elementary* when referring to the American materials. The evaluation of these two packages in relation to the model is presented in Table 14.1.

Table 14.1 indicates that neither package satisfied the model for exemplary professional development. Annenberg Learner would suit teachers in the United States reasonably well, but the materials are not directly relevant to Australian contexts, particularly in biology. All the ASTA materials were expected to be Australian, but materials from the United States were included, so again there is a contextual problem. Both packages contain variable materials; thus, although some parts are very good, others contain errors, lack relevance, or are outdated.

Each package is now described in more detail to elaborate why they did not satisfy the overall categories and the associated criteria in the model. The first and second authors responsible for evaluating the packages are both science educators. Some general comments are followed by specific comments. Karen Spence examined the physical science and the earth and space science components of each package, whereas Jenny Donovan examined the biological science and the chemical science components of each one.

The ASTA Package

ASTA is an association geared toward science teachers; as Australian science educators, we were predisposed to like this package and keen to evaluate it. ASTA requires teachers to create a free account and log in. This was a simple procedure, and the home page was easy to navigate. On first glance, it appeared to be a full package, with the requirement to enroll in each course. However, once that was achieved, the highly variable nature of the courses for primary and middle years schooling became apparent. Some, such as

TABLE 14.1

Applying the 4Cs Model to Evaluate Two Online Professional Development Packages for Science Teachers

Overall Category	Criterion	Australian Science Teachers Association	Annenberg
Content rich	Up to date and accurate	Okay, some minor errors	Okay, some minor errors
	Increases breadth and depth of teachers' science knowledge	Highly variable, some parts yes	Variable, some parts very detailed
	Utilizes familiar contexts	Some yes, but some not Australian	Yes for United States
	Authentic	Patchy	Patchy
	Relevant	Patchy	Patchy
	Addresses identified gaps	Not targeted	Very specific
	Focuses on how students learn	Patchy	Yes
	Provides immediate answers to teachers' questions	No, forums asynchronous	No, interactive workshops no longer open
	Balances teachers' science content knowledge and their science pedagogical content knowledge	No; also poor balance between science content strands in primary	Somewhat; each module attempts to address essential content knowledge and how to teach it
	Contributes new knowledge	No	Yes
	Encourages more monitoring of student work	Not in most materials	Not always
Cooperative	Innovative research-based strategies	In a few parts	In a few parts
	Strategies likely to enhance student learning	In a few parts	In a few parts
	Delivered using similar desirable strategies (do as I do)	No, mostly passive	No, mostly passive
	Minimum of passive tools (e.g., video)	No, mostly passive	No, mostly passive
	Observing others and being observed	Not mentioned	Mentioned
	Communal planning to implement new ideas	Not mentioned	Mentioned
	Opportunities to review student work	Not mentioned	Not mentioned
	Opportunities to present, lead, and write	Not mentioned	Not mentioned

(Continues)

TABLE 14.1 (*Continued*)

Overall Category	Criterion	Australian Science Teachers Association	Annenberg
Cooperative	Allows teachers to practice new behaviors in safe setting	Not mentioned	Mentioned
	Opportunities to receive peer feedback	Not mentioned	Not mentioned
	Opportunities to share expertise	Not mentioned	Not mentioned
	Synchronous communication preferable	No, forums are asynchronous	No
	Opportunities for communal learning	Some, but no sign of forum activity	Somewhat
	Fosters sustained collaboration in a community of practice	Provides forums	Somewhat
Coherent	Aligned with curriculum	Some with Australian curriculum but some materials from United States	Mostly with United States
	Aligned with quasi curriculum (e.g., textbooks)	Not obvious	Aligned with videos
	Aligned with research	Not obvious	Yes
	Builds on teachers' prior knowledge	May do	Possibly
	Provides a connected program	Definitely not	Somewhat
	Allows for advanced follow-up work	Not obvious	Somewhat
	Occurs over extended time periods	Yes, if you work through it all	Yes, if all units are covered
	Fosters lasting professional relationships	Unlikely	Possibly
Contextual	Supported by leaders and administrators	Depends on school	Depends on school
	Shared sense of need for change	Depends on teachers	Depends on teachers
	Aligned with research on learning	Not obvious	Yes
	Supportive of communal learning	Not obvious	Somewhat
	Encourages contextual teaching	Patchy	Somewhat
	May combine modes such as face-to-face, synchronous online, and asynchronous online resources	No, online only	Self-paced and online

Aboriginal Astronomy, were very scanty; some were cluttered and difficult to navigate. Others consisted solely of links to other projects, some of which were outside Australia, and some of these had fees for full access. Some links did not work, and some had document formats that did not open in Windows. Many images lacked citations, and some were irrelevant to the content.

The package's use of the term *course* and its use of Moodle as a platform set up our expectations that the resources would be packaged similarly to those in an online university course. We expected a suggested starting point and a pathway to follow, a variety of connected activities of increasing complexity, and an appropriate resolution. Most of the ASTA courses bore no resemblance to this. Instead, they were a jumble of items sourced from Creative Commons with little or no connectedness. Some, but not all, courses included science content and science PCK, and there was a video library on science teaching. Each course appeared to have an associated forum, but we saw minimal signs of activity. We received a welcome e-mail upon creation of the teacher account, but that was the only acknowledgment of our existence.

In general, the middle years' schooling materials were better because of the comprehensive resources added by one teacher, Mike McGarry. These were aligned to the *Australian Curriculum: Science* (Australian Curriculum, Assessment and Reporting Authority, n.d.) and made available for teachers to use with students in class, either with computers or printed and completed in hard copy. Our main criticism was that there were no answers provided for novice teachers. There were three courses for biology, four for chemistry, three for physics, one for earth and space science, and two integrated courses on sustainability (energy) and climate change but very little on science inquiry skills (data logging). No courses focused on the history of science or the nature of science.

Spence's Experience

The ASTA package covered the physical sciences with two courses for primary schooling that addressed the key concepts for electricity and the transfer of heat. However, the material was originally written for the Minnesota state curriculum and obtained under Creative Commons. A Shocking Adventure was developed for Year 4 students but did not connect with Electrical Interactions for middle school. The content of A Shocking Adventure covered insulators, conductors, series and parallel circuits, electromagnetism, generating heat, and the work of scientists in the area of electricity. The content of The Transfer of Heat was basic but covered the key concepts effectively for conduction, convection, and radiation and provided answers. Unfortunately, the modules contained some spelling errors, the content was repetitive, the glossary did not contain any entries, the Moodle tasks were irrelevant, and the pictures did not relate to the topic of electricity. The modules presented information from external sources, but many of these web links were broken or required redirection because it was not possible to access the demonstrations and activities.

Donovan's Experience

The first thing that I noticed was a lack of balance among the science disciplines. In the primary school materials, there were four courses for biology but only one for chemistry. The context chosen for the chemistry course, Science With Cinnamon, is unlikely to be familiar to many teachers. This could be seen as a positive, something new and different and yet easily available, but it could also be seen as a negative in that beginning teachers may find it difficult to extract the chemical principles from the activity to apply to other contexts. Four primary school courses targeted Science as a Human Endeavour, but only one targeted the Science Inquiry Skills as a curricular component, and two targeted the Nature of Science component. There was very little on the History of Science, but two courses tackled socio-scientific issues (Habitat Heroes and Year of Forests). Some attempted integration across disciplines, with the course titled Water Science being the most comprehensive by far.

Overall, the scientific and spelling accuracy of the biology and chemistry materials were satisfactory, but teachers could not rely on these materials to educate themselves sufficiently to teach these disciplines. Yet, with staffing situations in many Australian schools, we know that many primary school teachers lack background science knowledge. In the middle years, nonspecialist science teachers often have to teach some science. They need a more coherent and comprehensive package of materials than those currently provided by ASTA.

The Annenberg Learner Package

This package has a strong reputation, so we were curious to compare it to the Australian package. Annenberg Learner is ostensibly free but only if teachers have access to a substantial Internet account, as some of the view-on-demand video downloads are huge. DVDs were offered for sale but not outside the United States; therefore, Australian teachers must download everything that they want. Related print materials are available from publishers at variable costs. If teachers want to use the materials directly with students in a course (e.g., showing videos), a digital site license of $500 per series allows three years of usage. It was unclear whether such a license could be purchased from outside the United States.

Overall, this site was comprehensive, but some materials, although they were considered classics, were outdated and should be labeled as such. An example was A Private Universe, which dated from 1985 to 1994. The site was set out in strands and year levels and offered video series and lesson plans for most discipline areas. It claimed to be based on research on effective strategies; to connect to U.S. standards (it seemed to do this well); to provide examples in real classrooms through the videos and through linked websites; and to provide online texts, course and workshop guides, and background information. Lesson plans (resources), learner express modules (short videos on earth and space science), and 87 "interactives" sorted by grade were available. It took some time and persistence to navigate and locate all this information. However, lesson "plans" were brief general descriptions of how a teacher used the activity rather than detailed descriptions of how to conduct the activity with lists of materials, risk assessments, complete instructions, and indicative timing. It was difficult to see their relevance: They lacked sufficient detail for beginning teachers, and more experienced teachers would not generate worthwhile extra information from them.

There were about twice as many science content courses as those that focused on science PCK. However, 10 courses were aimed at high school students, college students, and adults, which was not our purview in this evaluation. There were only seven elementary or K–6 courses, and four listed as K–8. Five were listed as K–12, and one (A Private Universe) as listed as 5–12. Ultimately, this meant that the package was limited for elementary school teachers who needed to improve their background knowledge or for middle school teachers from other disciplines who had been asked to teach science.

Spence's Annenberg Package Experience

The Annenberg package covered the range of topics that would be required for Australian teachers to gain a depth of understanding for physics and earth and space sciences. Physics for the 21st Century was interesting and provided a contemporary approach to teaching traditional concepts: forces and motion, energy, and light. Unfortunately, especially for the beginning teacher, the section on light confused reflection and refraction. The earth and space sciences contained essential content knowledge for teachers, and some material was integrated with environmental science, such as the unit titled Habitable Planet. Most courses were usually based on approximately eight self-paced workshops. The Private Universe Project in Science was based on videos and discussion topics in a workshop format, but feedback on these workshops is now closed.

Donovan's Annenberg Package Experience

Biology and chemistry topic choices lacked expected topics such as cells, animal and plant classification, diversity, and atomic-molecular theory, yet there was one course on the brain, there was another on neuroscience, and atmospheric pollution was included as chemistry. The topics would not provide a balanced program for Australian teachers.

To evaluate the timeliness and accuracy of the science, I focused on my specialist area, DNA. I found the interactive outdated in that the package initially focused on past concepts of "one gene–one trait" (Mendel's work) and the notion of dominant and recessive forms of genes (alleles). Most traits are now known to be polygenic (the work of several genes), and some geneticists have called for the dominant–recessive dichotomy to be abandoned, as the reality is a more subtle interplay between alleles (e.g., Allchin, 2002; Dobyns, 2006). This interactive package perpetuated the myth that only two different alleles exist for each gene; this was particularly problematic given that the selected example was cystic fibrosis (CF). Presently, over 1,500 different alleles are known to bring about symptoms of CF, although each person has only two of these alleles. The interactive also used the terminology of *genes for* diseases such as CF and red-green color blindness. This was sloppy use of language, often seen in the mass media (Donovan & Venville, 2014). Causing disease is not the reason why we have a gene; genes are present to direct necessary functions. Disease results when faulty alleles yield a gene product incapable of correctly directing the intended function. The interactive mentioned a damaged copy of a gene without explanation.

Other misrepresentations and errors were found; for example, bacteria were confused with bugs. Many terms on diagrams, such as *histones*, *telomeres*, and *chromosomes*, were not explained. Concepts were presented in inappropriate sequences; for example, copying the DNA code, an essential step in the process of making proteins, was described before explaining what a protein is and why cells would need to make proteins. In all, the information perpetuated myths found in many textbooks and would not facilitate understanding, particularly by a naïve reader. Given that the study of DNA is a contemporary field, subject to considerable interest and research, I found this treatment of this exciting topic very disappointing.

Other packages considered selectively included the following:

- *The Australian Commonwealth Scientific and Industrial Research Organisation:* This site offers several programs, only limited elements of which are online. Programs include "Scientists in Schools," specialist assistance for registered Carbonkids schools, astronomy workshops (only face-to-face), and CREativity in Science and Technology (CREST) (support for teachers facilitating open inquiry investigations by their students). Of these, "Scientists in Schools" fosters ongoing face-to-face and e-mail relationships between the school and its scientists.
- *Science Teachers' Association of Queensland:* This site offers webinars. Currently, one webinar is offered for Year 7 science each term, each lasting about 90 minutes. Participants are e-mailed details of required resources one week prior. Each session includes a model investigation and aims to expose common misconceptions. The sessions are aligned with the four Science Understanding content subtopics (biological science, chemical science, physical science, and earth and space science) from *Australian Curriculum: Science* (Australian Curriculum, Assessment and Reporting Authority, n.d.). The cost for all four sessions is $116 AUD for member teachers and $195 AUD for nonmember teachers, which includes a digital membership.
- *Primary Teachers' Network, New South Wales:* This site offers free access to resources specifically for primary school teachers from New South Wales, but resources are available only through an interactive whiteboard. This may limit access for teachers in rural and remote areas.
- *Pearson Australia:* Although online is mentioned, most information appears to refer to one-day, face-to-face workshops on a variety of topics, with relatively little science. Webinars offered are very expensive ($199 AUD + GST [tax] each, or $499 AUD + GST for three).
- *Steve Spangler Science (United States):* In comparison with the fees for other packages, a registration fee of $199 USD for 30 ready-to-use, inquiry-based science activities seems reasonable. These activities use high-definition video, interactive learning prompts, handouts, and assessments; cover safety requirements; and integrate elements in popular children's literature. Certificates of completion are supplied.
- *Association for Supervision and Curriculum Development:* This organization claims to be the global leader in developing and delivering innovative programs, comprising 125,000 members from 138 countries. Despite that, its online offerings include only one science content and literacy course and one on science, technology, engineering, and mathematics (STEM) careers.

None of these packages offered teachers a coherent program or opportunities to engage in meaningful collaboration. Some had minimal science content, others did not have sufficient science PCK, and many relied on the passive viewing of videos. Collectively, they were so far removed from the model that they did not merit further evaluation.

Discussion

In this chapter, a model for evaluating online professional development packages for science teachers was developed by distilling overall categories and associated criteria identified from the literature. Two apparently comprehensive professional development packages, one from Australia and the other from the United States, were mapped against the model. The package from the United States, Annenberg Learner, outperformed the Australian package, ASTA Online Professional Learning, from ASTA, but neither satisfactorily aligned with the model.

Significant issues were lack of coherence, outdated and inaccurate science content, imbalances in the choice of topics, high reliance on passive delivery strategies, and limited fostering of teacher discussion and participation to enhance teachers' learning. An appropriate package would have to address all of these issues. Examples in the literature, such as the short courses examined by Marrero and colleagues (2010), indicated that professional development packages closer to meeting the requirements of the model have been achieved, although in a relatively limited capacity.

The proliferation of packages forming a piecemeal professional development landscape is not unexpected. When new technologies develop, many permutations of applications are trialed (Taylor & Taylor, 2012). Eventually, it is likely that the most successful applications will win through and that the variety will fall away. It is hoped that success will be measured in accordance with the research about what makes professional development work for teachers, so the end result will be an approach that better reflects our model.

It is important to note that this chapter does not reflect *all* the professional development available to Australian science teachers. Pioneering work by eminent educators such as professors Mark Hackling and Denis Goodrum brought "Primary Investigations," later redeveloped into "Primary Connections," and more recently "Science by Doing for Years 7–10" into Australian schools. However, at the time we wrote this chapter, these packages were not yet fully offered online, and we did not evaluate them. They have since been placed online (www.sciencebydoing.edu.au). Based on their previous hard-copy resources, it is likely that they will be the closest yet to satisfying the requirements of our model.

Conclusion

Science teachers need access to quality professional development, and in the contemporary world, using the online environment appears to be an obvious solution to the constraints of time, costs, and distance. However, at present, the packages available lack the essential qualities of coherence, targeted content, and strategies that promote contextual learning and foster cooperation among participants. These and other key features from the literature were encapsulated in the 4Cs model to facilitate the mapping and evaluation of professional development packages. We hope that future packages, such as the transition of "Science by Doing" to an online environment, will be more successful in meeting the needs of Australian science teachers and those in other countries as well.

References

Allchin, D. (2002). Dissolving dominance. In L. S. Parker & R. A. Ankeny (Eds.), *Mutating concepts, evolving disciplines: Genetics, medicine, and society* (pp. 43–61). Dordrecht, the Netherlands: Kluwer.

Australian Curriculum, Assessment and Reporting Authority. (n.d.). *Australian curriculum: Science* (v.7.2). Sydney, Australia: Author. Retrieved from www.australiancurriculum.edu.au/science/curriculum/f-10?layout=1

Desimone, L. M. (2009). Improving impact studies of teachers' professional development: Toward better conceptualizations and measures. *Educational Researcher, 38*(3), 181–199.

Dobyns, W. B. (2006). The pattern of inheritance of X-linked traits is not dominant or recessive, just X-linked. *Acta Pediatrica Supplement, 95*(S451), 11–15.

Donovan, J., & Venville, G. (2014). Blood and bones: The influence of the mass media on Australian primary school children's understandings of genes and DNA. *Science and Education, 23*(2), 325–360.

Duncan-Howell, J. (2007). *Online communities of practice and their role in the professional development of teachers* (Unpublished doctoral dissertation). Queensland University of Technology, Brisbane, Australia.

EdSurge. (2014, June). *How teachers are learning: Professional development remix: An in-depth report on the tools advancing teacher training.* Retrieved from d3e7x39d4i7wbe.cloudfront.net/uploads/report/pdf_free/6/PD-Remix-EdSurge-Report-2014.pdf

Garet, M. S., Porter, A. C., Desimone, L., Birman, B. F., & Yoon, K. S. (2001). What makes professional development effective? Results from a national sample of teachers. *American Educational Research Journal, 38*(4), 915–945.

Harwell, S. H. (2003). *Teacher professional development: It's not an event, it's a process.* Waco, TX: Center of Occupational Research and Development. Retrieved from www.cord.org/uploaded-files/harwellpaper.pdf

Lumpe, A., Czerniak, C., Haney, J., & Beltyukova, S. (2012). Beliefs about teaching science: The relationship between elementary teachers' participation in professional development and student achievement. *International Journal of Science Education, 34*(2), 153–166.

Marrero, M. E., Woodruff, K. A., Schuster, G. S., & Riccio, J. F. (2010). Live, online short-courses: A case study of innovative teacher professional development. *The International Review of Research in Open and Distance Learning, 11*(1), 1–8. Retrieved from www.irrodl.org/index.php/irrodl/article/view/758/1485

Taylor, M., & Taylor, A. (2012). The technology life cycle: Conceptualization and managerial implications. *International Journal of Production Economics, 140*(1), 541–553.

Wilson, S. M. (2013). Professional development for science teachers. *Science, 340*(6130), 310–313.

PART THREE

Summary and Future Trends

THE FUTURE STARTS TODAY

Dietmar K. Kennepohl
Athabasca University

We explore a tremendous amount of technology and science education in this book. It was Marshall McLuhan (1994, pp. 7–21) who famously noted, "The medium is the message." Indeed, that rich interplay between medium (technology) and message (learning) is well-known to science educators as they consider new technology-based methods of learning science (Dede & Barab, 2009). This technology–pedagogy interaction and integration is illustrated throughout this book. For example, in the chapters such as chapter 10 "Situated Science Learning for Higher Level Learning With Mobile Devices" and chapter 12 "Enabling Remote Activity: Widening Participation in Field Study Courses," we see how the technology of mobile devices has not only led to mobile learning in the class and situated learning in the field but also greatly reinforced vehicles for learning and outreach like citizen science. That implicit integration means we are continuously reinventing how we teach and learn. How we cope with and utilize those methods and those technologies is more important than ever. Change does appear to be the new constant in science education, but there are a few important pieces to keep an eye on for the near future. We complete our journey with a quick look at what is on the horizon.

Learning Analytics (Big Data and Personalized Learning)

We live in the age of information and are swimming in progressively larger pools of data. IBM estimates 90% of all the data in the world was created in the past two years, and as of 2014 we generated about 2.5 quintillion (2.5 × 10^{30}) bytes of new data every day (www-01.ibm.com/software/data/bigdata/what-is-big-data.html). Many scientists have already encountered large data sets in their research, but "big data" is also common in areas such as business, finance, security, and communications. As students carry out more of their learning in a digital environment, it is possible to track and analyze their activities and progress with the intention of informing decisions made by both learner and teacher (Siemens & Long, 2011). It may sound like Big Brother, but in the right hands, "learning analytics" can provide us direct insight into student choice, preference, and performance in a course without having to rely on proxy measures such as course satisfaction surveys, which mostly measure student perceptions. We already encountered learning analytics in chapter 6 "Practical Biology at a Distance: How Far Can We Go With Online Distance Learning?" and chapter 2 "Teaching Undergraduate Chemistry by Distance and Online: Lessons From the Front Line." At the moment, analysis is

225

mostly being used in a simple manual batch process to improve courses, identify students at risk, and determine preferred learning styles. However, some educators are looking at more automated and continuous processes with the goal of eventually developing courses that can literally adapt to students and provide a personalized learning environment (El-Bishouty, Saito, Chang, & Graf, 2015).

Open Educational Resources

The idea of science for all has reappeared several times throughout the past century of educational history in terms of augmenting science literacy and inspiring science curriculum reform (American Association for the Advancement of Science, 1989; Fensham, 1985; Smith, 2006; Uzzell, 1978). In its most recent configuration, the goal of open and universal access has undoubtedly been enhanced by new technologies and distance education. Leading that movement have been open educational resources (OERs), which offer an entirely new business model that is more collegial and affordable (Butcher & Hoosen, 2012). This model encourages resource sharing by permitting free access, use, adaptation, and redistribution of a wide variety of teaching, learning, and research materials. This may range from small discrete resources (reusable learning objects) such as a video, a test, or an applet to individual learning modules or even entire courses (open courseware). The two professional development courses reviewed for science educators in chapter 14 "Online Professional Development for Australian Science Teachers: Developing and Deploying a Curriculum Evaluation Model" are ostensibly free. We offer a brief word of caution for those considering using OERs. As with anything openly available on the Internet, the quality can vary greatly, so we advise discretion in selecting these resources. If we maintain that critical eye for quality, OERs can be especially useful for science-related disciplines, as buying or creating the needed resources can be very costly. Furthermore, OERs are ideal because of the universality and portability of scientific principles. The law of conservation of energy works just the same in Australia as it does in Zimbabwe, so you need not adjust the context and content of OERs based on political borders. We saw several examples in this book where authors employed OERs "as is" in their own teaching. Finally, OERs seem a natural fit with scientists, because the science culture of collaboration and pooling knowledge is fairly strong. We see this in areas such as sharing access to remote laboratories, discussed earlier in chapter 9 "Remote Access Laboratory Equipment for Undergraduate Science Education," and in the many emerging escience- (Bohle, 2013) and cyberinfrastructure-enhanced (National Science Foundation, 2012) science initiatives around the globe where huge data sets are generated, shared, and reused. Lately, a special subset of OERs has been in the college and university limelight and is worth a special note, namely, an entire course called a massive open online course (MOOC), which comprises thousands of students.

MOOCs

The hype around MOOCs in higher education has been incredible. Both the promise of open knowledge and free education for all and the threat of replacing faculty, and perhaps even entire institutions of learning, have generated controversy and active discussion (Waldrop & *Nature* Magazine, 2013). Those educators who have already been operating in the open distance learning (ODL) environment for some time and who have already realized the strong social mandate and the advantages accessibility and flexibility can bring learners are baffled, if not downright annoyed, by the sudden repackaging and marketing propaganda surrounding MOOCs. From an ODL perspective, MOOCs are not all that novel and certainly not as good (or bad) as some of the publicity they have received. We introduced MOOCs in our foundational chapter 3 "Developing Online Earth Science Courses" and chapter 1 "The Basics of Getting Biology Courses Online," as well as later in chapter 11 "Online Delivery of Field- and Laboratory-Based Environmental and Earth Sciences Curriculum." Haggard (2013) also provided an excellent overview of MOOCs, including their potential value, the search for business models, and the perspectives of both teachers and learners. Is this the next disruptive technology or just a natural extension of technologies that already exist? Whether you feel that the open online approach of MOOCs is revolutionary or not, it does pose an interesting and very important question regarding the role of the professor: In a world of ubiquitous knowledge, what added value do we provide as educators? Indeed, forcing this question on a generation of teachers may end up being MOOCs' biggest contribution to higher education.

Connectivism and Role of the Teacher

In 2005, George Siemens and Stephen Downes were at the heart of a new perspective on education that revolved around distributed knowledge with their idea of *connectivism* (Kop & Hill, 2008). Three years later, the first MOOC emerged, led by the two. It was titled Connectivism and Connective Knowledge (CCK08) and housed at the University of Manitoba. At its heart, connectivism sees knowledge as distributed over a network of connection points of information or "nodes," such as images, websites, individuals, data, communities, and so on. Learning then occurs as one links to those nodes and traverses that network (Downes, 2007). Some see connectivism as a new learning theory for a digital age of MOOCs and "onlinedness," whereas others are more critical and do not see it as a separate learning theory (Kop & Hill, 2008).

Educators have always been looking to find if there are preferred or better ways to learn. Over the years, this has generated a tremendous amount of research and innumerable learning theories. Some of the more recognizable theory groupings or paradigms include behaviorism, cognitivism, and constructivism (Schunk, 2012). In general, science educators tend to have a constructivist outlook. Bailey and Garratt (2002) provided an exceptional review of the theoretical underpinnings and their applications in chemical education, which is also a manageable introduction to learning theories that would be appreciated by any science educator. With a longer term view, one can see there are trends and fads in how learning is viewed and explained. Each new theory (or even paradigm) brings with it more insight. In that light, one should resist the temptation to see the latest theory as replacing all that has gone before. Connectivism speaks to our network digital world and underscores the idea of student-centered learning. The learner is autonomous and manages his or her own learning. So, where is the teacher in all this?

In the connectivist model, the teacher function is distributed over the network of nodes. Students are connecting with more than content; they are also meant to find and link with teachers, mentors, peers, and communities. It can work in a practical sense, but it requires fundamental experience and skills on the learners' part to be their own guide. A graduate student or senior undergraduate student would have a greater chance of success in this autonomous environment than the novice undergraduate. It is precisely here that the role of the teacher (and the institution) is so important and adds value by initially being that guide for learners and then also providing learners the necessary skills to effectively navigate a sea of knowledge.

Learning Outcomes, Assessment, and Prior Learning and Assessment

Although not the main theme of this book, readers should be aware of the role of learning outcomes, assessment, and perhaps also prior learning assessment and recognition (PLAR) in the design of their distance or online materials. With increased student mobility among institutions, open access to knowledge (including nonformal and informal learning), and increased institutional accountability, learning outcomes have become an integral part of the global trend in higher education reform. They are employed in the following interconnected areas: (a) quality assurance, (b) teaching and learning, and (c) transfer credit. There is a great deal in the literature around the learning outcomes and assessment cycle, including several helpful summaries and reviews (Nicholson, 2011; Tremblay, Lalancette, & Roseveare, 2012). We were introduced to the importance of learning outcomes in chapter 5 "Science Online: Bringing the Laboratory Home," whereas the role of assessment was mentioned in chapters 4 and 7 on physics, "Physics Teaching in Distance Education" and "Assessment in Physics Distance Education: Practical Lessons at Athabasca University." However, the importance of learning outcomes and their assessment in a multijurisdictional initiative was underscored in chapter 13 "Collaborative E-Learning in Pharmacy: Design, Evaluation, and Outcomes of a European Cross-Border Project." Not too far away on the horizon is PLAR, which is becoming more important as students seek recognition of their nontraditional routes to learning (Conrad, 2014). It is interesting to note that for most university graduates—including the science majors—science knowledge comes from outside the classroom (informal sources). Think of your own science knowledge, especially outside your scientific discipline—what did you learn formally at university and what did you pick up from informal sources such as museums, books, popular science magazines, conferences, television programs, and discussions with colleagues? PLAR raises two key points in our discussion. First, learning can and does take place outside the classroom. Second, because informal and nonformal learning do not possess the traditional educational "input" measures (e.g., textbook, course outline, contact hours), they must rely almost exclusively on learning outcomes and their assessment. So, as we consider new technologies and new approaches to learning in our own teaching, it is important that we continue to be aware of that full spectrum of learning (both inside and outside the classroom) and what that means in higher education in the twenty-first century.

Neuroscience

Popular science fiction may assert that space is the final frontier, but many believe it is very much closer to home, namely, the human brain. The intrigue is more than trying to understand the biological structure and function of the brain but also looking at the more psychological or metaphysical and philosophical questions such as, "What is a thought?"; "How is a thought created?"; "Is it spontaneous or willed?" As educators, we would be mostly interested in knowing how the brain learns and how our approach to teaching might take advantage of that. To be fair, the discipline of education has already been doing this for many years and has drawn heavily on other academic disciplines, including philosophy, psychology, biology, cognitive science, and sociology, to name a few. Along the way we have discovered characteristics of the brain that are useful for teaching. For example, too much information can lead to cognitive overload and ineffective learning (Sweller, Ayres, & Kalyuga, 2011), so for online design, one has to deal with issues such as inattentional blindness, attention capture, and selective amnesia (Rodrigues, 2011). On the positive side, there is a strong and established connection between play and learning (Kolb & Kolb, 2010), which has been leveraged in visualizations, gaming, and simulations, as we saw in chapter 8 "Computer-Based Laboratory Simulations for the New Digital Learning Environments." Despite this, our current knowledge about the human brain is still very rudimentary. However, two mega initiatives have been announced that might change all that. In January 2013, the Human Brain Project (funded by the European Union) was launched, with the aim to simulate the complete human brain on supercomputers to better understand how it functions (www.humanbrainproject.eu). The United States (April 2013) announced the Brain Research through Advancing Innovative Neurotechnologies (BRAIN) Initiative (or Brain Activity Map Project) that will map the activity of every neuron in the human brain (www.braininitiative.nih.gov/index .htm). Together, these multimillion dollar science projects have the potential to give us new insights in the next decade into how the human brain functions, including how we learn.

Teaching and building effective learning environments in the sciences are different from doing so in many other disciplines and can be challenging. This is especially true when online and at a distance. You are dealing with not only new technologies and rapid change of expectations from students and administrators, but also serious logistical considerations to contend with if there is a practical laboratory component. All the while you are trying to encourage and grow in students the genuine scientific methodology and culture needed within your own discipline. Throughout the pages of this book, we saw many examples of experienced science educators successfully exploring new approaches to teaching and learning. They inspire us to create learning environments that focus on activities rather than content, and they guide and engage self-directed learners so they can effectively access, understand, and use information they encounter—not just memorize it. It is really an exciting time for science education. Yes, there is a lot of chaos and work involved, but there is also opportunity to do more than we have ever done before. We just need to get going. Remember, the future doesn't start tomorrow—it starts today!

References

American Association for the Advancement of Science. (1989). *Science for all Americans: A project 2061 report on literacy goals in science, mathematics, and technology.* Washington, DC: Author.

Bailey, P. D., & Garratt, J. (2002). Chemical education: Theory and practice. *University Chemistry Education, 6*(2), 39–57.

Bohle, S. (2013). What is e-science and how should it be managed? *Spektrum der Wissenschaft (Scientific American) and Nature.com.* Retrieved from www.scilogs.com/scientific_and_medical_libraries/what-is-e-science-and-how-should-it-be-managed/

Butcher, N., & Hoosen, S. (2012). *Exploring the business case for open educational resources.* Retrieved from www.col.org/resources/exploring-business-case-open-educational-resources

Conrad, D. (2014). RPL in higher education: Past, present, and potential. In J. Harris, C. Wihak, & J. Van Kleef (Eds.), *Handbook of RPL: Research into practice.* Leicester, UK: National Institute of Adult Continuing Education.

Dede, C., & Barab, S. (2009). Emerging technologies for learning science: A time of rapid advances. *Journal of Science Education and Technology, 18*(4), 301–304.

Downes, S. (2007). What connectivism is [Web log]. Retrieved from halfanhour.blogspot.com/2007/02/what-connectivism-is.html

El-Bishouty, M. M., Saito, K., Chang, T., & Graf, S. (2015). Teaching improvement technologies for adaptive and personalized learning environments. In Kinshuk & R. Huang (Eds.), *Ubiquitous learning environments and technologies* (pp. 225–242). Berlin, Germany: Springer-Verlag.

Fensham, P. J. (1985). Science for all: A reflective essay. *Journal of Curriculum Studies, 17*(4), 415–435.

Haggard, S. (2013, September). *The maturing of the MOOC: Literature review of massive open online courses and other forms of online distance learning* (BIS Research Paper No. 130). London, UK: Department for Business, Innovation and Skills. Retrieved from www.gov.uk/government/uploads/system/uploads/attachment_data/file/240193/13-1173-maturing-of-the-mooc.pdf

Kolb, A. Y., & Kolb, D. A. (2010). Learning to play, playing to learn: A case study of a *ludic* learning space. *Journal of Organizational Change Management, 23*(1), 26–50.

Kop, R., & Hill, A. (2008). Connectivism: Learning theory of the future or vestige of the past? *The International Review of Research in Open and Distance Learning, 9*(3), 1–12.

McLuhan, M. (1994). *Understanding media: The extensions of man.* Cambridge, MA: MIT Press.

National Science Foundation. (2012). *A vision and strategy for software for science, engineering, and education: Cyberinfrastructure framework for the 21st century* (Doc. No. nsf12113). Retrieved from www.nsf.gov/pubs/2012/nsf12113/nsf12113.pdf

Nicholson, K. (2011). *Quality assurance in higher education: A review of the literature.* Retrieved from cll.mcmaster.ca/COU/pdf/Quality%20Assurance%20Literature%20Review.pdf

Rodrigues, S. (2011). Using chemistry simulations: Attention capture, selective amnesia and inattentional blindness. *Chemistry Education Research and Practice, 12*(1), 40–46.

Schunk, D. H. (2012). *Learning theories: An educational perspective* (6th ed.). Upper Saddle River, NJ: Pearson Education.

Siemens, G., & Long, P. (2011). Penetrating the fog: Analytics in learning and education. *EDUCAUSE Review, 46*(5). Retrieved from net.educause.edu/ir/library/pdf/ERM1151.pdf

Smith, D. V. (2006). *Scientists are also citizens: Science curriculum from the perspective of the new contractualism* (Unpublished EdD thesis). Monash University, Clayton Campus, Melbourne.

Sweller, J., Ayres, P., & Kalyuga, S. (2011). *Cognitive load theory.* New York, NY: Springer.

Tremblay, K., Lalancette, D., & Roseveare, D. (2012). *Assessment of higher education learning outcomes AHELO feasibility study report: Volume 1—Design and implementation* (pp. 15–38). Retrieved from www.oecd.org/edu/skills-beyond-school/AHELOFSReportVolume1.pdf

Uzzell, P. (1978). The changing aims of science teaching. *School Science Review, 60*(210), 7–20.

Waldrop, M. M., & *Nature* Magazine. (2013, March 13). Massive open online courses, aka MOOCs, transform higher education and science. *Scientific American.* Retrieved from www .scientificamerican.com/article/massive-open-online-courses-transform-higher-education-and-science/

APPENDIX A: ONLINE VERSUS FACE-TO-FACE APPROACHES FOR VARIOUS LEARNING ACTIVITIES

Learning Activity	Comments	
	Online	Face-to-Face (F2F)
Examination	Digitized, so it can potentially automate some grading and keep records. Remote invigilation is just developing and not trusted everywhere.	Handwritten in-person invigilation is most universally accepted. In-person invigilation of online work is a good emerging option.
Reading	It is device dependent and usually not appealing for longer text. It is an excellent option for changing or continually updated pieces.	Print has good resolution, access, and portability. Information is fixed, and if several sources or larger volumes are needed, it can be a physical challenge.
Assignment or laboratory report	This could potentially automate grading and feedback of digital submissions. An assignment drop box system could track progress and keep records.	Print submissions mean manually handling all work in the grading process.
Practice examination	Sample exams are similar to print ones, but they can also offer more interactive and varying formats. They are easier to obtain than similar course exams from elsewhere.	Sample printed course exams are easily accessed for independent work. Printed sample exams from other institutions are more difficult to obtain.
Lecture	Longer video lectures (live or recorded) are usually not engaging. For recordings, smaller modules that are indexed and searchable are useful. Students can control what and how often something is viewed.	Longer lectures are usually not engaging and often require a strong personality and varying the presentation to the class. The direct human interaction can be compelling, but it is a onetime event.
Flash cards or drills or quizzes	These can provide excellent variation of questions and can adapt to student skills and instant feedback.	Print versions are good but are fixed, do not vary, and require manually checking the answers.

Learning Activity	Comments	
	Online	*Face-to-Face (F2F)*
Group project	Social and then cognitive presence needs to be fostered and managed. There is more flexibility than F2F to get together, and any written communication tends to be more articulate than verbal.	Social and then cognitive presence needs to be fostered and managed. Direct human interaction is greatly valued.
Self-test	Automation provides instant feedback on performance or insight on ability or potential success (e.g., self-diagnostic).	This requires manually checking answers.
Laboratory experiments and fieldwork	Simulations are good, safe, and inexpensive, but learning is more effective when combined with F2F. Remote labs and self-guided field trips with mobile devices are much better but can be complex and costly at the start. Home lab kits are less costly but are limited to work that does not require direct supervision.	Full experience of reality is achieved, but learning is more effective when combined with other modes such as simulations. This can be overwhelming for the novice. It can also have safety issues and carries the highest cost of any mode of delivery.

Note. Although the particular mix of teaching and learning modes is really dependent on the specific situation, experience has shown that certain learning activities are better suited to different approaches. To assist you in finding your own right mix, Appendix A provides a first glimpse of some issues to take into account for the learning activities in your course. It is far from exhaustive but is illustrative of some of the many considerations you may have in forming your own approach.

APPENDIX B: SELECTED ONLINE RESOURCES

General Science

Bozemanscience, Paul Andersen (www.bozemanscience.com): This site offers a series of freely available videos in various STEM disciplines. They are done by an advanced placement high school teacher but are useful at the introductory undergraduate level.

Crash Course, John and Hank Green (www.youtube.com/user/crashcourse/featured): This offers a series of up-tempo videos teaching courses such as astronomy, ecology, biology, and chemistry at the high school and introductory undergraduate levels.

FutureLearn MOOC, The Open University and other partners (www.futurelearn.com): This is a massive open online course platform delivered by over 50 partners from the United Kingdom and elsewhere, including university and other education providers (e.g., the British Museum and the National Film and Television School). A broad range of topics is covered, including science and technology. Courses are free for learners and can be taken by individuals or used as additional resources or for specific skills development by established courses. The majority of courses are desktop based, though some also offer the opportunity to explore science at home (e.g., the Kitchen Chemistry course offered by the University of East Anglia).

Khan Academy (www.khanacademy.org): This website provides freely available videos of hand drawings with audio overlay on targeted topics in undergraduate math, chemistry, physics, computing, health, medicine, cosmology, astronomy, and biology. Presentations are detailed and slow, so they may not be ideal to use exclusively for teaching. However, they are a good vehicle to introduce a specific topic and for remedial work and problem areas.

Late Nite Labs, Macmillan (www.latenitelabs.com): This site provides educational institutions with commercial virtual online simulations for various science subjects.

Merlot II, California State University (www.merlot.org/merlot/index.htm): The goal of this website is to provide a quick conduit to online resources for teaching and learning in the science, technology, engineering, and math (STEM) areas and others. This website provides a rich database for earth science resources similar to The National Science Digital Laboratory. Merlot II has useful filters for obtaining a particular type of educational material and extracting higher quality peer-reviewed learning resources in the earth sciences.

Molecular Workbench, The Concord Consortium (mw.concord.org/modeler/showcase/chemistry.html): This site offers open source simulation software, modeling tools, an authoring system, and molecular simulations in the areas of physics, chemistry, biology, biotechnology, and nanotechnology.

North American Network of Science Labs Online (wiche.edu/nanslo): This is an international remote lab consortium enabling access to high-quality, modular, openly licensed courseware, integrating immersive web-based labs with software, video, and robotics for the study of science courses.

OpenLearn, The Open University (www.open.edu/openlearn/science-maths-technology): This site provides a range of free distance learning materials and resources from The Open University. The OpenLearn site is organized by topic areas; the Science, Maths, and Technology area includes a broad selection of science materials. Each item is cataloged according to educational level, the intended duration (i.e., study hours), and the date the materials were last updated. The OpenLearn site also supports keyword searches.

PhET Interactive Simulations, University of Colorado Boulder (phet.colorado.edu): This website provides fun, free, interactive, research-based science and mathematics simulations.

The National Science Digital Library, University Corporation for Atmospheric Research (nsdl .oercommons.org): This website is a meta-database that mediates a broad array of physical and earth science resource links. The resources submitted must adhere to a set of standards providing good quality control. This site is a very useful tool for quickly determining what educationally reliable resources are available on a particular earth science topic, from lesson plans to simulations and other rich multimedia. The search allows users to search by educational level, which is particularly helpful in culling resources inappropriate for higher education.

The OpenScience Laboratory, The Open University (www.open.ac.uk/researchprojects/open-science): This is a repository of all the assets made by the Open University, ranging from citizen science projects, to remote experiments, to interactive screen experiments suitable for undergraduates. Many are completely open access; others invite partnerships of some kind. The collection covers all the sciences.

Virtual Labs, Pearson (www.phschool.com/sales_support/marketing_websites/virtual_lab_center/index .html): This website provides various commercial laboratory simulations in chemistry, biology, physics, and planetary motion at both school and higher education levels. Developed at Brigham Young University, tours of the different products and additional information is provided on their website (chemlab.byu.edu).

Primary and Elementary Science

Beyond Penguins and Polar Bears, The Ohio State University (beyondpenguins.ehe.osu.edu/issue/ category/professional-learning/unit-plans): This website has information about the 5Es (the five stages of a sequence for teaching and learning: Engage, Explore, Explain, Extend or Elaborate, and Evaluate) misconceptions, and the inquiry approach to teaching science with literacy. This in an online magazine for elementary teachers that has a wealth of resources and 5Es unit outlines on a variety of thematic issues.

Beyond Weather and the Water Cycle, The Ohio State University (beyondweather.ehe.osu.edu/issue/ category/in-the-classroom/unit-plan): This is an online magazine for elementary teachers with professional learning and classroom resources.

Biology4Kids, Andrew Rader Studios (www.biology4kids.com): This site covers a range of biology topics in clear, conversational language (more information than activities).

Biology for Kids, A2Z Home's Cool (homeschooling.gomilpitas.com/directory/Biology.htm): This site is an annotated bibliography to a wide range of activities. The annotations indicate the level of reading and understanding required to complete the activity successfully.

Changing Circuits, BBC Schools Science Clips (www.bbc.co.uk/schools/scienceclips/ages/10_11/ changing_circuits.shtml): This interactive learning activity lets students construct virtual circuits and explore the notions of parallel and series circuits.

Chem4Kids, Andrew Rader Studios (www.chem4kids.com): This site offers more information than activities, but the language is clear, conversational, and up to date (e.g., includes Bose-Einstein condensates as a state of matter).

Cosmos4Kids, Andrew Rader Studios (www.cosmos4kids.com): This site offers more information than activities, but as with the other "4kids" sites, the language is clear and conversational so very readable. Some topics have videos.

Engineering Interact (www.engineeringinteract.org/resources/parkworldplot/parkworldplotlink.htm): This is a free educational resource for 9- to 11-year-olds that introduces students to science and engineering concepts. It contains a number of interactive modules, split into 3 sections: learning, testing, and engineering applications.

How Light Works, How Stuff Works (science.howstuffworks.com/light.htm): These interactive websites explore light energy. There is a series of explanations, images, and video clips to describe how light works.

Indigenous Weather Knowledge, Australian Bureau of Meteorology (www.bom.gov.au/iwk): Indigenous Australians have long held their own seasonal calendars based on the local sequence of natural events. The map of Australia showcases Indigenous weather knowledge for some sites around Australia, with hyperlinks to the corresponding seasonal calendars for given regions.

NASA Kids' Club (www.nasa.gov/audience/forkids/kidsclub/flash/index.html): This website is designed for kids, with facts, interviews, games, and activities about space and space exploration.

Physics4Kids, Andrew Rader Studios (www.physics4kids.com): This site has information in an accessible form.

Scienceworks, Melbourne Planetarium (museumvictoria.com.au/scienceworks/education): This site is full of information about the sky, earth, moon, planets, and stars, including science facts.

Working Scientifically, Deakin University (www.deakin.edu.au/arts-ed/education/sci-enviro-ed/early-years/pdfs/intro.pdf): This article provides a rationale for working scientifically, key concepts and misconceptions about working scientifically, and a number of activities based on consumer science aligned to appropriate years.

Biology

Amazon Interactive (www.eduweb.com/amazon.html): This is a fun site to explore the geography of the Ecuadorian Amazon and is great to illustrate concepts around human–ecosystem interactions.

Biology Online (www.biology-online.org): This site includes a very useful dictionary, plus links to text-based tutorials.

Biology Teaching and Learning Resources, D. G. Mackean (www.biology-resources.com): This is a useful source of images and illustrations.

Cell Size and Scale, University of Utah (learn.genetics.utah.edu/content/cells/scale): This site is excellent for demonstrating differences in scale.

Douchy's Biology, EvolvEducation (www.evolveducation.com.au/biology.html): This site offers free podcasts dealing with the senior secondary school biology curriculum (in Victoria, Australia). It is also useful for first-year undergraduate students who have a weak or no background in biology.

EDU Tree of Life (etreeoflife.com): This website is useful to illustrate concepts of phylogeny and relatedness, evolution, speciation, and extinction.

iSpot, The Open University (www.ispotnature.org/communities/global): This is a citizen science project that employs crowdsourcing to identify organisms through automation and connecting beginners with experts.

Royal Society of Biology, Open Education Resources (heteaching.rsb.org.uk/heteaching-home): This collection is focused on the biosciences and supports teaching practical biology at the higher education level. All the resources are peer reviewed. This site is easily searchable and contains links to other online repositories. It also invites new submissions.

The Biology Project, University of Arizona (www.biology.arizona.edu): This website provides text-based tutorials and summaries of key topics and concepts.

The Scale of the Universe (www.htwins.net/scale2): This site is also great for illustrating scale and goes beyond the scale of cells and molecules in both directions.

Chemistry

ChemCollective, Carnegie Mellon University (www.chemcollective.org): This is a collection of virtual labs, scenario-based learning activities, tutorials, and concept tests organized by a group of faculty and staff at Carnegie Mellon who are interested in using, assessing, and creating engaging online activities for chemistry education.

ChemEd DL (www.chemeddl.org): This site provides digital resources, tools, and online services for teaching and learning chemistry.

Chemistry Now, NBC Learn (www.nsf.gov/news/special_reports/chemistrynow): This site offers a video series on the science of everyday things, developed by the National Science Foundation and National Science Teachers Association for the International Year of Chemistry 2011.

ChemWiki, Delmar Larsen (chemwiki.ucdavis.edu): This open access textbook is funded by the National Science Foundation and hosted at the University of California, Davis. It is a dynamic hypertext that is constantly being updated by students and teachers. Currently it covers five fields: organic chemistry, inorganic chemistry, biochemistry, physical chemistry, and analytical chemistry. This is part of the larger STEMWiki initiative to generate open access e-texts such as the BioWiki, the GeoWiki, the StatWiki, the PhysWiki, and the MathWiki.

Higher Education Resources, Royal Society of Chemistry (www.rsc.org/learn-chemistry/collections/higher-education/he-resources/teaching-and-learning-chemistry): This RSC website features searchable downloads, links, and information related to higher education chemistry teaching.

Illustrated Glossary of Organic Chemistry, Steven A. Hardinger (www.chem.ucla.edu/harding/IGOC/IGOC.html): This site is a searchable index of organic chemistry terms with illustrated definitions and provides links to both related terms and Wikipedia. A link to this site is a must for any online organic chemistry course.

JCE Web Software Collection (www.jce.divched.org/jce-products): This is a suite of subscription online tools for *Journal of Chemical Education* (ACS) Xchange subscribers.

Labshare (www.labshare.edu.au): Labshare is a consortium of Australian universities promoting the sharing of remotely accessed science and engineering laboratories.

Master Organic Chemistry, James Ashenhurst (www.masterorganicchemistry.com/getting-started): This blog offers excellent instructional articles on introductory organic chemistry, as well as commercial materials such as study guides and summary sheets. The Resource Guide (www.masterorganicchemistry.com/resource-guide) is particularly useful, as it lists and links to a wide range of resources from entire courses to specific learning activities.

MERLOT Chemistry (chemistry.merlot.org): MERLOT (Multimedia Educational Resource for Learning and Online Teaching), a program of the California State University System, is a free and open peer-reviewed collection of online teaching and learning materials.

VisChem (www.vischem.com.au): This is a research and development project to study the effectiveness of molecular-level visualization, produce animations of chemical structures and processes at this level, and develop effective learning designs for a deep understanding of chemistry.

Weblabs (como.cheng.cam.ac.uk/index.php?Page=Research&Section=Weblabs): Weblabs is a University of Cambridge group producing remotely accessed laboratories.

Earth Sciences

Academic Earth (academicearth.org/earth-sciences): This website provides some earth sciences lectures on several topics (rather than complete courses).

Earth Science Simulations–Sciencecourseware, the National Science Foundation and California State University (www.sciencecourseware.org/eecindex.php): This excellent website provides more advanced simulations and learning materials in the earth and environmental sciences that are useful in developing online labs or for supplementing learning. In particular, the site provides a rather comprehensive set of simulations supporting standard geology labs.

Enabling Remote Activity, The Open University (projects.kmi.open.ac.uk/era): The Enabling Remote Activity (ERA) project provides opportunities for students with mobility impairments to fully participate in fieldwork learning activities. By using mobile and communications technologies, ERA provides practical solutions to the challenges of fieldwork accessibility.

Exploring Earth, TERC (www.classzone.com/books/earth_science/terc/navigation/home.cfm): This website was originally built as a companion to a general textbook on the earth sciences. It is particularly useful in providing rich media on a broad array of earth science topics. The resources are arranged, as might be expected, in a logical and sequential style for basic earth science instruction.

Glossary of Soil Science Terms, Soil Science Society of America (www.soils.org/publications/soils-glossary): This site provides a single online searchable glossary of terms for the various disciplines of soil science.

On the Cutting Edge: Strong Undergraduate Teaching, National Association of Geoscience Teachers (serc.carleton.edu/NAGTWorkshops/index.html): This project provides teaching lessons and ideas from geoscience teachers for geoscience teachers. Lessons on the site have undergone review by peers, and top-rated lessons have been fully vetted by the teaching community.

Study.com (study.com/articles/List_of_Free_Online_Earth_Science_Courses_and_Classes.html): This site provides a list of free online earth science courses and classes.

Teaching Geoscience Online (serc.carleton.edu/NAGTWorkshops/online/index.html): The materials presented are designed to help geoscience faculty improve their online teaching and to provide guidance to those who are considering venturing into the online classroom.

The Paleontology Portal, University of California Museum of Paleontology, Paleontology Society, Society of Vertebrate Paleontology, and U.S. Geological Survey (paleoportal.org): This website is exemplary in demonstrating a "one-stop shopping" approach to coalescing online resources in a discipline-specific area in the earth sciences. The resources linked in the site span various multimedia types and teaching levels and do an especially good job of integrating online public resources from museums. As such, instructors can easily facilitate the use of informal learning resources available through linked institutions with rich media online.

University of Nebraska, Lincoln, Plant and Soil Sciences eLibrary (passel.unl.edu/pages/index2col.php?cat=1): This online educational portal has a collection of useful modules on soils, agriculture, and plant sciences, including peer-reviewed online lessons, including some lessons directed to Spanish-speaking learners.

The following agencies offer earth science materials and data that can be used for instruction at the university level. Typically these are not lectures, but the components can be incorporated into courses.

- U.S. Geological Survey (education.usgs.gov/undergraduate.html)
- British Geological Survey (www.bgs.ac.uk/data/home.html?src=topNav)
- Geological Survey of Canada (www.nrcan.gc.ca/earth-sciences/science/geology/gsc/17100)
- Geoscience Australia (www.ga.gov.au)

Physics

AAPT ComPADRE Digital Library (www.compadre.org): This site is a network of free online resource collections supporting faculty, students, and teachers in physics and astronomy education.

American Institute of Physics (www.aip.org): This website represents a federation of various physics societies and contains links to numerous physics programs and resources with excellent educational materials around the history of modern physics.

HyperPhysics, Georgia State University (hyperphysics.phy-astr.gsu.edu/hbase/hph.html): This site provides a visually oriented exploration environment for concepts in physics, employs concept maps, and is interconnected with thousands of links.

Physlets, Wolfgang Christian (webphysics.davidson.edu/applets/applets.html): This site presents small, flexible Java applets designed for science education that are freely available for noncommercial use. The links on the right contain tutorials, download instructions, and example problems to help you use Physlets (*Phys*ics app*lets*) in your teaching.

The Mechanical University, Annenburg Learner (www.learner.org/resources/series42.html): This website offers a video series with excellent real-life examples for introductory physics.

The Physics Classroom, Tom Henderson (www.physicsclassroom.com): This free-to-use physics website is developed primarily for beginning physics students and their teachers. The website features a variety of sections intended to support both teachers and students in the tasks of learning and teaching physics.

Editor

Dietmar K. Kennepohl, BSc (Hons), PhD, FCIC (dietmark@athabascau.ca), is professor of chemistry and former associate vice president, at Athabasca University. Most of his teaching experience has been in a distributed and online setting. He holds both university and national teaching awards. Over the years, he has published in chemical education, as well as petroleum, main group, and coordination chemistry. His research in chemical education concentrates on the use of innovative distance delivery methods for undergraduate laboratory work.

Contributors

Farook Al-Shamali, BSc (Hons), MSc, PhD (farooka@athabascau.ca), is academic coordinator of physics courses at Athabasca University. He has teaching experience in conventional and distance education systems and publications in particle physics, geo-magnetism, and physics education. Current interests include the design of online courses and the development of multimedia material and low-cost home labs.

Paul Bennett, BS, PhD (Paul.Bennett@cccs.edu), earned his PhD at the University of Colorado Boulder in 2006 in molecular, cellular, and developmental biology. He has been involved in STEM reform efforts since 2007. He is the laboratory technology manager for the North American Network of Science Labs Online facility in Denver, Colorado.

Nicholas Braithwaite, DPhil, FInstP (n.s.braithwaite@open.ac.uk), is professor of engineering physics and director of The OpenScience Laboratory at The Open University. He has taught widely in engineering, materials, and physical sciences, mostly in a distance learning context. In recent years, he has used research-related experience of robotic experiments to develop online practical work for globally accessible undergraduate laboratories.

Daniel M. Branan, BS, MS, PhD (Daniel.Branan@cccs.edu), earned his PhD at the University of Denver in 2003 and MSc in chemistry at The Ohio State University in 1996. He has taught traditional and online chemistry courses since 1996. He is director of the North American Network of Science Labs Online facility in Denver, Colorado.

Marion Bruhn-Suhr, Diplom-Mathematikerin, PhD (m.bruhn-suhr@gmx.de), managed the e-learning activities in the center for continuing university and distance education of the University of Hamburg (*Arbeitsstelle für wissenschaftliche Weiterbildung*) until the end of March 2012, when she retired. From 1996 to 2012 she was also the local representative of The Open University, United Kingdom, in northern Germany and managed all activities based on a cooperation between the two universities.

Trevor Collins, BEng (Hons), MSc, PhD (trevor.collins@open.ac.uk), is a research fellow in the Knowledge Media Institute at The Open University, United Kingdom. His research in educational technology focuses on exploring the ways in which technologies can be designed and developed collaboratively with stakeholders to create scalable, sustainable, and usable tools for learning.

Martin Connors, BSc (Hons), MSc, PhD, PPhys (martinc@athabascau.ca), is a researcher in astronomy and physics and pioneered new methods in distance education science education, with an emphasis on bringing laboratory experiences to home-study students. Primarily active at Athabasca University, he has taught at the University of California, Los Angeles and collaborated on Massachusetts Institute of Technology's online Vibrations and Waves course.

P. A. Danaher, BEd, BA, BA (Hons), GradDipTertEd, MLitt, PhD (Patrick.Danaher@usq.edu.au), teaches education research ethics and methods in his role as professor in educational research at the University of Southern Queensland, Australia. He is also adjunct professor at Central Queensland University, Australia.

Dorothee Dartsch, PhD (d.dartsch@campus-pharmazie.de), is a licensed pharmacist and director and cofounder of CaP Campus Pharmazie GmbH. As assistant professor at the University of Hamburg, she established the novel subject of clinical pharmacy there and is well published in this area, as well as in toxicology, drug development, and medication management. She was the lead on the European collaborative project described in this book.

Sarah Davies, BSc (Hons), MA, PhD (sarah.davies@open.ac.uk), is a senior lecturer in the Department of Environment, Earth and Ecosystems at The Open University, United Kingdom. Her research focuses on technology-enhanced learning, with particular reference to fieldwork learning and new blends of physical and digital networked resources for STEM learning.

Jennifer Donovan, BSc, GradCertEd (tertiary teaching), PhD (jennifer.donovan@usq.edu.au), brings nearly 40 years of experience in teaching science at high school and various Western Australian Universities to her role as lecturer in science education at the University of Southern Queensland, Australia.

Kevin F. Downing, PhD (KDOWNING@depaul.edu), is a professor at DePaul University in Chicago, Illinois, where he has regularly designed and taught online earth science, biological, and paleontology courses since 1998. In addition to research on best practices in online science learning, his field investigations focus on Cenozoic fossil mammals and Pleistocene corals.

Mark Gaved, PhD (mark.gaved@open.ac.uk), is a lecturer in the Institute of Educational Technology, at The Open University, United Kingdom. His research includes field-based and mobile learning and teaching and how networked technologies may alter existing educational practices. He is also exploring how personal devices such as smartphones can enable informal learning.

Jasmin Hamadeh, MA (j.hamadeh@campus-pharmazie.de), is an e-learning consultant and director and cofounder of CaP Campus Pharmazie GmbH. Since 1999, she has been involved in online teaching, course design, and e-learning, specifically consulting in academies, universities, and corporate training contexts and setting up the Train the e-Trainer online course at the University of Hamburg to qualify teachers for designing and moderating online or blended learning processes.

Mark C. Hirst, BSc, PhD, FRSB (mark.hirst@open.ac.uk), is senior lecturer in human genetics at The Open University, United Kingdom where he works on the underlying molecular consequences of triplet instability in human disease, notably in fragile X syndrome and Huntington's disease. He is an expert in the pedagogy and practice of online learning, especially in the design of tools for teaching practical biology.

Robert Lambourne, BSc, PhD, FRAS, FInstP (robert.lambourne@open.ac.uk), is professor of educational physics at The Open University, United Kingdom. He is chair of the International Commission on Physics Education and former chair of the Physics Education Division of the European Physical Society. In addition to formal university teaching, he has a broad involvement with informal education and efforts to encourage public engagement with science.

Peter Lye, BSc, PhD, GradCertHEd, CChem, MRACI (plye@une.edu.au), is a senior lecturer in chemistry at the University of New England in Australia. He has developed and taught tertiary-level chemistry courses for on- and off-campus students for more than 12 years. During this period, he has seen great change in terms of resources and online development of chemical education.

Hilary A. MacQueen, BSc, PhD, FRSB (hilary.macqueen@open.ac.uk), is professor in health sciences at The Open University, United Kingdom, where she has designed and taught more than 20 distance modules across a broad range of health sciences, from microbiology to human nutrition. She has a particular interest in online assessment as a teaching tool and has devised innovative quizzes to assess both theoretical and practical learning.

Mary V. Mawn, BS, MEd, PhD (Mary.Mawn@esc.edu), is an associate professor in the Center for Distance Learning at SUNY Empire State College, Saratoga Springs, New York, where she coordinates and teaches online courses in biology. Her research interests focus on online laboratories, scientific inquiry, and the online professional development of science teachers.

Brett McCollum, BSc, PhD (bmccollum@mtroyal.ca), is associate professor in the Department of Chemistry at Mount Royal University (Calgary, Alberta), a Nexen Scholar of Teaching and Learning, and an Apple Distinguished Educator. He has published in the areas of chemistry education, interdisciplinary teaching, and radical chemistry using the exotic muonium atom. His research in chemistry education focuses on effective uses of technology for student engagement, collaboration, and learning, and he has authored chemistry learning objects for mobile devices.

Jennifer Mosse, BSc (Hons), MBiotech, DipEd, BEd, GradCertHEd (jennifer.mosse@federation.edu.au), is associate professor in biomedical science at Federation University Australia and has been teaching both on-campus and distance students for over 25 years. Her research interests include methods to improve access of regional and remote students to STEM education.

Barbara C. Panther, BAppSci, GradCertHEd, MAppSci, MEd, PhD (barbie.panther@federation.edu.au), is the associate dean of learning and teaching in the Faculty of Science and Technology at Federation University Australia. Panther has been teaching online and off campus for many years and is particularly interested in how the online environment can be used to improve the teaching of chemistry.

Ron Reuter, BS, MS, PhD (ron.reuter@oregonstate.edu), is an associate professor of natural resources in the Department of Forest Ecosystems and Society and teaches courses for Oregon State University (OSU)–Cascades and OSU Ecampus. He is engaged in research in the areas of effective distance education technology and ecosystem processes in the Pacific Northwest of the United States.

Erica Smith, BSc, MSc, PhD, CChem, MRACI (erica.smith@une.edu.au), is a senior lecturer in chemistry at the University of New England in Australia. She has been a tertiary-level chemistry instructor for over 10 years, with a particular expertise in teaching first-year chemistry. Since commencing at the University of New England in 2010, she has been developing and adapting her pedagogical skills and course delivery for online and distance education students.

Karen Spence, BSc (Hons), GradDipSecEd, PhD (Karen.Spence@usq.edu.au), is a lecturer in science education at the University of Southern Queensland in Australia. She has a background in microbiology and secondary science teaching.

Richard Swan, BA, MS, PhD (richard_swan@byu.edu), is associate director of the Center for Teaching and Learning at Brigham Young University. He received a BA in film studies at the University of Utah and an MS in instructional science and a PhD in instructional psychology and technology from Brigham Young University.

Jessie Webb, BS (jessiemwebb@gmail.com), is a graduate student at Brigham Young University studying chemistry with an emphasis in chemistry education. She graduated from Brigham Young University with a BS in chemistry in 2013 and desires to teach chemistry.

Brian F. Woodfield, BS, MS, PhD (brian_woodfield@byu.edu), is a professor of chemistry at Brigham Young University. He received both a BS and an MS in chemistry from Brigham Young University; a PhD in physical chemistry from the University of California, Berkeley, in 1995; and a National Research Council Postdoctoral Fellowship at the Naval Research Laboratory. He is the creator and project director for Pearson's virtual laboratory suite.

Wendy Wright, BSc (Hons), CertHEd, PhD (wendy.wright@federation.edu.au), teaches introductory cell and systems biology in on- and off-campus modes at the Gippsland Campus of Federation University Australia. The campus has a long history of mixed-mode teaching. Wright also teaches ecology at upper levels and is an active researcher in the fields of ecology and education.

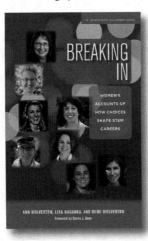